The Specialised Lexicographical Approach: A Step further in Dictionary-making

Linguistic Insights

Studies in Language and Communication

Edited by Maurizio Gotti,
University of Bergamo

Volume 102

PETER LANG
Bern · Berlin · Bruxelles · Frankfurt am Main · New York · Oxford · Wien

Nuria Edo Marzá

The Specialised Lexicographical Approach: A Step further in Dictionary-making

PETER LANG
Bern · Berlin · Bruxelles · Frankfurt am Main · New York · Oxford · Wien

Bibliographic information published by Die Deutsche Bibliothek
Die Deutsche Bibliothek lists this publication in the Deutsche Nationalbibliografie; detailed bibliographic data is available on the Internet at ‹http://dnb.ddb.de›.

British Library and Library of Congress Cataloguing-in-Publication Data:
A catalogue record for this book is available from *The British Library,* Great Britain.

Library of Congress Cataloging-in-Publication Data

Edo Marzá, Nuria.
The specialised lexicographical approach : a step further in dictionary-making / Nuria Edo Marzá.
p. cm. – (Linguistic insights, ISSN 1424-8689 ; v. 102)
Includes bibliographical references.
ISBN 978-3-0343-0043-8 (alk. paper)
1. Terms and phrases–Lexicography. 2. Lexicography. 3. Corpora (Linguistics)
I. Title.
P305.E36 2009
413.028–dc22
2009025156

ISSN 1424-8689
ISBN 978-3-0343-0043-8

Hochfeldstrasse 32, CH-3012 Bern, Switzerland
info@peterlang.com, www.peterlang.com, www.peterlang.net

Printed in Germany

To my parents

To Nacho

Contents

List of acronyms and abreviations

ASCER	Asociación Española de Fabricantes de Azulejos y Pavimentos Cerámicos
ASTM	American Society for Testing and Materials
CTT	Communicative Theory of Terminology
EAGLES	European Advisory Group on Language Engineering Standard
GTT	General Theory of Terminology
GL	General language
ICT	Information and Communication Technologies
IEC	International Electrotechnical Commission
IEV	International Electrotecnnical Vocabulary
IPA	Inglés Profesional y Académico (Profesional and Academic English)
ISA	International Standardisation Association
ISO	International Organisation for Standardisation
IULA	Instituto Universitario de Lingüística Aplicada
IVEX	Instituto Valenciano de la Exportación
KWIC	Key Word in context
LGP	Laguage for General Purposes
LSP	Language for Specific Purposes
LU	Lexical unit
MI	Mutual Information
OCR	Optical Character Recognition
PAE	Professional and Academic English
PAL	Professional and Academic Language
PAS	Professional and Academic Spanish
SLA	Specialised Lexicographical Approach
TIC	Tecnologías de la Información y la Comunicación (Information and Communication Technologies)
TU	Terminological unit
WST	WordSmith Tools 4.0

I. Theorical Framework

Approach each new problem
not with a view of finding what you hope will be there,
but to get the truth,
the realities that must be grappled with.
You may not like what you find.
In that case you are entitled to try to change it.
Bernard M. Baruch

1. Introducing the specialised lexicographical approach (SLA)

This book is the result of many years of research and reflection in specialised dictionary-making. As such, it tries to coherently summarise and put forward the main aspects considered for the creation of a bilingual corpus-based specialised active dictionary of the ceramic industry within what I have called the "specialised lexicographical approach" (SLA). The specialised lexicographical approach involves dictionary-making from a natural, communicative perspective; it implies the study of terminology from a *continuum* view of language and an integrating perspective; it is a corpus-based approach towards the study of specialised languages and the presentation of their terminology in dictionaries; it adopts an active, user-friendly and user-focused perspective in specialised dictionary-making; it implies correct undestanding and accurate use; it makes necessary the inclusion of different and varied pieces of linguistic and pragmatic data; it goes beyond the mere compilation of terms; it implies thinking about the "how", "what for", and "for whom" we make specialised dictionaries.

This book has tried thus to describe and analyse the development process of a specialised dictionary from this approach in a progressive way, and pains have been taken to make the resulting specialised lexicographical work comprehensive, coherent, systematic and close to the reality it seeks to characterise from a terminological point of view.

The first section of this book offers a comprehensive theoretical framework accounting for the objectives, principles and methods on which this work is sustained. These basic aspects are presented in a progressive, integrating fashion with the aim of facilitating the global comprehension of this framework. In order to understand the relevance of all these reflections and their appropriateness for the correct understanding of this work, figure 1 shows a graphic representation of the way in which these theoretical issues have been approached from a theoretical perspective.

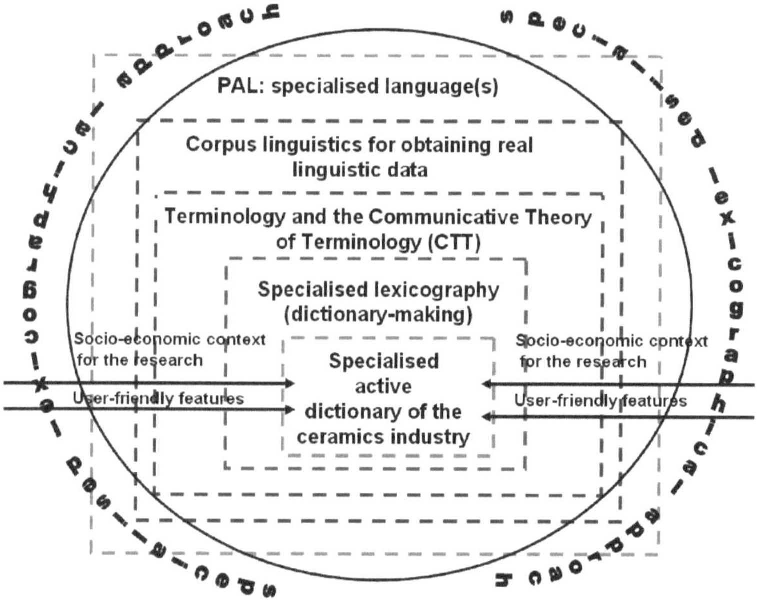

Figure 1. Structure of the theoretical aspects involved in the SLA and how they have been progressively approached in this book with the final aim of creating an active, specialised dictionary of the ceramics industry.

Closely linked to the development of the SLA is the fact that in recent years it has been increasingly urged that dictionaries should be designed to meet the specific needs of the groups of users for whom they are intended (Kromann, Riiber, Rosbach, 1991). In this sense, Cowie (1979, in Kromann, Riiber, Rosbach, 1991) noticed that the scope, organisation and meta-language of dictionaries should analyse and reflect more closely the reference needs (and levels of sophistication) of the classes of user for whom they are intended.

Therefore, a key issue before starting to undertake the elaboration of any specialised dictionary is the consideration of how to meet the needs of prospective users so that decisions on whether to create a monolingual or bilingual dictionary, a descriptive or prescriptive one, etc. are taken appropriately. The SLA tries to consider and meaningfully combine all the aspects involved in the correct treatment of terminology. With this aim and from a theoretical point of view, it is grounded on an adequate understanding of general and specialised language, on the communicative dimension of terminology, on its use in real world (corpus-based studies), on a correct understanding of those disciplines in charge of the study of lexicon (specialised or not) and on the socio-economic dimension of speciality domains. Terminology, as a subject that deals with the compilation, description, management and presentation of the terms that belong to the speciality fields of one or more languages, is not a practical activity that can be justified in itself but within a wider scope – in this case the ceramic industrial district. Terminology has thus been conceived throughout this work as a field of knowledge aimed at solving social needs and linked to the optimisation of the communication between specialists and professionals, something which, up to now, has not been done in the ceramic tile industry. From a practical/applied perspective, the theoretical aspects of the SLA give way to a method for specialised dictionary-making that goes a step further compared to terminography.

Hence, this research came to light as a proposal aimed at "filling a gap" in specialised communication and specialised dictionary-making, contributing to the improvement of the communication between, in this case, specialists in the ceramic industrial district. In this way, a bilingual specialised lexicographical work like this based on the results of a deep needs analysis from the linguistic point of view was believed to be necessary.

Taking all these factors into account the main objective of this book can be easily summarised as to progressively disclose the SLA from a theoretical perspective in order to, subsequently, illustrate it by showing the development of a bilingual (English-Spanish, Spanish-English) dictionary of the ceramic industry.

In this specific work, the great number of aspects involved in the SLA has made it necessary:

- To show the importance of terminology in the study of specialised languages/Professional and Academic Language (PAL) and to analyse, describe, highlight and explain the benefits of a corpus as a tool for the extraction and observation of real, natural terminological data.
- To justify the reason for presenting the Communicative Theory of Terminology (CTT) as the most realistic and suitable way of approaching terminology, in opposition to other theories like the GTT, by pointing out the shortcomings and flaws of previous conceptions in lexicographical and terminographical works.
- To provide a detailed account of the communicative nature of terminology and its interdisciplinarity and present a study which integrates the theoretical aspects of terminology with a coherent practice of it.
- To analyse and examine in depth the context of use of the specialised lexicographical tool to be designed (needs analysis) so as to ascertain and show the necessity to create a dictionary that satisfies the specific demands of the ceramic industrial sector and that realistically responds to "what is needed".
- To create a user-friendly, active dictionary which realistically reflects the terminological reality analysed and which fulfils the expectations and needs of prospective users; consequently, to explain the appropriateness of using the label "specialised lexicography" to define a work like this.

To sum up, all through these pages attempts have been made to provide a coherent approach – from both the theoretical and the applied points of view – to the development of a specialised lexicographical tool (specialised dictionary) which meets the expectations and needs of the prospective user for whom it has been designed. The following chapters present the theoretical aspects involved in the SLA.

Language is not an abstract construction
of the learned, or of dictionary makers, but
is something arising out of the work, needs, ties, joys,
affections, tastes, of long generations of humanity,
and has its bases broad and low, close to the ground.
Noah Webster

2. Professional and academic language/ specialised languages

One of the primary considerations when undertaking a linguistic work of any kind is the understanding of this very same linguistic reality and our positioning towards it. As its own name indicates, the specialised lexicographical approach (SLA) works with specialised languages as its "raw material" for subsequently elaborating specialised dictionaries like the one here presented. However, the way of conceiving language as a whole affected and integrated by several aspects has never been a matter of universal agreement. The following sections in this chapter will try to put forward the way the SLA understands language and its specialised instances in an attempt to show the benefits and convenience of a *continuum* perspective.

> El intercambio permanente entre lenguaje especializado y lengua común, así como los problemas que de él se derivan requieren una mediación consciente entre ambas áreas. Sólo es posible asegurar o facilitar la comunicación entre expertos y legos y entre los expertos de distintas áreas, si un número cada vez mayor de partícipes en el proceso comunicativo se esfuerza activamente por lograr esa comunicación y se ocupa de las cuestiones lingüísticas que se plantean. (Arntz and Picht, 1995: 42)
>
> [The permanent interchange between specialised language and common language, as well as the problems arising from it, make a conscious mediation between both areas necessary. It is only possible to assure or facilitate communication between experts and laymen and between experts from distinct areas if a growing number of participants in the communicative process actively makes an effort to achieve such communication and deals with the linguistic questions posed. (Arntz and Picht, 1995: 42)]

2.1. Language and how to detect specialisation: is there a clear-cut boundary between the general and the specialised?

As happens in almost every aspect of life, there is more than one possible way to approach the issue of whether the general and the specialised (in terms of language) are delimited by a clear-cut boundary which allows for an easy distinction. Two main viewpoints thus appear in this respect:

- On the one hand, the view of those supporting the idea that a clear, sharp line can be drawn between the general and the specific or specialised, and that a criterion justifying such a distinction can be established. For them, the main criterion allowing this division is the specialisation of the addresser, that is, the fact that a given discourse or text has been produced by a specialist addresser that conceptually controls the subject matter:

  > We may want to postulate the separate system at the grammatical, semantic or pragmatic level or any combination of these. There are many reasons for establishing a separate pragmatic dimension, e. g. separate user groups, different topics, different situations. On the semantic level the situation is less clear as we have separate lexical items, but also many common ones, and we know that considerable variation exists in the use of special lexical items as indeed there is variation in what we attribute to the lexicon of a special subject. On the grammatical level we may have some syntactic, morphological and phonological differences between general and special and between special languages but we would wish to stress the similarities in order to preserve a unified notion of a language in the same way as we define dialects as variations of a national language and do not normally go beyond national language boundaries. (Sager *et al.*, 1980: 2)

- On the other hand, the view of those who believe that between the specialised and the non-specialised there is a continuum, since the difference between general and specialised is a matter of degree. For them, it is neither adequate nor natural to force a limit between what is considered to be specialised or not, since many factors have an influence on it. This is why they consider it more sensible to talk about discourse, texts, documents or languages being specialised to a greater or lesser extent, depending on some parameters or on others.

Bearing these considerations in mind, the SLA adopts an integrating version of both views that is closer to the second one, but sets out from the fact that it is not so much languages that are specialised but the use made of them in specialised contexts, which may range from a discourse markedly specialised to a variety of "border-discourse" close to common language.

Basically, cognitive factors are responsible for establishing a dividing line that allows a general text to be differentiated from a specialised one. However, this issue of tracing a dividing line is a very controversial one that is not at all easy to establish, and is what has led many scholars to resort to the notion of the *specialisation continuum*. However, this difficulty does not necessarily imply that a specialist in a subject matter is unable to establish what is specialised for him/her, since there seems to be a prototypicality index with respect to the so-called specialised discourses created in terms of their thematic area, goal, the field in which they are used, and so forth.

> Por ejemplo, los discursos de la física, la química, la biología, la geología, [...] serían más prototípicos de lo especializado que los de la banca, la bolsa, el comercio o las finanzas; y más periféricos aún serían los discursos [...], la peluquería [...], los deportes [...]. No obstante, si mantenemos que sólo las condiciones cognitivas (el control sobre la estructura conceptual del ámbito) determinan que una producción discursiva es especializada, lo que hace variar la percepción de más o menos especializado en dos producciones del más alto nivel de especialización será la mayor o menor opacidad de la temática, producto de que sea más o menos difundida socialmente. (IULA, 2007 c)

> [For instance, the discourse of physics, chemistry, biology, geology [...] would be more prototypical of "the specialised" than those of banking, the stock exchange, trade or finance, and those of hairdressing [...], sports [...] would be even more peripheral. Nonetheless, if we maintain that only cognitive conditions (the control over the conceptual structure of the domain) determine that a discourse is specialised, what will vary the perception of two productions with the highest specialisation level being more or less specialised will be the greater or lesser opacity of the subject matter resulting from being more or less socially widespread.] (IULA, 2007 c)

If, according to what has been discussed so far, we accept the fact that between the specialised and the non-specialised there may be a boundary (more or less precise or acute), as different authors claim, then obviously the next question that has to be posed in this research is how can specialised languages be differentiated from non-specialised ones? That is to say, how can "specialisation" be detected? Following the IULA (2007 c), for a text to be considered as specialised, together with the lexicon criterion, other pragmatic, functional, thematic, textual-linguistic and cognitive criteria must also concur:

1) From a pragmatic point of view, it can be said that the factors that characterise the production, transmission and reception process of specialised discourse are determined by the following aspects:

- the producer or addresser; a specialist or a person with a high degree of competence in the subject matter;
- the addressee, who expects to be informed;
- the predominant function (informative);
- the tone, which is formal, although different levels of formality are accepted;
- the situation, which is always professional.

2) From a functional point of view there is also a series of common traits shared by every language that is considered to be specialised: their basic function is the transmission of information and their respective terminologies are used to denominate the concepts of a specialised area.

3) From the point of view of the topic, texts that are normally specialised usually belong to the following disciplines (although exceptions are possible): scientific-technical subjects, exact sciences, experimental sciences, social sciences, human sciences, professions and specialised activities.

4) From the textual point of view, specialised texts possess an overall specific configuration that characterises them and makes them easy to differentiate from the configuration that characterises

other kinds of texts.[1] They also present a regular style (scientific-technical style) which shows variations depending on the topic and on the different levels on which it is dealt with. To sum up, these texts are:

- concise (with little redundancy);
- precise (with no ambiguity);
- objective or depersonalised (not very or not at all emotive).

5) Finally, the IULA (2007 c) points out that the most intrinsic trait is that, from a cognitive point of view, texts are specialised when they convey precise knowledge resulting from a very specific process of conceptualisation of reality undertaken and validated by consensus among specialists in the field.

Hence, depending on the degree of accomplishment of these factors, "specialisation" in language can be detected and measured, something which has allowed me to establish some sort of delimitation in this respect, but always from a continuum point of view which does not (cannot) abruptly separate general from specialised language as has been explained in subsequent sections.

2.2. General/common language vs. specialised language(s)

> Las lenguas especializadas surgen dentro de la lengua común pero se diferencian de ella en que su objetivo último es el cubrir las necesidades específicas de comunicación formal y funcional que se plantean en cada una de las profesiones u oficios de los diversos ámbitos técnicos y científicos. (Gómez de Enterría, 1998: 30)
>
> [Specialised languages come up within common language but are differentiated from it in the fact that their ultimate aim is to cover the specific needs of formal and functional communication that arise in each of the professions or jobs from the different technical and scientific domains.] (Gómez de Enterría, 1998: 30)

1 Literary texts, religious texts, advertising texts, etc.

As Arntz and Picht (1995) state, the fundamental importance of general language for specialised language is obvious. As these authors explain, in the same way that formalised language (such as a mathematical formula) cannot exist without natural language, neither can specialised language be conceived without common, general language, in spite of the fact that the latter can survive on its own. However, it is a fact that the influence of specialised language on common/general language is not new at all and nowadays the influence is even greater due to the increasing presence of science and technology in everyday life.

At the same time that specialised language becomes more precise and concise, it progressively loses the capacity to be widely or generally understood. This leads to a situation in which fewer and fewer people are capable of understanding texts about highly specialised areas to which they do not regularly devote their efforts.

> La principal justificación de la existencia de los lenguajes especializados y de su desarrollo consiste en exigir a los científicos y técnicos que se esfuercen en la precisión incluso en el ámbito lingüístico. Nuevas ideas y nuevos objetos requieren denominaciones que aún no estén "adjudicadas", o sea, que no puedan confundirse con otras. La lengua común, si es que puede librarse del peligro de confusión, sólo lograría hacerlo mediante paráfrasis excesivamente largas [...] Pero la descripción exhaustiva no resultaría adecuada para la comunicación especializada, que a la vez exige concisión y claridad. Por esto son imprescindibles unos medios especiales, convenidos entre los interlocutores afectados, para hacer posible la comunicación en y sobre su área especializada. (Arntz and Picht, 1995: 42)
>
> [The main justification for the existence and development of specialised languages is to demand scientists and technicians to make an effort in order to achieve precision even in the linguistic field. New ideas and new objects require new denominations that are not yet "allocated", that is, that cannot be mixed up with others. Common language, in case it can avoid confusion, would only be able to do it by means of excessively long paraphrases [...]. However, exhaustive descriptions would not be adequate for specialised communication, which at the same time demands concision and clarity. That is why special means, agreed among the affected interlocutors in order to make communication in and about their speciality area possible, are essential.] (Arntz and Picht, 1995: 42)

This book presents – from the SLA – the development and a sample of the results of a corpus-based dictionary on ceramic industry terminology and, consequently, this implies that a specific or specialised "kind" of language has been dealt with.

Hence, one of the main aims in this section has been to show how to "prepare the ground" – from a theoretical point of view – for a work like this by reflecting on and identifying the different pragmatic and linguistic features that characterise this kind of specialised language and make it different from the non-specialised one. Once these features have been identified, it is also easier to create a model for accurately and correctly representing the specialised language as such and its terminology from a communicative perspective in order to finally develop a specialised lexicographical work. The knowledge of what specialised languages are and imply has also contributed to create a more accurate corpus that was specifically designed for the purposes previously established and from which it has been possible to extract the terms that presumably conform the terminological panorama of the field of industrial ceramics.

Alcaraz (2000) defines language as the instrument by which a community communicates and, as such, it is not solely used in everyday communication but also in specialised contexts – what Alcaraz (2000) calls "professional contexts". The language used in everyday communication has been traditionally known as general or common language, whereas the language used in professional or specific contexts is usually known as specialised, special or speciality language. The general or common language is made up of a series of subcodes that are selected by speakers throughout the communicative process, depending on what they want to express and the communicative situation, or context, in which they are immersed. For this same author, the term *lengua de especialidad* (specialised language), derived from the French term *langue de spécialité*, refers to the specific language used by some specialists and professionals in order to transmit information and negotiate the terms, concepts and knowledge of a given field of knowledge, that is to say, to confirm the existing terms by delimiting their field of application and modifying them, whether totally or partially (Alcaraz, 2000). The term "specialised language" has also received a number of alternative names that may be considered, in general terms, as being synonymous: the already-mentioned special language, speciality language, special subject language and language for specific purposes (LSP),[2] although this last denomination is better applied, according to its origin, to the field of teaching (Sager *et al.*, 1980).[3]

Alcaraz (2000) also adds to his definition of specialised language a shade of meaning because, as he points out, this "kind" of language has also been called "technolect", although he concedes it is more restrictive[4] and less preferable than the label "specialised language". In spite of this, in Alcaraz's (2000) view, the term specialised language and the grouping of some of these specialised languages under the aforementioned label of LSP is better and more accurately expressed in the case of English by the acronym IPA (*Inglés Profesional y Académico*), what I have called PAE[5] (Professional and Academic English) in English. Vargas (2005) explains that Alcaraz (2000) coins this term to refer to the modality of English that includes the grouping of the different specialised languages that arise in the academic world and during the practice of the corresponding professions.

> Existen muchas lenguas de especialidad, tantas como actividades humanas (la de los políticos, los militares, los comerciantes (…)). Con un buen número de ellas se ha formado un núcleo de subvariedades llamado "inglés profesional y académico (IPA)", que coincide en líneas generales con lo que en inglés se llama ESP (English for Specific Purposes), y en español, IFE (inglés para fines específicos). Utilizamos el nombre de "inglés profesional y académico" porque nos parece mucho más concreto que el de "inglés para fines específicos" (...) Así lo estima también Widdowson (1998: 3-4), para quien cualquier uso que hagamos del lenguaje siempre será "específico", porque servirá para un fin concreto. (Alcaraz, 2000: 15)
>
> [There are many speciality languages, as many as human activities (the language of politicians, soldiers, traders (…). With a great number of them, a nucleus of subvarieties called "*inglés profesional y académico*, Professional and Academic Language (IPA in Spanish, PAL in English)" has been formed.

---

2 In opposition to Language for General Purposes (LGP).

3 Throughout this study, the denomination "specialised language" (referring to the specific case of the ceramic industry) is the preferred one, and it is considered to belong to the wider category of PAL.

4 It is more restrictive because it only comprises the subcode made up of the lexicon of a given discipline.

5 Together with PAE, we may also have PAS (Professional and Academic Spanish), which would be another dimension of PAL (Professional and Academic Language).

> In broad terms, it coincides with what has been called in English ESP (English for Specific Purposes) and in Spanish IFE (*inglés para fines específicos*). We use the name, "Professional and Academic Language" because we consider it to be much more specific than that of "English for Specific Purposes" (...) This is also Widdowson's view (1998: 3-4), for whom any use made of language will always be "specific" since it will be used for a specific aim.] (Alcaraz, 2000: 15)

Consequently, from this reflection arises what I have called (following Alcaraz's (2000) and Aguado's (2001) proposal) PAL[6] (Professional and Academic Language), understood as being a way to concentrate specialised languages under a single denomination. Accordingly, in order to follow a consistent and coherent way to refer to this linguistic phenomenon, in general, throughout this work the term "specialised language" has been the most commonly used to refer to a single specific specialised language (in this case, the one used in the ceramics industry), whereas PAL has been the preferred denomination to refer to specialised languages as a whole. Taking all this into account and in accordance with the integrating view between general and specialised languages outlined in the previous section, the way the SLA conceives language as a whole and in its different integrating aspects could be presented as the diagrammatic structure in figure 2. This diagram conceives specialised language both as a *continuum* made up of inclusive relationships which go from the general to the specific in terms of language and as a somehow independent phenomenon with certain peculiarities with respect to general language. Despite this, these inclusive dimensions do not constitute closed, clear-cut, absolute boundaries because the very nature of language does not allow this to be so, as far as I conceive it. This is the reason why the diagram is represented with discontinuous lines:

6 Aguado (2001) points out that the result of the investigations in this field can be extended to every language and give as a result what would be called LPAs ("Lenguajes Profesionales y Académicos) what I have called in English PAL(s) (Professional and Academic Language(s)).

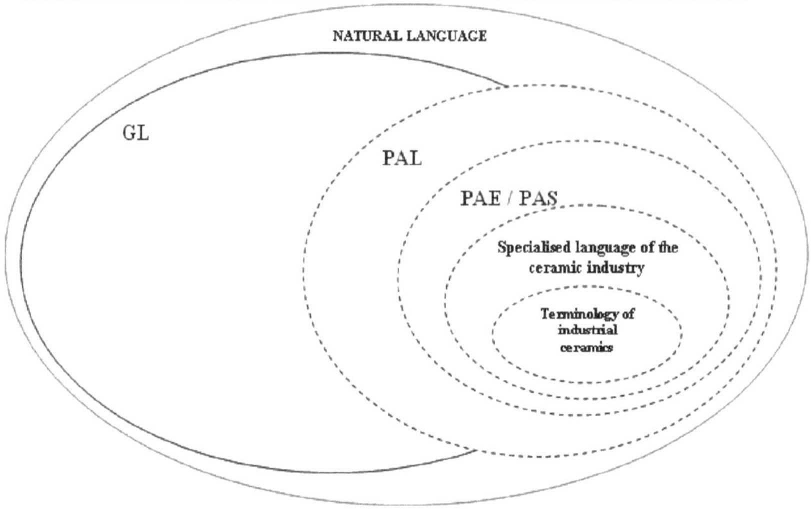

Figure 2. Figure illustrating the integrating consideration of specialised and general language in the specialised lexicographical approach (SLA). GL: General Language; PAL: Professional and Academic Language; PAE: Professional and Academic English; PAS: Professional and Academic Spanish.

Directly related to this is the fact that many times every day, as we participate in different communicative situations, we use a wide range of varieties of language. These situations may range from talking to a friend to reading a research article or from having a business meeting to speaking to a child. These varieties of language that we use in different situations are referred to as registers.

Therefore, a register may be defined as the variety of a language aimed at accomplishing a communicative goal in a specific professional or academic framework, so that in general terms, it can be stated that the concept of "register" also refers to the concept expressed by *langue de spécialité* or specialised language.

For Cabré (1993: 127), a particular language is made of a diverse group of subcodes that speakers use "according to their dialectal modalities", and which they select according to the expressive necessities and the particular characteristics of the communicative context in which they are located. However, even with these codes that make language a complex system with multiple varieties, each general language consists of a set of rules and units (phonological, morphological, lexical, semantic and discursive) that are common to every speaker of this language. The group of rules, units and restrictions that form part of the knowledge of the majority of the speakers of a language constitutes the so-called common or general language, and the units of this common language are used in situations that can be described as "unmarked".

In contrast, specialised languages are used to refer to "a group of subcodes (which partially coincide with the subcode of the common language) characterised by a series of "special" peculiarities. These traits are specific to each speciality language and can refer to the topic, the kind of interlocutor, the communicative situation, the speaker's intention, the medium in which the communicative interchange takes place and so on. Therefore, the situations in which specialised languages are used can be considered as "marked". However, even when, according to this, general language and specialised languages may (at least in theory) seem clearly delimited in their fields of work, in reality this is not so. Closely related to what has been discussed in section 2.1, Vargas (2005) states that establishing a neat dividing line between general and specialised language or between specialised languages is a controversial issue from which two main theories arise (Ciapuscio and Kugel, 2002). The first is that of the linguists who try to clearly fix the limits and boundaries between the two kinds of languages in their works (Sager *et al.*, 1980) and the second is that of the linguists who, unable to clearly establish these boundaries, prefer the notion of *continuum* to account for this phenomenon. In Balboni's (1986: 3) words, "from simple LSP to the most formal LSP there is a continuum" because, in spite of the fact that there exist specific features of different types (textual, functional, and so forth) for each specialised language, these traits are not enough "to make a razor to cut the continuum" (*ibid.*: 4).

To go deeper into the diverging views on this topic, figure 3 below illustrates the many different conceptions this issue gives rise to. Ahmad (1995, in Pérez 2002) summarises the different views on the topic by regarding the relationship between the natural language and specialised languages in the three different models represented in figure 3.

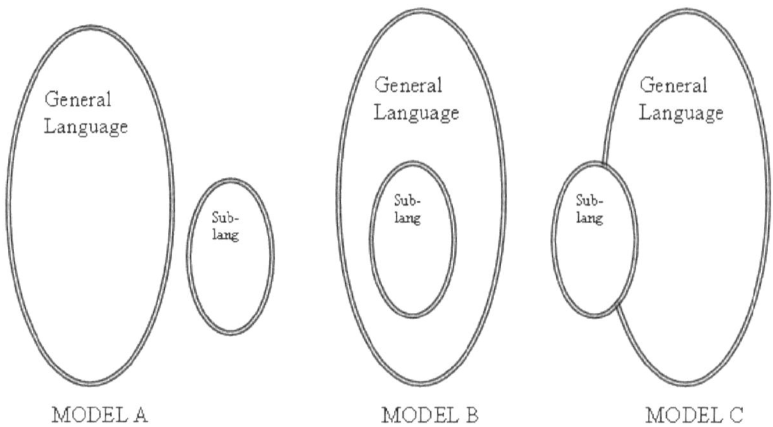

Figure 3. Illustrative view of the possible relations that can be established between the general language and specialised languages (sub-languages).

The viewpoint of this author (the same as that of the SLA) is closer to model C because he believes that the relations between the general language and the specialised language must be considered not as the juxtaposition of both or as a subsystem of the general language, but as the "merging of a subset of the general language with a set of specific elements of its own" (Pérez, 2002).

According to Bergenholtz and Tarp (1995), most linguists make a basic distinction between language for general purposes and language for special (or specific) purposes: language for general purposes (LGP) may be seen as a synonym of standard language, and all languages for specific/special purposes are regarded as elements of the general language. This corresponds to the view that a certain language system is determined by the general-language system and that, to a greater or lesser extent, all LSPs make use of the general-language system and can be found within it. They illustrate this approach as reproduced in figure 4 (Bergenholtz and Tarp, 1995: 17).

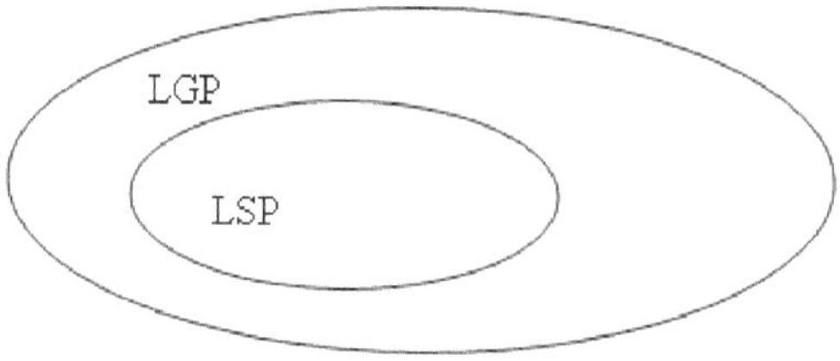

Figure 4. Relations between Language for General Purposes (LGP) and Language for Specific Purposes (LSP).

However, other linguists take the opposite view. For them, all general language expressions are also found in special languages and according to this lexically-oriented approach, LGP is a subset of LSP (Bergenholtz and Tarp, 1995: 17). Figure 5 illustrates this view.

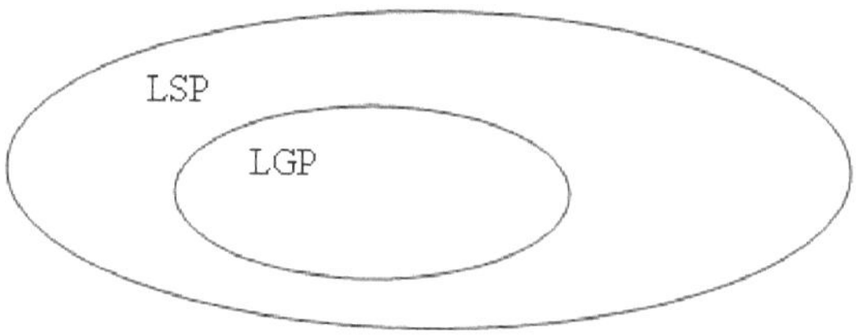

Figure 5. Relation between Language for General Purposes (LGP) and Language for Specific Purposes (LSP) contrary to the one illustrated in figure 4.

According to Bergenholtz and Tarp (1995), and from a communicative point of view, LGP and LSP are used in completely different situations. LSP refers to the language used by experts for communicating within their areas of expertise but, as expert knowledge cannot be presupposed in daily communication, general language must be resorted to. Although it is to a certain extent possible to refer to the same things by using general language, communication runs the risk of becoming so oversimplified that the whole can no longer be considered LSP. Thus, LSP and LGP are equal, yet distinct phenomena, as illustrated by the model (Bergenholtz and Tarp, 1995: 17) in figure 6.

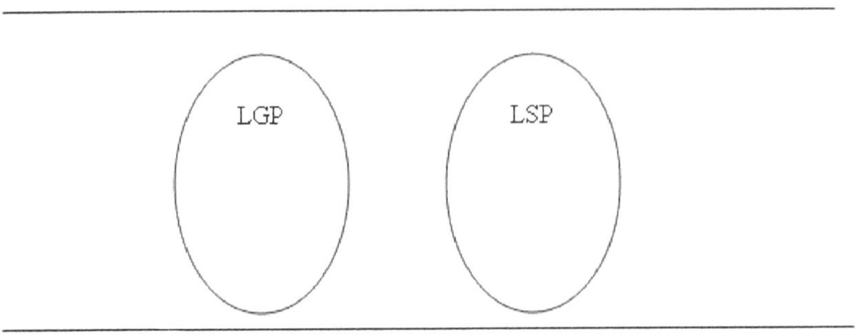

Figure 6. LGP and LSP as perfectly differentiated linguistic realities.

Delving again into Cabré's (1993: 148) views in this respect, "algunos autores han concebido los lenguajes especializados por la temática como sistemas totalmente diferenciados de la lengua común. Esta afirmación, en términos absolutos no parece muy adecuada".[7] According to this author, the autonomy this approach defends would only be possible if after the comparison of two texts, one general and one specialised, they did not present any kind of linguistic coincidence and therefore the idea that they come from isolated systems could be coherently defended. Cabré (1993) stresses the fact that both texts will show highly significant linguistic coincidences that reveal that they have been constructed on the basis of a common system. At the same time, however, she also declares that the texts would also present important differences that could lead us to conclude that, in certain aspects, they come from different codes: the code that unifies them is the common language, and the code that diversifies them is the specialised language. In conclusion, both codes share an intersection relation that partially coincides with model C proposed by Ahmad (1995) in figure 3 and which is in accordance with the integrating view supported by the SLA and consequently adopted for this research.

In general, LSP will make use of (only) part of this assumed general language, such as certain possible grammatical constructions

7 "Some authors have conceived languages specialised by the subject matter as systems completely differentiated from common language. In absolute terms, this statement does not seem much adequate."

and not all general-language words; nevertheless, special technical terms and, in some cases, also register-specific structures are also used. This is shown by the model in figure 7, in which the intersection (INT) between LGP and LSP is made up of structures and elements occurring in both LGP and LSP. This intersection is another possible way of illustrating a conception of LGP and LSP (specialised language) that is very similar to the one adopted in this work. From the point of view of lemma selection, the intersection comprises those words in specialised texts (here referred to as "common words") which are not normally lemmatised in LSP dictionaries (Bergenholtz and Tarp, 1995: 18-19).

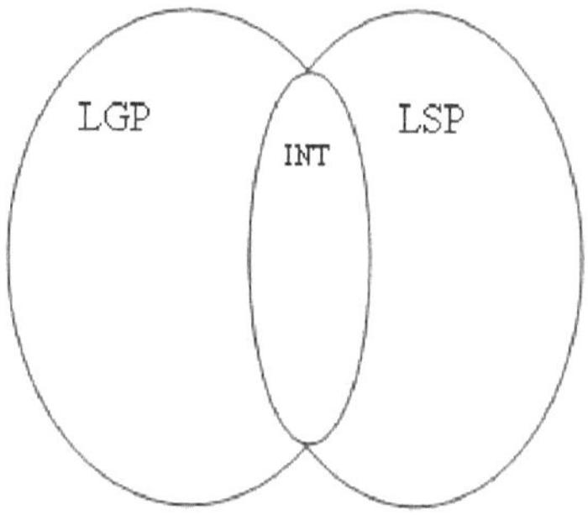

Figure 7. Intersection between LGP and LSP.

Finally, another possibility is to dismiss the existence of LGP as a phenomenon in its own right altogether, assuming instead that each usage is specific to a certain situation. This approach implies that every language variety is an LSP (Bergenholtz and Tarp, 1995: 18).

If the views in this respect of other researchers on the field are considered, the IULA (2007 c) states, for instance, that the frequent use of the denomination specialised or special language implies accepting that the communicative resources used in certain circumstances present some idiosyncrasy (something "special" or "different"). However, if the concept of language is analysed in depth and if the real features of every specialised language are observed, most of their differences and peculiarities would not allow us to differentiate them from the linguistic resources used in non-specialised language or general language. Consequently, the claim that a different specialised language exists would make no sense. However, this is not the only possible interpretation of this topic and, as this research group goes on to explain, three different views coexist in this respect:

1) the view of those who consider specialised languages to be codes that can be completely differentiated from general or non-specialised language:

> (...) cada llenguatge d'especialitat seria un mitjà de comunicació relativament independent i, respecte del llenguatge comú (llenguatge global), seria el mateix que el particular és al general; la seva particularitat es trobaria només en la selecció i la disposició dels recursos lingüístics per a un objectiu determinat i no en els recursos lingüístics per ells mateixos. (Hoffmann, 1998: 48) (...) Un llenguatge d'especialitat és el conjunt de tots el recursos lingüístics que s'utilitzen en un àmbit comunicatiu (delimitable pel que fa a l'especialitat) per tal de garantir la comprensió entre les persones que treballen en aquest àmbit. (Hoffmann, 1998: 51)
>
> [(...) each speciality language would be a relatively independent means of communication and, regarding common language (global language), it would be the same as the particular is to the general; its particularity would only lie in the selection and layout of linguistic resources for a particular aim and not in the linguistic resources as such. (Hoffmann, 1998: 48) (...) A speciality language is the set of all the linguistic resources that are used in a communicative field (which can be delimited regarding the speciality) in order to guarantee the comprehension among the people working in that field.] (Hoffmann, 1998: 51)

2) the view of those who believe that the only difference between specialised languages and general language lies in the specialised lexicon used by the former:

> (...) une délimitation rigoureuse entre technique et non-technique se révèle toujours délicate en matière de langage, ce dont témoignent les hésitations des faiseurs de dictionnaires depuis qu'ils opèrent cette discrimination nécessaire. (Quemada, 1978: 1148-1149)
>
> [(…) a rigorous delimitation between technical and non-technical is always revealed on the basis of language, as dictionary authors' doubts show when establishing this necessary discrimination.] (Quemada, 1978: 1148-1149)

3) the view of those who believe that specialised language is a functional register that constitutes a subgroup within the general code of language:

> (...) los lenguajes de especialidad o lenguajes especializados son registros funcionales caracterizados por una temática específica "tratada de determinada manera", o mejor aún, conceptualizada de forma específica. Y todo ello producido en situaciones de comunicación en las que el emisor o los emisores son específicos (personas que han adquirido conscientemente un conocimiento especializado, fundamentalmente los especialistas de una determinada materia), el tipo de situación también lo es (fundamentalmente profesional y siempre dentro de un nivel de formalidad aunque esta formalidad admita grados distintos) y la función comunicativa que les es inherente es la informativa, sin menoscabo que cada producción use estrategias discursivas distintas. (Cabré, 2004: 2)

> [(...) speciality or specialised languages are functional registers characterised by a specific subject matter "dealt with in a certain way" or, even better, conceptualised in a specific way. All of this produced in communicative situations in which the addresser or addressers are specific (people who have consciously acquired a specialised knowledge, mainly specialists in a given subject field), the situation is specific as well (fundamentally professional and always within a level of formality, even when this formality allows different degrees) and their inherent communicative function is informative, without undermining the fact that each production uses different discursive strategies.] (Cabré, 2004: 2)

In this work, and according to what has been stated previously, the third view has been the one adopted to frame the whole research and thus to start characterising the SLA, assuming thus that specialised languages do not constitute a code that is totally or completely differentiated from general language, although, as the IULA (2007 c) states, the expression "languages" is used because of tradition and metaphorical sense. Accordingly, specialised languages are conceived as, or are believed to be, functional varieties of general language, which are, however, differentiated from it by a group of characteristics that are activated when a series of specific communicative circumstances are given: the topic is specialised, the speakers are specialists, the situation is formal and professional, from a discursive point of view some information is trying to be transmitted, and so on.

> En definitiva, se mantiene el término lenguaje, pero utilizado en el sentido de discurso, discurso que se desarrolla en un contexto y con una determinada finalidad comunicativa. De hecho, son estas circunstancias comunicativas las que permiten la actualización de un conjunto de características lingüísticas (entre ellas las léxicas, pero también morfológicas, sintácticas, rutinas discursivas, etc.) que confieren al texto su carácter especializado. Estas características se activan unas en detrimento de otras en función de la situación pragmática y comunicativa. (IULA, 2007 c)
>
> [In short, the term language is maintained but referring to/meaning discourse, a discourse that is given in a context and with a specific communicative purpose. In fact, these communicative circumstances are the ones that make possible the updating of a series of linguistic features (the lexical ones among them, but also the morphological and syntactic ones, discursive routines, etc.) that confer the text its specialised character. These features are activated to the detriment of the others depending on the pragmatic and communicative situation.] (IULA, 2007 c)

To end this discussion, it may be interesting to analyse in some depth the adjective "specialised", which, when applied to language, can be said to have an ambiguous character since it may report two different realities:

1. A language is specialised when it deals with a specialised topic, that is to say, the adjective refers to the specificity of the topic dealt with, which does not belong to the general or common domain. In this way, specialised languages would correspond to those used in the different academic and technical disciplines and professional activities.

According to the IULA (2007 c), this does not imply, however, that a language such as that of chemistry or physics is more specialised than the language of cooking or games. It is more accurate, however, to talk about tendencies and state that a chemistry text, because of its subject matter, is more likely to be specialised than one about cooking, but the topic is not an indispensable condition or a decisive one. Hence, if any scientific content is codified and transmitted without precision and adequacy, without any referential purpose, it becomes non-specialised communication. In the same way, any object from common reality can be dealt with as specialised knowledge if objectively and accurately dealt with.

This means that the context of a cooking text can be dealt with in a highly specialised way and, consequently, can be more specialised than a popularising chemistry text.

2. A language is specialised (or special or specific) in relation to the different communicative factors that it may present with respect to general language. Thus, here the label refers to the possibility of intrinsic variation that a language has.

With respect to this second point, there are a series of variables that may be different and, depending on how they overlap, give rise to different functional registers:

- channel, basis for the differentiation of oral and written languages;
- topic, which allows general and specialised topics to be delimited;
- degree of formality between the speakers;
- the communicative purpose, the basis for establishing the different discursive functions in a text and related with the communicative purpose in each specific case: expound, argue, classify, explain, describe, etc.

Following the IULA (2007 c), according to these variables, a language would be specialised because of its deviation with respect to the standard of communication that would correspond to or coincide with spontaneous oral discourse on a non-specialised topic that is fairly formal and with a basically referential function.

However, before going any further with the general language-specialised language dichotomy, and on the basis of the variables mentioned above, Cabré (2002) refers to the notions of horizontal and vertical variation and contends that there are two basic factors which allow both the characterisation of specialised languages and the creation of a typology of the texts considered to be specialised. These essential factors are subject matter and degree of specialisation:

- Subject matter[8] (horizontal variation). According to this criterion, texts can be typologised depending on the discipline or field of knowledge they deal with. In this sense, Hoffman (1998: 62) states that establishing the communicative spheres and their corresponding speciality languages leads to a given structure [see figure 8] that will be called "horizontal division".
- Degree or level of specialisation or abstraction to be found in the content of a message (vertical variation).

The fundamental criterion according to which texts are typologised vertically is the level of specialisation: according to this criterion, texts have been classified as "highly specialised", "fairly specialised" and "with a low level of specialisation (Cabré, 2002). The correlation between this classification and the kind of texts, according to their knowledge transmission function, gives as a result the distinction between texts that transmit knowledge from specialist to specialist, from specialist to novice, and popularising texts for a public that may be interested in the topic without being a specialist or a novice in the field.

Hoffman (1987, in Cabré, 2002: 31) combines four variables of analysis for the characterisation of specialised texts as illustrated in figure 8:

	Abstraction level	*Linguistic form*	*Field /sphere*	*Participants in the communicative situation*
A	Highest	Artificial symbols for elements and relations	Fundamental and theoretical sciences	Scientist <-> scientist
B	Very high	Artificial symbols for elements; general language for relations (syntax)	Experimental sciences	Scientist (technician) <-> scientist (technician)

8 This criterion, however, has never been as crystal-clear or easy to apply to specialised texts as expected, especially when this speciality concept has widened so much in the last few decades and has surpassed the boundaries of the traditional scientific-technical disciplines (Cabré, 2002).

C	High	Natural language with specialised terminology and highly controlled syntax	Applied sciences and technology	Scientist (technician) <-> scientific-technical manager of the material production
D	Low	Natural language with specialised terminology and relatively free syntax	Material production	scientific-technical manager of the material production <-> masters <-> specialised workers
E	Very low	Natural language with some specialised terms and free syntax	Consumption	Trade representatives <-> consumers <-> consumers

Figure 8. Adaptation of Hoffman's (1987) characterisation of specialised texts according to vertical and horizontal variation.

Thus, by means of horizontal variation, specialised languages can be classified according to the topics dealt with, whereas vertical variation accounts for the fact that each speciality topic or subject matter can be expressed in texts with different levels of specialisation. Therefore, every level would be determined by the degree of abstraction in which a subject matter is presented and by its cognitive adequacy to the addressee and the communicative situation.

Consequently, one may argue that there are different specialised languages depending on the subject matter dealt with and in the way of dealing with them, thus allowing thematically specialised texts to be produced. Moreover, depending on the degree of abstraction that these contents present, texts can show different levels of specialisation. However, specialised languages usually present common features, that is, a homogeneous and general group of features that justify the generalisation and the proposal of an abstract field called "specialised language" that allows the production of specialised discourse.

2.3. Professional and Academic Language (PAL)/ specialised languages: their characterisation

Now that some light has been shed on how language as a whole and language specialisation in particular is understood in the SLA, in the following subsections the key aspects of specialised languages or PAL(s) are analysed in order to provide a comprehensive characterisation of them within the SLA.

2.3.1. General features

According to what has been explained hitherto in previous sections and as summarised by Schröder (1991, in Vargas, 2005), the features that best characterise Professional and Academic Language in general or the different specialised languages in particular are:

- They are not defined in opposition to common or general language (GL). They are sublanguages that belong to a specific field of specialised communication and use the communicative and linguistic resources of a specific linguistic and cultural system. They do so depending on the content, the goal and the communicative situation of the text or discourse.
- They are differentiated according to two variables: a) through a horizontal division in which the different specialised discourses are classified depending on the topic being treated; and b) through a vertical division which pays attention to the different levels of communication produced within the frame of a specialised field;
- They are functional languages whose main objective is to make specialised communication as effective as possible.
- They present and undergo variations over time.
- They are not just stylistic variants or terminological subsystems Because all the basic features that characterise specialised texts must be considered.
- They include the use of non-linguistic elements in the stage of text formulation, so that the concept of specialised communication

would be more precise than the concept of language for specific purposes.

In addition to this, specialised languages present the following traits that allow us to identify and characterise them:

> a) Cuentan con una conceptualización previa bastante controlada;
> b) no suelen admitir (en teoría) nuevas unidades si no están establecidas y conceptualizadas previamente;
> c) no tienen (en teoría) términos polisémicos; la polisemia del léxico común deviene homonimia en el léxico especializado;
> d) la forma escrita de los términos es prioritaria sobre su forma oral;
> e) los términos especializados tienden a tener validez supranacional en muchos casos;
> f) no suelen materializar ni la función emotiva ni la función poética del lenguaje, al menos en el grado en que ocurre en los textos del lenguaje general.
>
> (Cabré, 1993: 131-132)

> a) [They have a rather controlled previous conceptualisation;
> b) they do not normally admit (in theory) new units if they are not previously established and conceptualised;
> c) they do not have (in theory) polysemic terms; the polysemy of common lexicon becomes homonymy in specialised lexicon;
> d) the written form of terms is a priority over its oral form;
> e) specialised terms tend to have supranational validity in many cases;
> f) they do not normally embody the emotive or poetic function of language, at least not in the degree in which it is given in texts from general language.]
>
> (Cabré, 1993: 131-132)

Hoffman (1985) is the author of a series of studies on the specific linguistic characteristics that differentiate specialised texts from non-specialised ones. With this aim in mind, Hoffman (1985) compiled a large corpus with a huge variety of texts from the main European languages. In this way he identified a series of features common to all, or at least to a great number of, specialised languages. Regarding the morphosyntactic traits of these specialised languages, Hoffman (1985: 105ff) summarised the results he obtained as follows:

- The verb loses its specific temporal reference and is nearly always used in the present tense, especially in the third person singular.
- Often the verb is the passive form.
- The verb as a lexical category plays a rather secondary role.
- The noun plays an important role.
- Singular forms are given with more frequency than plural ones.
- The adjective appears quite frequently.

With regard to the lexical features of specialised languages, that is to say, to the structure of specialised lexicon, the boundaries between the two (i.e. specialised and non-specialised vocabulary) admit many different interpretations.

However, in spite of possible interpretations or conceptions of specialised languages, what must be kept as a mainstay is that specialised language is not only limited to and characterised by the use of specialised vocabulary, but also by presenting another series of (mainly syntactic and structural) traits at text level. Nevertheless, if there is something that shapes and characterises specialised discourse, it is the lexical dimension of its specialised texts, that is to say, their terminology, as is explained throughout section 4.

As has already been mentioned, one of the meanings of the adjective "specialised" applied to language has to do with the "different" characteristics that a given language presents with respect or in relation to general language. From all the defining features that specialised languages possess, the most inherent to the very notion of "specialised" is the conceptual control of information (IULA, 2007 c). Accordingly, those with the highest conceptual control are the specialists in the field, and their knowledge is consolidated by means of the discourse they use in order to communicate with other specialists and by means of the terminological works created to cover such necessities (dictionaries, glossaries, vocabularies, etc.)

However, there are many other traits that allow the specialised character of a given discourse to be established, and these traits are very often of a linguistic nature.

2.3.2. Definition and general features of the specialised text

Specialised discourse is normally and advisably given and analysed in the form of specialised texts that are mainly (although not exclusively) characterised by "special" lexical features. Regarding the shaping of specialised languages into specific linguistic instances, that is to say, specialised texts, Hoffmann (1991: 61) defines them as follows:

> The LSP text is the instrument and at the same time the result of a communicative activity carried out in connection with a specified professional (e.g. scientific) activity; it consists of a finite, ordered set of pragmatically, semantically and syntactically coherent/cohesive sentences/utterances (textemes) or units equivalent to them, which, being complex language signs, correspond to complex propositions in human thinking and to complex states of affairs in reality. (Hoffmann, 1991: 61)

From Hoffman's (1991) definition it can be extracted that this kind of texts have a series of specific features of a pragmatic, syntactic and semantic nature that characterise their discourse communities and which give them a specificity within the whole group of texts produced in a language:

- These texts are originated within a situation of communication of specialised knowledge (socio-productive activity).
- They are, at the same time, the tool for undertaking the communication of such specialised knowledge.
- The languages within which specialised texts are produced make use of complex linguistic signs to reflect an objective reality.

Vargas (2005) explains that linguists and, more particularly, terminologists coincide in the view that specialised discourses operate with a particular lexicon responsible for the "representation of reality" (Alcaraz, 2000). Following Varantola (1986), some linguists consider that the only aspect that deserves attention in the analysis of these discourses is terminology, or the group of specialised words of a given field of knowledge or activity. However, even when traditionally the lexical component has been the element that more clearly differentiates specialised languages among them and with respect to general language, the distinctive traits that specialised discourse present do not only comprehend the use of a specific lexicon but also a series of pragmatic-communicative aspects.

Nevertheless, it can be stated that the specific terminology of each speciality field is one of the elements that better "delimits" and differentiates general language from specialised language (Vargas, 2005). As Cabré (1993) states, terminology plays a fundamental role when it comes to characterising specialised language and to classifying the different speciality languages.

Thus, in Alcaraz's (2000: 42) words, "al vocabulario de las 'lenguas de especialidad' se le llama metalenguaje o terminología",[9] which is what the specialised dictionary whose development process is presented here has tried to analyse in the field of ceramics as the paradigmatic (but not the only) aspect of specialised language.

The degree of specialisation of a text varies depending on various factors and it is therefore not enough to just determine what can be considered to be specialised or not – it is also necessary to ascertain the degree of speciality it displays. Vargas (2005) summarises the criteria established by various authors in order to "measure" the level of specialisation of a text, as illustrated in figure 9.

Author /criteria	*Cognitive/Pragmatic criteria*	*Linguistic criteria*
Hoffmann (1998)	Abstraction degree	Number of terms
	Field	Number of symbols
	Participants in the communicative situation	Kind of syntax (+ or - rigid)
Arntz (1995)	Field	Number of terms
		Complexity of the terms
		Frequency and complexity of the paralinguistic communicative elements

9 "The vocabulary of 'speciality languages' is called metalanguage or terminology".

Cabré and Doménech (2001)	Topic perspective	Number of words that form part of an UCE (Unidad de Conocimiento Especializado. In English, USK: Unit of Specialised Knowledge)
		Number of different UCE (Unidad de Conocimiento Especializado. In English, USK: Unit of Specialised Knowledge)
	Addresser/addressee	Presence of synonymy and paraphrasis

Figure 9. English version of Vargas' (2005: 70) synthesis of different criteria for determining the level of specialisation of texts.

According to the premises of the SLA, the best way to structure a work like the one presented here is to consider that the system of communication that interlocutors use in a specific field of knowledge includes, on the one hand, the general language (from which syntax, morphology and part of the lexicon are used) and, on the other hand, the subcode that is characteristic of the speciality field as such, which contains the terminology that is specific to that field. In addition to this, a focus on pragmatic issues (an aspect neglected and even forgotten for many years) is also necessary. If terms, as key components of specialised languages, are considered, for Cabré (1993) they are units that appear in combination with one another and with other units from the common language or from a different speciality area, thus constituting the specialised discourse. Apart from presenting a threefold character (formal, conceptual and functional) that makes them part of a grammatical system, terms (which could be defined as the communication units of specialised discourse) are also pragmatic units of communication and reference, and as such they appear in specific discourses undertaken in specific communication situations and by individuals with different features. This pragmatic perspective is the one which best establishes the differences between common lexicon and terminology to be found in a text. Cabré (1993) refers to the five main features that, in her opinion, allow common lexicon to be differentiated from terminology (see figure 10):

- The basic function proposed.
- The subject matter they deal with.
- The users.
- The communicative situation.
- The kinds of discourse.

COMMON LEXICON		TERMINOLOGY	
Basic function	Conative, emotive, and others	Basic function	Referential
Subject matter	Generic	Subject matter	Specific
Users	General	Users	Specialised
Communicative situation	- Formalised	Communicative situation	+ Formalised
Discourse	General	Discourse	Professioinal and scientific

Figure 10. Cabré's (1993: 22) pragmatic factors to distinguish between common lexicon and terminology.

To sum up, one of the main conclusions to the sections we have seen so far is that in the SLA the boundaries between PAL and general language are not clearly established because, although there are many different features that characterise them, these are not enough to trace a perfectly delimited and neat dividing line (probably because no such line exists). Although I am not going to deal with this phenomenon in depth, this impossibility to delimit the boundaries between a specialised language and general language in an absolute way is made apparent, for instance, on the lexical level, where one may find that the lexical units of a given specialised language or from GL are transferred from one field to another. Although in theory, terminology and general or common words are quite easily differentiated, in practice these differences are not so clearly established, as the discontinuous lines in figure 2 showed and as the "intersection theory" between the two defends.

2.3.3. The construction of specialised discourse: pragmatic, communicative and discursive aspects

Because of the central role played by the communicative aspect of specialised languages in general and teminology in particular within the specialised lexicographical approach, it is important to point out that, in order to have/acquire real cognitive competence and lexical or terminological competence, we need to know the pragmatic variables that may influence every speciality field (IULA, 2007 c). Hence, it is necessary to delve into the aspects presented by each discourse regarding addressees, topics, channels, means, functions, communicative purposes and so on. These aspects are necessary because, as happens in every communicative phenomenon, specialised communication varies with respect to the situation, use and circumstances in which it takes place. All these aspects are important since, according to the Communicative Theory of Terminology (CTT) (see section 4.2), communicative success does not only depend on the correct use of the linguistic resources that define any good specialised discourse but also on the fact that such discourse is pragmatically adequate in the context in which it is given (Cabré, 1999 a).

Thus, in this section the linguistic-discursive aspects that constitute a prototypical specialised discourse have been dealt with. These aspects include:

- It must be conceptually controlled and adapted to the speciality field.
- It must be precise (without ambiguity). A discourse is precise when it conveys knowledge which is also precise and which is the result of a very specific process of conceptualisation of reality, i.e. the one undertaken and validated by consensus among the specialists of a field. In this aspect, the terminology established by specialists plays a fundamental role. Precision has to do with correctness and systematicity and is opposed to the vagueness

that could lead to misinterpretations or cause problems in understanding.

- It must be concise (without redundancy), that is to say, concision is opposed to informative redundancy, or additional information which does not add any content, so that ideas are presented without rhetorical artifices, thus expressing what is relevant and doing so in a straightforward, concise way.
- It must be objective as regards the necessary degree of depersonalisation. Hence, the addresser must try to separate him or herself from what is being said, using all the necessary linguistic resources to achieve this.
- It must be systematic (with a control of denominative variation) and use the most adequate or accurate denominative forms. The degree of denominative variation will depend on the level of specialisation and on the discursive purposes of each text.

Bearing this in mind, the next section deals with the most prototypical aspect of specialised languages – terminology – whose study and correct characterisation within dictionaries are one of the mainstays of the SLA.

2.3.4. Terminology as the main articulator of specialised discourse

Obviously, terminology is the most evident, visible and easily "palpable" characteristic of specialised discourses (or, if preferred, of specialised languages or texts). Researchers in the IULA (2007 b) contend that specialised lexicon is a key element that allows the different specialised discourses to be characterised. This is so since terms are, on most occasions, the best way to identify a speciality area or to distinguish among different domains since terms represent concepts and the acquisition of the key concepts of a subject matter implies, in the long run, the command (total or partial) of this subject matter.

Going a little bit deeper into this topic, it can be said that terminology is a fundamental element in the study of specialised languages, that is to say, a key issue for the characterisation of specialised discourse, and there are three main reasons for this:

1) Terms are perfectly delimited by a community of specialists, who are the people communicating and producing the discourses of a speciality field.
2) Terms are the units that best concentrate specialised knowledge and the ones that best represent and transfer the concepts (the content) of a speciality.
3) From a semantic and conceptual point of view, terms are the linguistic elements that best guarantee the precision required in every specialised communication, that is, the exchange of knowledge among the members of a professional community, no matter what their source language may be.

Hence, as can be deduced, not only does terminology guarantee the acquisition of knowledge and the concepts of the speciality field, but it also plays a crucial role in the transfer of knowledge and in the discursive productions of the speciality:

However, to gain a correct understanding of the cognitive structure of a text or the functioning of terminology, it is not enough to study terms in isolation. This is the reason why three important aspects must be included in the study of terminology:

1) The conceptual relations existing between the terminological units.

In terminology, it is important to account for not only isolated terms but for the structure and conceptual relations among them. This is useful because in real communication, that is, in a text or discourse from a speciality area, terms (understood as cognitive knots) are linked by different relations which make them form an interrelated cognitive whole.

As explained in section 8.3, these relations have been established for the dictionary of industrial ceramics mainly by creating the field diagram of the domain.

2) The morphological aspects of terminological units.

> Las unidades terminológicas presentan diferentes estructuras que corresponden a determinados procesos de formación morfológica: las composiciones cultas en medicina, cierto tipo de sufijación en química, etc. (IULA, 2007 a)

[Terminological units present different structures that correspond to certain processes of morphological formation: learned formations in medicine, certain kinds of suffixation in chemistry, etc.] (IULA, 2007 a)

This aspect is particularly interesting in this work if we consider that the user of the dictionary may benefit from it and more easily understand the semantics of many terminological units as well as use this morphological knowledge in the future for the semantic decoding of new terms (neologisms), especially in a constantly changing and evolving field like the one considered here.

3) Syntactic combinatorial aspects of the terminological units.

As happens with general language, in speciality contexts there are phenomena involving the restricted combination of lexical units (IULA, 2007 b). Hence, although it is often not impossible to decode the meaning of the combination from the sum of the meanings of its components, a non-specialist is frequently unaware of the units that must be used within the specialised discourse to express a given meaning. Closely related to this is the notion of "collocation" – in ts widest sense meaning words in habitual company – a key aspect in the dictionary entries elaborated in this research and a fundamental piece of information to be included in them according to the active use of language the SLA tries to foster.

Another key aspect for the correct understanding and use of terminology is what has been called in studies on the didactics of specialised languages "subtechnical lexicon", which is opposed to purely technical lexicon in the sense that the latter is the exclusive lexicon of each specialised discourse. In fact, the best way to understand the phenomenon of subtechnical lexicon is to acknowledge that each field has a terminology that is exclusive of it and a terminology which is shared with other specialities or with general language. In fact, as Vangehuchten (2003) states, in the field of didactics applied to the teaching of language for specific purposes it seems as if the belief exists that teaching needs to devote more time to the so called subtechnical lexicon than to technical lexicon as such, the latter being considered as monosemic and universal.

As has already been mentioned, according to the *continuum* view of language supported here, language presents different degrees of specialisation and subtechnical lexicon is a clear example of this. Its inclusion in a specialised lexicographical work is necessary since subtechnical lexical units do also form part of the linguistic characterisation of the domain and are necessary for the user in order to understand other more technical LU. The next chapter describes the kind of method adopted by the SLA in order to obtain the real, terminological data, both technical and subtechnical, for its specialised lexicographical works, corpus linguistics.

Knowledge of the world is only to be acquired in the world, and not in a closet.
Lord Chesterfield

3. Corpus linguistics

3.1. Corpus linguistics: an empirical approach to the description and analysis of language in use

Every science aiming at the formulation and rejection or corroboration of hypotheses to account for certain aspects of reality must be strongly based on the data that this same reality offers. This kind of data is commonly known in natural sciences as empirical data and in spite of its (at least apparently) more scientific nature, human sciences can also take them as their foundation. These empirical data come from and reflect the aspect of reality they are trying to describe, thus making the validation or the rejection of hypotheses possible. In this light, it seems coherent to think that those studies – like this one – aimed at explaining or showing a portion of reality are better undertaken if they set out from empirical data which reflect and form part of this very same reality. Therefore, linguistics needs elements of true reference as much as natural sciences do in order to provide a real and realistic view of language and to confirm hypotheses about language, its use and also to show its behaviour in context. Corpora are essential to the SLA because of the quality, objective and exploitable data they provide but in order to progressively delve into this issue, I have first introduced the theoretical hints necessary to understand the way this research has been approached as a whole from corpus linguistics. Corpus linguistics is a discipline whose importance and influence in linguistic studies is constantly increasing and developing nowadays. Its use is being extended to a wide range of linguistic disciplines and it is characterised by two basic aspects (Vargas, 2005): a) the aforementioned empirical study of language in use with the aim of describing it, and b) the use of a computer for data storage and analysis, as explained in detail in section 3.2.3.

In the elaboration of a specialised lexicographical work like the one here described, the point of departure is the identification and subsequent characterisation of the specialised lexical units (terms) that shape the speciality field of the ceramic industrial district and to present them taking into account their communicative dimension of use (pragmatic aspects and real contexts). As reality shows, only a good corpus can provide us with these data and only through it can all the terminological features that must be known for effective, accurate and proper communication in this speciality field be determined. The corpus used in this study has allowed us to identify the terms belonging to the speciality domain analysed, and also to detect their frequencies of use, their most characteristic collocations and the way in which these specialised lexical units or terminological units[10] are used in real communication and shape the speciality field of industrial ceramics.

Consequently, the decision to adopt a corpus-based approach in this research instead of another approach to linguistic analysis was mainly due to the scope and reliability of the analyses that corpus-linguistics offers because of its intrinsic characteristics, which were specified by Biber, Conrad and Reppen (1998) as the fact that:

- It uses a large and principled collection of natural texts (the "corpus"), as the basis for the analysis.
- It is empirical, so that it allows the analysis of actual patterns of language use in natural texts.
- It makes extensive use of computers for analysis, using both automatic and interactive techniques that facilitate and make the work more reliable.
- It depends on both quantitative and qualitative analytical techniques.

Terminology benefits greatly from the use of linguistic corpora since a corpus is conceived as a more powerful methodology from the

10 Also called UCE (*Unidad de Conocimiento Especializado*) in Cabré and Estopà's (2002) terms and USK (Unit of Specialised Knowledge) in my English adaptation of their denomination.

point of view of the scientific method, because it is open to objective verification of results (Leech, 1992). Hence, terminology (and even more specialised lexicography) benefits from the information that a corpus may provide when it comes to elaborating terminographical applications like dictionaries. Thanks to the use of corpora, the task of discovering neologisms or words with a low frequency of use, observing the different meanings a lexical form may have, detecting collocations or linguistic patterns and obtaining real examples of use, is easier and much more feasible and reliable.

What can be deduced from previous information is that there is a constant necessity to work with authentic texts that allow the terminographer to study the real use made of language both in oral and written discourse, especially if we consider the increasing influence and importance granted to contextual and pragmatic factors in current linguistic studies. However, as is explained in subsequent sections, although the statistical and empirical analysis of the language had started even before the 1950s and had to go through many upheavals until it could continue to spread and grow, with the astonishing developments in computer science, it is living its "golden age". Thanks to this positive evolution, the management of the data contained in corpora has become a more feasible task, from which very significant results can be obtained. In this way, although technological advancements have substantially changed for the better the way of approaching corpus linguistics and the benefits coming directly from it (statistical and empirical analysis of the language), it can be stated that the essence of this kind of research remains faithful to that with which it started more than half a century ago.

This tendency of analysing language in context was originated in the views of authors prior to the advent of corpus linguistics as such. Firth (1935: 38), for instance, put forward the notion that data had to be extracted from "speech sequences operating in contexts of situation which are typical, recurrent, and repeatedly observable". Nearly 60 years later and in the same way, Stubbs (1993: 2) added certain elements to this statement and systematised it in a principle (the second one of the eight he proposes): "Language should be studied in actual, attested, authentic instances of use, not as intuitive, invented, isolated sentences".

This second principle leads easily onto the third of Stubb's (1993: 3) principles, which states that "the unit of study must be the whole text". As is observed throughout section 7.3, all these principles and views on which corpus linguistics is grounded are directly related with the conception and elaboration of active dictionaries like the one we have developed throughout this study.

However, like almost any discipline or approach, corpus linguistics is not an instance of universal agreement and has also encountered "enemies" who have proclaimed its lacks and failures, Chomsky (1964, 1965 and 1968) being the most salient opponent to early corpus linguistics.

Nevertheless, in spite of Chomsky's reservations, experience shows every day that using samples of the actual language employed in naturally occurring texts is highly beneficial, in the specific case of this study, for determining the kind of linguistic-terminological needs of the prospective users of the specialised dictionary of ceramics terminology, and therefore for selecting the terms to be included in it and the way of presenting them. This can also be coherently associated with the aim of creating an active dictionary intended at providing the user with all the information necessary in real-world communication, emphasising not so much other more theoretical aspects but those more directly related with real and true users' demands:

> Corpus-linguistics shows how an analysis of language use goes beyond traditional grammatical description to ask why the language should have multiple structures that are so similar in their grammatical function and meaning.
> Until recently many investigations of language use were either unfeasible or simply impossible. The corpus-based approach, however, provides a means of handling large amounts of language and keeping track of many contextual factors at the same time. It therefore has opened the way to a multitude of new investigations of language use. (Biber, Conrad and Reppen, 1998: 3)

Corpus linguistics is thus presented in this book as the best way to determine language use and to create tools (like the dictionary of ceramics terminology) that make effective communication possible even in highly specialised contexts like the one under study. Despite this, it is not a simple task, since large amounts of language collected from many sources have had to be analysed in order to make sure that conclusions were not wrongly based on the idiosyncrasies of just a few speakers. This is probably the most important strength and, at the same time, the most difficult-to-avoid weakness in corpus linguistics. Comprehensive studies of use require the empirical analysis of large databases extracted from authentic texts (like the ones a corpus-based approach offers) since comprehensive studies of use cannot rely on intuition, anecdotal evidence or small samples. In this respect, in the section devoted to criteria for corpus design and compilation (section 8.2.1) the aspects considered for selecting a representative corpus of the field of ceramics have been specified.

There are many areas of linguistics that can be addressed with the corpus-based approach. In the particular case of specialised lexicography (or its previous "stadium" terminography), and more specifically for "specialised dictionary makers", the use of corpora makes it possible to examine the linguistic and non-linguistic associations of a given word as well as to include information about the most common uses, frequency of related words, collocates/collocations-phraseological units, and the contexts in which words and meanings are most commonly found. In addition to this, grammatical structures can also be analysed from the perspective of their use by means of corpus-based techniques. The enormous development this has represented in modern lexicography can be easily understood if we think about the past, in which "dictionary makers" generally limited, or had to limit, their task to identifying the possible meanings of a word. In order to better illustrate these facts, part of the information that can be obtained from the analysis of the corpus this study is based on is explained in more detail in the second part of this book.

3.2. A historical overview on the evolution of language study: the rise of corpus linguistics

The first time the term *corpus linguistics* as such appears in the linguistic arena was during the 1980s, after the first generation of electronic[11] corpora. This term aims to cover a new approach in linguistics, i.e. the study of large quantities of text through computer tools. As Leech (1992: 105) puts it:

> The term "corpus linguistics" made only occasional appearances until the publication of a book of that title [Corpus Linguistics: recent Developments in the Use of Computer Corpora in English Language Research] edited by Aarts and Meijs (1984).

In a brief and simple way, Corpus Linguistics refers to those linguistic studies that are mainly based on the analysis of textual corpora (Pérez, 2002), but this definition lacks certain aspects that can be successfully completed with the help of other authors' definitions. According to Sinclair (1991: 171), "(…) a corpus is a collection of naturally-occurring language text, chosen to characterise a state or variety of a language". Some years later, Sinclair (1996: 4) offered another definition of corpus which constitutes a step forward in the conception of this discipline: "a collection of pieces of language that are selected and ordered according to explicit linguistic criteria in order to be used as a sample of the language". However, these definitions still lack certain aspects underlying the work undertaken within corpus linguistics nowadays, something that Sanchez's (1995) definition of corpus completes with the inclusion of the computer component:

> Un corpus lingüístico es un conjunto de datos lingüísticos (pertenecientes al uso oral o escrito de la lengua, o ambos) sistematizados según determinados criterios suficientemente extensos (…) de manera que sean representativos del

11 The adjective "electronic" is not really necessary nowadays for referring to or to make explicit this characteristic of a corpus since it is implicit in the modern concept of corpus. However, it should be borne in mind that "electronic" means "computerised".

> total del uso lingüístico o de algunos de sus ámbitos, y dispuestos de tal modo que puedan ser procesados mediante ordenador con el fin de obtener resultados varios y útiles para la descripción y el análisis. (Sánchez *et al.*, 1995: 8-9)
>
> [A linguistic corpus is a group of linguistic data (belonging to the oral or written use of language, or both) systematised according to certain criteria wide enough (…) so that it is representative of the linguistic use as a whole or of some of its fields and structured in such a way that can be processed by means of the computer with the aim of obtaining various and useful results for description and analysis.] (Sánchez *et al.*, 1995: 8-9)

Indeed, the technological dimension of corpora nowadays cannot be forgotten in the definition of corpus. In fact, working with large corpora (some of which can reach several million words) using only manual methods is an altogether unrealistic feat today. In this sense, Hunston (2002: 2) also adds a technological dimension to the traditional concept of corpus and affirms that corpora are "collections of texts (or parts of texts) that are stored and accessed electronically".

In spite of this, the second definition of corpus provided by Sinclair (1996) above can be considered to be the official one, since it has been adopted by EAGLES (European Advisory Group on Language Engineering Standard). In broad terms (leaving aside the fact that it does not include the computer element) Sinclair's (1996) definition is highly representative and complete, since it contains some fundamental aspects that must be included in any definition of corpus for it to be a complete and comprehensive one. Two of these essential features are the fact that the texts that form part of a corpus must belong to real situations (pieces of real discourse and consequently containing real language) and their inclusion in the corpus must be determined by a series of explicit linguistic criteria aimed at ensuring that these texts can be used as representative samples of a language. Nevertheless, in spite of the benefits that corpus linguistics presents at first sight, it is also true that its way through history has not been as easy as might be thought. In the following subsections a global view of the evolution of corpus linguistics has been provided in order to better understand the current (rather privileged, I would say) situation of corpus linguistics. Corpus linguistics has evolved in three different stages, in each of which its role has also been radically different: early corpus linguistics, the advent of its main critic, Noam Chomsky, and a revival era closely related to ICT[12] whose plenitude has been reached nowadays with the huge number of possibilities offered for the exploitation of corpora.

3.2.1. Early corpus linguistics

"Early corpus linguistics" is the term used by McEnery and Wilson (2001) to describe these linguistic studies before the advent of Chomsky, that is to say, corpus-based studies prior to 1950.

The idea of using real examples and studying the language in context is not new at all. Lexicographers, for instance, have been gathering textual quotations for a long time and, already in the 1950s, linguists like Jespersen or Harris in America openly supported this way of approaching the study of a language. Even earlier, field linguists like Boas (1940), who studied American-Indian languages, and later linguists from the structuralist tradition used a corpus-based methodology (McEnery and Wilson, 2001), although the term "corpus linguistics" as such was not yet used at the time. However, the first works that originated what is known nowadays as corpus linguistics as such were those of Firth (1935) in Great Britain, followed by those undertaken by his disciples Halliday and Sinclair. Firth (1935) was first influenced by the work of the English ethnologist Malinowski (1923), who observed through his studies how language could not be understood outside the culture and the social context of the statement. This observation originated the appearance of the term *context of situation*,[13] which, in Firth's (1935: 37) words, is the means through which meaning is achieved: "the complete meaning of a word is always contextual, and no study of meaning apart from a complete context can be taken seriously".

In order to show a wider and more complete panorama of early corpus linguistics it may be interesting to also provide a brief overview of some other interesting and specific investigations in the arena of corpus-based studies predating 1950. Significantly, language acquisition

12 Information and Communication Technologies (ICT); in Spanish TIC (*Tecnologías de la Información y la Comunicación*).

13 This term refers to "the environment of the text" (Halliday and Hassan, 1985: 5) and is the leitmotiv of the COBUILD dictionaries.

in children, for instance, was roughly studied back in the years between 1876 and 1926 through the analysis of carefully compiled and composed parental diaries which gathered and recorded children's locutions. Even nowadays, things have not changed that much in this respect and it is not strange to find diary studies for language acquisition research. In this way, these "primitive corpora" can be said to constitute the genesis of corpus studies applied to, for instance, acquisitional issues, such as the ones undertaken by Ingram (1978). In this same field, after this period of diary studies, corpora compilation and collection diversified giving way to the appearance of large sample studies, mainly in the period between 1927 and 1957, in which corpora were collected from a large number of children with the aim of contributing to language acquisition research by establishing norms of development.

Another interesting corpus-based study predating 1950 was that dealing with spelling conventions, in which Kading (1897) made use of an 11-million-word corpus of German to "collocate frequency distributions of letters and sequences of letters in German" (McEnery and Wilson, 2001). If we consider the technical media available at the time, the size of the corpus is impressive (it is a really large and impressive corpus even nowadays) and is not far at all from modern corpora in terms of size.

The field of foreign language pedagogy was also studied by means of corpus-based studies. Linguists such as Fries and Traver (1940) and Bongers (1947) used corpora with such aims in mind. In fact, as Kennedy (1992) noted, the link between corpus and second language pedagogy in the early half of the 20th century was so strong that vocabulary lists for foreign learners were often extracted or derived from corpora.

3.2.2. Corpus linguistics questioned: the advent of Noam Chomsky

If "early corpus linguistics" is the term used to refer to this linguistic discipline before the advent of Noam Chomsky, the key question is why and how this author constituted such a turning point in linguistics at the time. This was so mainly because he changed the empirical direction linguistics was adopting with early corpus linguistics towards what has been called "rationalism". He was the main precursor of this change which, moreover and surprisingly, was undertaken in a relatively short period of time and in which he invalidated and denied the action and value of corpus linguistics as a reliable source for extracting linguistic evidence and making linguistic enquiries. Hence, although corpus linguistics was becoming increasingly accepted and used in early corpus linguistics, that is to say, before the advent of Chomsky, it is a fact that it experimented a period (in the 60s and 70s) in which this acceptance was not so because at that time the linguistics defended by Chomsky was the preferred trend in the linguistic panorama.

Therefore, Noam Chomsky, the main representative of Generativism, was the linguist who spoke out most strongly against the use of textual corpora in linguistic research and the one who endangered its development and prevalence the most. The main reason he alleged for introducing such a radical change in the evolution that linguistics was experimenting was that, according to his views, the corpus could never be a useful tool for the linguist since the linguist must seek to model language competence rather than performance (Chomsky, 1965 in McEnery and Wilson, 2001).

In order to understand better the multiple shortcomings Chomsky found in corpus linguistics, it may be necessary to make explicit what is meant by "competence" and "performance". Competence can be described as the tacit, internalised knowledge of a language a speaker has, whereas "performance" is considered to be the "material", external evidence of such competence and the usage made of it on particular occasions when factors other than linguistic ones may affect its forms. For Chomsky (1965), competence is the key factor for explaining, characterising and, hence, analysing a speaker's knowledge of a language, whereas performance is just a minor issue to consider, a poor aspect of language if compared with the potential offered by competence. Thus, the main and initial criticism Chomsky exerted over corpus linguistics was on the basis that "a corpus is by its very nature a collection of externalised utterances – it is performance data and is therefore a poor guide for modelling linguistic competence" (Chomsky, 1965 in McEnery and Wilson, 2001) and this is so because there are many factors that can alter the way we speak (performance) on any particular occasion, i.e. speaking after drinking too much.

Chomsky made further criticisms on the work of early corpus linguistics on the basis of two fundamental, although flawed, assumptions, i.e. for early corpus linguists, the sentences of a natural language were finite and could be collected and enumerated.

Hence, in its early years "linguists ... regarded the corpus as the sole explicandum of linguistics" (Leech, 1991 in McEnery and Wilson, 2001), thus considering such a corpus as the unique source of evidence for a new linguistic theory, Chomsky claimed that the number of sentences in a natural language is not just and merely arbitrarily large, but potentially infinite since the total number of combinatorial choices (both lexical and syntactic) to be made when producing a sentence allow the creation of an infinite number of them. Hence, early generativist trends departed from the idea that the number of statements of a language is non-finite, so that the existence of a finite data repertoire that was adequate enough to explain all the mechanisms of linguistic production was not possible. In Chomsky's (1965: 4) words "linguistic theory is mentalistic, since it is concerned with discovering the mental reality underlying actual behaviour". In this way, a rationalist approach with an introspective basis was preferred, according to which an ideal speaker with a linguistic competence that allows him/her to produce statements in his/her language was the best way to describe language. Following Vargas (2005), for Chomsky (1965), the object of study of linguistic investigation is the "underlying mental reality" (Alcaraz, 1990: 90) and so he does not give any importance to observation, invalidating the corpus as a source of true data in linguistic research. In Chomsky's (1965) view, the linguist must aim at the creation of theoretical models that explain linguistic competence, not performance (contrary to what Halliday and Sinclair propose).

However, it would not be fair either to oversimplify the issue by stating as a general claim that every single linguist working with corpus linguistics agreed with the two flawed statements discussed above. Although Harris (1951) is probably the most characteristic defender of these views of early corpus linguistics, according to which the sentences in a natural language had a finite nature that meant they could be collected and enumerated, other linguists like Hocket (1948) suggested that "the purpose of the linguist working in the structuralist tradition "is not simply to account for utterances which comprise his corpus" but rather to "account for utterances which are not in his corpus at a given time" (Leech, 1991 in McEnery and Wilson, 2001).

In this sense, Chomsky's criticism to early corpus linguistics is coherent and well-grounded since a number of linguistic phenomena corroborate the non-finite nature of language: centre embedding, for instance can give rise to an infinite number of sentences of this sort: "the child that killed the bird that ate the fly that saw the cat…". Accordingly and in Chomsky's views, the only way to provide a complete account for the grammar of a language is through the description of its rules, which in the case of syntactic ones are considered to be finite by Chomsky even when they can and in fact do give way to an infinite number of sentences.

In addition to this, Chomsky also put forward the disregarded value assigned to introspection as another of its main criticisms to corpus linguistics. Chomsky based such criticism on a fact as simple as: if our finite corpus does not contain the sentence *he shines Tony books*, on what basis can we conclude that it is ungrammatical if, in addition, there may be sentences in the corpus such as *he gives Tony books, he lends Tony books* or *he owes Tony books*, which suggest that it is grammatically correct and acceptable? (McEnery and Wilson, 2001). Hence, although early corpus linguistics denied its use, introspection seems to be the best way to get to grips with cases of this nature. Even in the case of a common linguistic phenomenon like ambiguity, the most successful way to disambiguate misleading structures seems to be not only the observation of physical form but the consideration of introspective judgements and knowledge (the terminologist's intuition is a key factor for term extraction and analysis). McEnery and Wilson (2001) propose the following example containing ambiguous structures in order to illustrate how it is only through introspection (speakers' reflections and intuitions of the language) that we know that Fido is the name of a dog so that it is Fido the one eating the dog food and Tony the one who reads the book:

> Tony and Fido sat down – he read a book of recipes
> Tony and Fido sat down – he ate a can of dog food

Hence, for Chomsky, at times the very same intuition the speakers of a language possess can save time and work, making it unnecessary to search in a corpus if we delve into our own linguistic competence.

Apart from the aspects earlier, there are some other aspects of corpus linguistics that have also been criticised: its probabilistic view of language, the technique used and the status of corpus linguistics as an independent discipline or as a methodology. At this point, in order to provide a brief summary of the main points that have been mentioned to distinguish between Corpus Linguistics and Generativism, Vargas' (2005) summary of the topic has been included in figure 11:

	Corpus Linguistics	Generativism
Method	EMPIRICISM	RATIONALISM
Linguistic data	CORPUS	INTUITION
Object of study	PERFORMANCE	COMPETENCE

Figure 11. Adapted from Vargas (2005). *Basic differences between Corpus Linguistics and Generativism.*

Taking up again what has already been mentioned at the beginning of this section, on the one hand, Corpus Linguistics uses an empiricist method consisting in the construction of knowledge through experience. From a linguistic point of view, this implies giving prevalence to the observation of the linguistic data in real-use situations, these data being gathered in the form of a corpus. On the other hand, however, Generativism imposes rationalism as the method that should lead scientific investigations related to language. This rationalism claims that knowledge comes from principles established *a priori*. According to this paradigm, language is observed through the "intuitive and introspective" judgements (Alcaraz, 1990) of the researcher, who, at the same time, will be the one in charge of explaining the linguistic intuitions that every speaker has about his/her language (Levin, 1963).

In spite of the prominent role played by Chomsky against corpus linguistics, which led him to be considered as the "architect" of the crisis it suffered at the time, there were other linguists who also showed their rejection of it. Although Chomsky's criticisms were more theoretical, there were also problems of the practicality of corpus linguistics, which linguists like Abercrombie (1963) summarised with the definition of the corpus-based approach as a sum of "pseudo-procedures". In order to understand this criticism better, McEnery and Wilson (2001) ask their readers to imagine searching through Kading's (1879) 11-million-word corpus with the sole help of their eyes. Obviously, analysing an 11-million-word corpus with purely human means is prohibitively time-consuming and exhausting, as well as error-prone and expensive, so that Abercrombie's criticism seems to have a sensible and coherent basis after all. It is a fact that early corpus linguistics required a series of data processing abilities which, although available nowadays thanks to technology, did not exist at that time.

Consequently, the impact these criticisms made on corpus-linguistics inflicted such an influential, immediate and profound "wound" that corpus linguistics was almost abandoned in the 1950s, though it never completely disappeared or died.

3.2.3. The revival of corpus linguistics: Chomsky questioned and the fundamental role of computer technology in corpus analysis

In spite of the harmful repercussion Chomsky's criticisms had on corpus linguistics, not all corpus-based work stopped with Chomsky's advent. In fields such as language acquisition the gathering and observation of naturally occurring evidence remained the dominant approach to the field since, obviously, in the case of children who were just a few months old, it would be almost impossible to make them express their introspective judgements to the linguist/psychologist; according to McEnery and Wilson (2001) "introspective judgements are only available to us when our meta-linguistic awareness has developed", which is not the case with small children. In the case of phonetics, naturally observed data were also the dominant source of evidence ahead of introspections of any kind. In this sense it is also significant that even Chomsky (1964) recognised the importance of performance data as a source of evidence for language acquisition studies.

Hence, introspective data also present weak points, which make the benefits that Chomsky claimed so strongly for (in detriment of corpus data) not so crystal-clear. Thus, following McEnery and Wilson (2001), Chomsky's proposal of introspective data prevalence was not ideal either since:

1) Naturally occurring data is observable and verifiable by everyone. Introspective judgements are unobservable, and therefore much more difficult to verify.
2) Introspective data is artificial. Sampson (1992) argues that the type of sentence analysed by the introspective linguist is a long way from the type of evidence

we tend to see typically occurring in a corpus. By artificially manipulating the informant, we artificially manipulate the data itself.

3) Human beings have only the vaguest notion of the frequency of a construct or a word. Corpora are sources of quantitative information beyond comparison. However, frequency-based data is not available via introspective means.

In this light, the benefits of corpus data started to become clearer again and corpus linguistics re-emerged with renewed strength and fewer flaws. In this regard:

1. A corpus is open to the objective verification of results, which makes it a more powerful methodology, especially from the point of view of the scientific method (Leech 1992).

2. Contrary to what Chomsky argued – that is to say, that language production (performance) was a poor reflection of language competence – Labov (1969) pointed out the grammatical character of the majority of utterances in all contexts. As McEnery and Wilson (2001) put it, "we are not saying that all sentences in a corpus are grammatically acceptable, but it seems probable that Chomsky's (1968: 88) claim that performance data is 'degenerate' is an exaggeration".

3. In spite of Chomsky's rejection, quantitative data has proved to be useful to linguistics. Many studies undertaken years ago such as Svartvik's (1996) study of passivisation already relied on quantitative data extracted from corpora.

4. Although Abercrombie's appreciation of the time-consuming, expensive and error-prone nature of corpus linguistics was quite realistic in early corpus linguistics, this is no longer so thanks to the technological development the field has undergone in recent times. Nowadays, the advancement of computer science has given way to powerful computer aids and software capable of carrying out work with no errors and processing large corpora in just a few seconds.

Hence, although it must be acknowledged that early corpus linguistics presented many failures and shortcomings that led to its being questioned by authors like Chomsky, it is also true that many of Chomsky's appreciations can also be tinged and questioned.

Chomsky's impact on linguistics has been enormous and the influence his views had on corpus linguistics is undeniable. However, as has been stated at the beginning of this section, corpus linguistics was never entirely abandoned in the 1950s (and neither did it suddenly and spontaneously re-appear in the 1980s – it was more of a process). There were a series of important pioneer corpus linguists who went on with their research during the "Chomskian influx years"; Quirk (1960), for example, started his ambitious Survey of English Usage (SEU) in 1961 and in that same year Francis and Kucera began to work (the process took them 20 years) on the famous Brown Corpus. The same happened with the already-mentioned work undertaken by Svartvik in 1975, the purpose of which was to construct the London-Lund corpus. Hence, although these linguists and their corpus-based works were in a minority situation at the time (the approach used for undertaking their research being almost an exception), it is also true that they never let corpus linguistics completely disappear and thanks to them, and to others who followed their lead afterwards, corpus linguistics managed to revive in subsequent years.

Despite this, the "boom" experimented by corpus linguistics has been relatively recent and mainly caused by the technological advancements experimented by computer science, which can be considered the mainstay of corpus linguistics: "the availability of the computerised corpus and the wider availability of institutional and private computing facilities do seem to have provided a spur to the revival of corpus linguistics" (McEnery and Wilson, 2001).

In the late 70s and early 80s, personal computers became a relatively easy-access tool and it was then that the use of corpora, together with computer tools for their processing and exploitation, merged and began to develop towards the boom we know today. This new technological context made an important contribution to the revival of corpus linguistics after the Generativists' attacks, since "the resurgence of corpus linguistics can be measured in terms of the increasing power of computers and of the exponentially increasing size of corpora" (Leech, 1991: 9-10).

Therefore, corpus linguistics is directly and intrinsically connected with computer technology and benefits from its development and evolution, especially due to the large amounts of data to be dealt with, which would be difficult if not impossible to handle with only traditional/manual methods.

Looking into this in more detail, the connection between computers and the compilation and creation of large corpora has been a key element for overcoming some of the theoretical and practical criticism targeted towards corpus linguistics. This link has even originated the already mentioned fact that nowadays the term "corpus linguistics" implicitly or explicitly contains the characteristic of being computer-readable as a defining trait. In this respect, it would be enough to mention again Hunston's (2002) or Sánchez's (1995) definitions of the concept of corpus (see section 3.2), which incorporate a technological dimension that makes of corpora collections of texts (or parts of texts) that are stored and accessed electronically.

Regarding the general contributions of computer science to corpus linguistics in general and to the methodology used in this research in particular, it is important to highlight the influence and advantages with which it contributes to almost any stage in the compilation and management of terminologies. The automatic analysis of texts and the possibility of dealing effectively with huge amounts of information have changed the basis of terminological compilation and terminographical/specialised lexicographical analysis for the better. Hence, the possibility of analysing huge amounts of data has also modified the conception and management of terminological work. In fact, computer science offers resources and tools that make the most repetitive tasks (data search, retrieval and treatment, etc.) much easier, quicker, and even more accurate in almost every stage of a terminological work, but this has been dealt with in more detail in section 5.2, devoted to *terminotics*.

Electronic corpora have thus become an essential means for the investigation of the structure of the language in use, for proving linguistic hypotheses, for knowing the different meanings that words acquire depending on the context in which they appear, and for developing technologies for the processing of natural language (Vargas, 2005). They are thus absolutely crucial in the SLA.

Accordingly, one of the characteristics of modern corpus-based analysis is its extensive use of computers for undertaking such analyses; several of the advantages of this approach stem from the fact that this use of computers allows the linguistic researcher to quickly identify and analyse complex patterns of language use, while at the same time allowing an impressive amount of data storage. Apart from this, computers can also be used interactively, allowing the human specialist to make difficult linguistic judgements or to make decisions while the computer saves the data. Moreover, computers provide reliable and consistent analyses that are not affected by human traits such as changing one's mind or getting tired.

Nowadays, an empirical approach to language would be unfeasible in its wider instances without the technological developments that allow the creation and exploitation of increasingly extensive and complex corpora. Therefore, in this work, the kind of corpus used has been, according to Rafel and Soler (2003), an automated one, that is, a corpus that has been codified in a standard and homogeneous way for different tasks of information retrieval.

The corpora used before computers were introduced were limited by a series of circumstances arising directly from the manual treatment of the information, namely, the lack of sistematicity in the treatment of information, the participation of non-specialists in the tasks of corpus constitution (resulting in errors of analysis and classification of the linguistic data) and the use of intuitive criteria. However,

> La utilización del ordenador permite una mayor sistematicidad en el tratamiento de grandes volúmenes de datos, de manera que no es necesario recurrir a ciertos tratamientos manuales ni a la aplicación de criterios intuitivos que pueden desviar o enmascarar los datos que se desean estudiar.
> La introducción de los medios informáticos en la constitución, el procesamiento y la explotación de corpus ha permitido tratar grandes volúmenes de información de una manera sistemática y objetiva, sin la intervención de factores externos que no tienen que formar parte de la investigación, como por ejemplo la intuición del lingüista. (Rafel and Soler 2003: 47)
>
> [The use of computers allows the user to obtain a greater systematicity in the treatment of big amounts of data so that it is not necessary to resort to manual treatment or to the application of intuitive criteria that may 'disguise' the data under study.

> The introduction of computer media for the compilation, processing and exploitation of corpora has allowed the user to deal with great amounts of information in a systematic and objective way, without the influence of external factors that must not be a part of the research, such as the linguist's intuition.] (Rafel and Soler 2003: 47)

Consequently, "whatever philosophical advantages we may eventually see in a corpus, it is the computer which allows us to exploit corpora on a large scale with speed and accuracy" (McEnery and Wilson, 2001). In addition, as is put forward in the section devoted to method, the use of computer tools is inherent to the SLA and the only way of adequately retrieving and processing the large amounts of data necessary for correctly characterising specialised lexical units in dictionary entries.

As has already been mentioned and as is explained in detail in subsequent sections, nowadays, the term *corpus* is almost a synonym of the term "electronic corpus" or "computer-readable corpus". Such a quasi-equivalent relationship is mainly due to the crucial role played by computer technology for corpora processing and analysis nowadays. In comparison to a human being, the time and effort a computer needs to carry out various processes at the same time are almost negligible if compared with humans. Hence, this machine-readable feature assigned to corpora nowadays is basically due to what has been called the "marriage of machine and corpus", which allows the user to search for any word in the corpus, to retrieve all the examples of such a word in just a second and to explore thousands or millions of words easily, quickly and successfully. Machines can also perform difficult calculations, display the data in different and diverse forms which may be adapted to the kind of research undertaken, they can sort data according to certain parameters or filters and they may arrange the data alphabetically or according to frequency parameters. Moreover, thanks to them, we can analyse words in their naturally occurring environments (contexts of use) in the form of concordance lines, which make it much easier to analyse collocates.

All the things enumerated above can be achieved easily thanks to powerful computers and adequate software. The specific software and the method used in this study for the exploitation of the corpus and the storage of data (with specialised lexicographical objectives) are explained in detail in section II of this book.

3.3. Corpus defining traits and types of corpora

In the same way as a good meal needs good ingredients, a good corpus needs good texts. However, the notion of corpus[14] runs the risk of being confused with the examination of single texts. This is so because any collection of more than one text can, in principle at least and according to early corpus linguistics, be considered a corpus. However, nowadays, when we are immersed in modern linguistics, the term corpus has evolved and added certain features and connotations to the more simple definition of "a collection of texts" as has already been explained in section 3.2. There are four basic features inherent to the concept of corpus in modern corpus linguistics. These defining traits of modern corpus linguistics are, according to McEnery and Wilson (2001): sampling and representativeness, finite size, machine-readable form and a standard reference.

According to Ahmad and Davies (1992: 22):

> A corpus-based approach enables the terminologist to identify, study and record terms in their natural habitat, and translators, as users of the term bank, to have customised access to a full set of information about all the terms and related terminological data of a domain.

However, before starting to use any corpus, linguists must be aware of the importance of designing a good corpus that constitutes a smaller but representative sample of the linguistic phenomenon, variety or language under study.

If one intends to work with a corpus, then two possibilities are presented: to work with an already elaborated corpus or to elaborate the corpus so that it can be designed in the way that best fits the objectives and necessities set out at the beginning. In both cases, the quality of the corpus will determine the results of the linguistic research and so it is worth taking into account a series of parameters that can guarantee this quality up to a certain extent (and also guarantee that a corpus is so and can be called so, and is not just a collection of texts

14 CORPUS: from the Latin for "body", so a corpus "is", literally, any body of text.

gathered at random). In accordance with this, there are certain issues that must be taken into account for the design of a corpus and these features are considered as forming part not only of the corpus as such but also of the methodology used for corpus compilation (however, this methodology is analysed in more detail in the section devoted to corpora in the second part of this book).

Starting from the fact that a corpus is not just a collection of randomly selected and gathered texts, but a collection of texts that seeks to represent a part of a language, the appropriateness of this corpus will be mainly determined by its representativeness in terms of the area under study. "The appropriate design for a corpus therefore depends upon what it is meant to represent" (Biber, Conrad and Reppen, 1998: 246).

What seems obvious, whatever the topic area or the research objectives of a given corpus might be, is that the representativeness criterion is crucial in the compilation and design stage since it will determine the kind of research questions to be posed, as well as the level of generalisability and reliability that can be given to the results of the research. However, representing a language or a part of it is not an easy issue at all because it is impossible to know "the full extent of variation in language or all the contextual variables that need to be covered in order to capture all variation in texts" (Biber, Conrad and Reppen, 1998: 246). Closely related to this is the criticism of the corpus approach made by Chomsky which states that, if language is assumed to be infinite, then any corpus will be skewed and insufficient. The implications of such criticism are then clear: with a corpus-based approach to language study it is more than probable that some utterances are excluded because of being rare and others which may be far more common might be excluded simply by chance or at random. In the same way, however, and also due to probability or chance, extremely rare utterances might be included several times in a corpus, the result being a frequency that is not exactly representative of, for instance, a variety of language. This criticism made by Chomsky leads us directly to acknowledge the importance of representativeness, since taking into account and measuring the representativeness of the linguistic samples that go to make up a corpus is the only way to obtain a corpus that realistically describes a linguistic variety or a language. This need to look for representativeness has also been favoured by modern computer technology, since not only does it allow researchers to collect and compile much larger corpora than those Chomsky could think about in the 1950s, but also to construct less biased and much more representative corpora.

Following McEnery and Wilson (2001):

> We are therefore interested in creating a corpus which is maximally representative of the variety under examination, that is, which provides us with an as accurate a picture as possible of the tendencies of that variety, as well as their proportions. What we are looking for is a broad range of authors and genres which, when taken together, may be considered to "average out" and provide a reasonably accurate picture of the entire language population in which we are interested.

These key features (authenticity, representativeness and size) are analysed in depth in the section devoted to considerations for work preparation and corpus compilation (see section 8.2) but, apart from these, there are other characteristics that have already been mentioned that nowadays shape modern corpora, such as finite size, machine-readable form and standard reference. It is obvious that the generative potential of a language is immense, so that the number of utterances that can be constructed in a language is infinite. However, as McEnery and Wilson (2001) state, the term "corpus" also implies a body of text of finite size, with the exception of monitor corpora.[15] For instance, at Birmingham University, John Sinclair's COBUILD team have been engaged in the construction of one of these monitor corpora, the main advantages of which are their non-static character, since new texts can always be added (unlike the synchronic cut provided by finite corpora), and their scope, due to the fact they are constantly absorbing new samples and thus becoming larger and larger. However, these monitor corpora are not such a reliable source of quantitative data (as opposed to qualitative data) since changes in their size are constant and they are normally less rigorously sampled than finite corpora.

With this exception of monitor corpora in mind, it can be said, however, that it is much more common for a corpus to consist of a finite number of words. For example, the Brown Corpus contains 1,000,000

15 A monitor corpus is an open-ended entity or "collection of texts" (as Sinclair's team prefers to call it), that is to say, a corpus in which texts are constantly being added so that it gets bigger and bigger.

words and the common thing to do is to establish beforehand, prior to beginning a corpus-based project, the approximate size such a corpus will have and thus the amount of data to work with. In this way, it is commonplace that, unlike in a monitor corpus, once a corpus reaches its intended size (a certain number of running words of text) no more textual samples are added and the corpus stops increasing in size. An interesting exception to this is, however, the case of the London-Lund corpus, which saw its number of integrating textual samples and hence its size increase in the mid-1970s in order to cover a wider and more modern variety of genres.

In addition to this, it may be important to mention again the fact that, nowadays, the modern term "corpus" carries almost implicitly with it the feature "machine-readable". This was not the case before the "computer boom" experienced in the last two decades and the term "corpus" was only used in reference to manually compiled printed text. This machine-readable feature is what determines the main advantages that modern corpora display with respect to written or spoken formats, since they offer the possibility of being searched and manipulated at high speeds and can easily be enriched with extra information.

Apart from the features of modern corpora we have already mentioned, McEnery and Wilson (2001) also state that there is often a *tacit* understanding that a corpus constitutes a standard reference for the language variety that it represents, supposing that it will be widely available to other researchers as happens with many corpora, such as the Brown corpus, the LOB corpus and the London-Lund corpus. A number of areas of language study have greatly benefited from the exploitation of corpus data. This has been and is so because of four main advantages with which these corpus data may contribute to different and varied areas of language study. Thus, following McEnery and Wilson (2001), from a general point of view, the main characteristics and advantages of corpora are as follows:

- Sampling and quantification. According to what has been mentioned with respect to representativeness, a corpus is sampled always bearing in mind that one of the major goals is that it must represent the population to the maximum degree possible, so that any findings extracted from the corpus can be generalised to the larger population. Consequently, this fact of representing the population makes quantification in corpus linguistics really meaningful, since it comprises representative information about a variety of a language as a whole and not just about the fraction of language analysed at a given moment.

- Ease of access. It is obvious that dealing with already elaborated corpora may save researchers a lot of time and work. This is so because they do not have to go through the issues of sampling, collecting and encoding. In addition to this, once corpora have been obtained (which, in general, is not difficult since most corpora are either free or low-cost) current technological advancements in the form of concordance programs make it easy and fast to access, manage and analyse the data a corpus may contain.

- Enriched data. Although this is not the case of the corpus used in this study, it is a reality that many corpora are enriched with additional linguistic information. An example of this additional information would be, for instance, part-of-speech annotation, parsing and prosodic transcription, thus giving rise to annotated corpora, which can be easier to interpret and more specific than other corpora which have not been annotated.

- Naturalistic data. This feature is probably one of the greatest potentials of corpora since it allows, for the most part, access to unmonitored, naturalistic data which are the product of real social contexts, thus constituting one of the most (if not *the* most) powerful and reliable suppliers of data to be examined. The most important factor of corpus linguistics for the study of language is the usage of empirical data that enable the linguist to make objective statements rather than subjective ones. Empirical data allow investigations to be based not only on the researcher's perceptions or intuitions or on the individual's own internalised cognitive perception of language, but on real data extracted from real discourse.

Regarding the types of corpora that can be compiled, the most characteristic and probably the most widely known and used kinds of corpora are reference corpora. These **reference corpora** contain the standard vocabulary of a language and so they can be used for a multitude of purposes mainly because, among other things, if they are large enough, they reveal the contexts in which words are embedded and with which other words give rise to collocations with other words. Accordingly:

> A typical reference corpus will represent what the discourse community agrees to be what a fairly educated member of the middle class would read outside of work, mostly in printed form, but also handwritten or typed; and, in principle at least, it should also contain a sample of what they would hear, in conversations, at more formal social events, or on the radio. (Teubert and Cermáková, 2004: 118)

Hence, reference corpora are carefully construed and have a deliberate composition, the British National Corpus with its 100 million words being a good example. However, reference corpora may be construed with another goal – that of being benchmarks for special corpora, which leads us to another category in this corpora typology. These **special corpora**, which are normally smaller than reference ones (generally a million words or so) are compiled in order to fit a specific, specialised research focus or goal, that is to say, they are compiled to undertake research in which the objective is not the analysis of standard language as a whole, but the analysis of some special phenomenon (accordingly, this is the kind of corpus used in this study).

Another kind of corpus in the typology, an alternative to the reference one, is the *opportunistic* or *cannibalistic corpus*, based on the assumption that every corpus is imbalanced, so it does not claim to represent a language or to reflect discourse. This assumption makes it possible to manage the problem of balance or representativeness from a different angle and, as Teubert and Cermakova state (2004: 120), the opportunistic corpus is the result of collecting all the documents one can lay hands upon (which makes them open-ended and, in certain aspects such as intentionality, rather different from what has been considered a proper corpus in this study). In this sense, the best cannibalistic or opportunistic corpus is the one that is documented in the most comprehensive way and, furthermore, the larger it is, the better.

Another corpus in this typology is the **monitor corpus**, which is a corpus that monitors language change. This kind of corpus is especially useful for lexical change studies since it is, in principle at least, regularly updated and open-ended, and this study of lexical change is translated into the more specific possibility of undertaking research not only on the introduction of new words into the discourse, which is the most obvious one, but on other factors that Teubert and Cermakova enumerate as (2004: 121):

- The change of frequency of words or other units of meaning (compounds, multi-word units, collocations, set-phrases), which is often indicative of a change in meaning or in the domain in which words are used;
- The occurrence of new words;
- The occurrence of new larger units of meaning;
- Changing context profiles, i.e. changes in the frequencies of words occurring in the contexts of words or other units of meaning.

Another important kind of corpus is the *parallel corpus* or what in certain contexts is also known as a translation corpus. This kind of corpus can be defined as a corpus of original texts in one language and their translations into another or several other languages. However, sometimes parallel corpora do not contain texts in the original language but only translations of the same text in different languages. This is the reason why a subtype of parallel corpora consists of reciprocal parallel corpora, which contain original texts and translated texts in all the languages involved. In general, and for most applications, sentence alignment will be necessary so that a unit in one language corresponds to the equivalent unit in another language. However, this sentence alignment, which at first used to be done by hand, is not easy at all even with the automatic means available nowadays because alignment is a time-consuming process which requires substantial human intervention due to the reasons given below:

- Firstly, although it may not seem so, it is rather difficult to identify sentence endings automatically since full stops also designate abbreviations (*etc.* standing for etcetera, *2.* standing for second, and so forth), which do not necessarily occur at the end of a sentence.

- Secondly, as may be easily noticed, one sentence in a source language may correspond to two or even more sentences in a target language or the other way round so that the instability of sentences as units is quite clearly shown. The translator's whim also has much to do with things in this sense, since it is a common practice even to omit sentences in a translation or introduce new ones.

These are probably the reasons for the scarce number of parallel corpora of a considerable size (more than 5 million words per language) existing nowadays. In spite of this, there is an aspect which is even trickier for alignment and that is the lexical level. This is so because ideally, each unit of meaning in the source corpus should be linked to the equivalent in the target one but this, as reality shows, is not always so. In Teubert and Cermakova's (2004: 124) words:

> Lexical alignment uses statistical procedures and/or lexicon look-up. Neither is very reliable. It is because bilingual dictionaries (and the lexicons derived from them) are not very instructive that we turned to parallel corpora in the first place. [...] We will still be given both *work* and *labour* and also some other words like *employment* or *job* as equivalent of French *travail*. If we want to find out more, we have to look at the contexts in which *travail* is embedded when it is translated as *work*, as opposed to the contexts in which *travail* is embedded when it is translated as *labour*. Thus, if we have to translate *travaux* followed by the adjective *préparatoires*, our parallel corpus tells us that this phrase is never translated as *preparatory labours* but always as *preparatory work* (with a singular phrase in English corresponding to the French plural phrase).

Finally, I would like to mention another "type" of corpus which is acquiring an increasing and pre-eminent role among linguists: the Internet as a virtual corpus. The Internet, due to the billions of texts contained in it, is by far the largest existing library nowadays (although it is not infinite, it is certainly inexhaustible) and turns out to be particularly useful for finding out if a word is in current use or if a word or phrase we have heard of really exists. However, one must be cautious with the information to be found on the net since the freedom it offers allows anyone to add his/her contributions, regardless of their quality. The Internet is a virtual corpus and, like the discourse of any language community, we cannot expect to access it as a whole (Teubert and Cermakova, 2004: 125).

The SLA needs corpus data as the source from which to retrieve and analyse the linguistic material of speciality domains. The in-depth, pragmatic characterisation of terminology carried out by specialised lexicography would not be feasible without a solid, real base such as the one provided by a corpus.

If names are not correct,
language will not be in accordance
with the truth of things.
Confucius

4. Terminology: A key element in the study of PAL/ Specialised Languages

Following Cabré (1993, in Hoffman, 1998), despite the fact that not all the specialists share the same ideas about specialised languages (or PAL), there are a couple of points of universal agreement amongst them. These points are, first of all, the fact that the communications produced within this "framework" refer to very specific areas of knowledge and secondly that, according to this point of view, every speciality area, as well as academic disciplines, jobs and professions would be considered areas of specialised knowledge. Consequently, the expression and transmission of such knowledge could require the use of specific units and rules and it is in this sense that one may talk about special or specialised languages and their terminologies.

As has already been dealt with, terminology is a key element in the study of PAL or specialised discourse because it is a fundamental integrating part of it, that is, the most prototypical "feature" of specialised language. Terminology – understood as specialised vocabulary – is also the basis of the specialised lexicographical work. Nonetheless, as this chapter will disclose, terminology does not only refer to a specific set of specialised vocabulary items. Given the name of the approach put forward in this book, the reader could be wondering why the term "terminology" is being constantly used instead of the notion "specialised lexicology". It is necessary to go through this chapter in order to understand what is really meant by specialised lexicography, what makes it "a step-further" with respect to terminography and how all these disciplines have been conceived. Nonetheless, what is clear from the very beginning is that the term "terminology" implies a wider dimension and acceptance than that of "specialised lexicology". No one refers to the lexicon of, for instance, chemistry, as the "specialised lexicology" of chemistry but as the "terminology" of chemistry. As this chapter shows, the notion "terminology" makes reference to three realities perfectly established in current linguistics: it refers to the discipline and grounding principles in charge of the study of terms, to the very same group of terms or specific vocabulary of a domain, and to the practical study of terms, normally shaped in the elaboration of speciality dictionaries (what has been normally called terminography). Currently, however, when referring to "specialised lexicology" most linguists could recognise the discipline and grounding principles underlying the study of specialised lexical units (terms) but no one would identify it with the set of specific vocabulary belonging to specialised languages. In order to avoid an unnecessary denominative confusion and because of its wider scope, the traditional denomination "terminology" has been the one adopted throughout this study.

In this book, two main ways of approaching and conceiving terminology have been put forward and analysed as opposite views: in the first one, called the General Theory of Terminology (GTT), a static and normalising view of the terms (adopted from the Vienna School) was proposed whereas in the second one, the Communicative Theory of Terminology, we find those linguists who conceive terms as elements from the natural language found in specialised texts. According to the SLA and the active features it promotes, in this book the second view has been endorsed as the most realistic way to approach terminology.

4.1. Terminology: a historical review

To better understand terminology and the way the specialised lexicographical approach conceives it, it is necessary to have a look at its evolution. Although the systematisation of terminology and the fixing of its scientific status are very recent (that is to say, terminology started to take shape as a discipline relatively few years ago) terminological practice dates back a lot further in time (Cabré, 1993). This is not strange at all if we consider that, from a practical point of view, terminology has always existed as the means through which the communicative necessity of referring to any concept belonging to a specialised field can be solved.

Already in the 18th century the works undertaken by Lavoisier and Berthold in chemistry, or Linnaeus in botany or zoology highlighted the interest that the fixing of the denominations of scientific concepts has always had for its true and real protagonists, i.e. specialists. However, although the "soul" of terminology was present in these denominations, the work carried out by these authors was known as "nomenclatures" (not yet terminology), Versalius being the precursor of these "scientific nomenclatures".

The word "nomenclature" was defined by the naturalist Duhamel du Montceau in 1785 as "the art of classifying the objects of a science and naming them" until the word "terminology" was first used by the German Christian Gottfried Schütz (1747-1832) as an alternative to "nomenclature", (the adjective *terminologisch* was first used in 1788).

Hence, in the early 19th century, more specifically in 1801, and mainly due to the progressive internationalisation of science, scientists began to suggest the need to have rules for term formation for each discipline, and it was at that time that terminology started to be named and used as such in France. It was then when terminology started to be considered and conceived as an organised practice regulated by a set of work norms. In this respect, as Cabré (1999 a) concedes, the compilation and study of the specialised lexical units of different professional fields has, since distant times, been carried out within the scope of lexicography and dialectology. Nonetheless, it was not until the unification and regulation of the vocabulary of various scientific disciplines, during the 17th and 18th centuries, that these endeavours began to be consciously conceived as an organised and coherent activity.

However, while in the 18th and 19th century scientists were the ones leading the concern for terminology, in the 20th century technicians were showing greater involvement in terminology-related issues, probably due to the high degree of specialisation of their fields of knowledge and the communicative necessities arising from them. The accelerated progress of the different technical branches and the rapid development of technology created a demand from the very beginning (and even more nowadays), not only to denominate the new concepts that appeared as a consequence of this progress but mainly to harmonise the new denominations in order to provide some sort of unified, coherent and consistent system of denomination. The scientific development and the progress experimented through the centuries, together with the increasing use of the languages in each country, led to scientists' and specialists' creating terms for the different concepts of their fields of knowledge. In Rey's (1995: 49) words:

> During the simultaneous expansion of knowledge and the growth of technology and communication in the eighteenth century, terminology was seen as a necessary tool for overcoming some of the difficulties associated with these multiple developments.

The first works that really and accurately warranted the denomination of *terminological* date back to 1906. They were undertaken by the International Electrotechnical Commission (IEC) and were finished in 1938, thirty years later, with the appearance of the *International Electrotechnical Vocabulary* (IEV). It was during the 1930s that what is considered to be modern terminology as such appeared and numerous efforts were made to establish its linguistic grounds. These efforts were especially significant in Germany, Austria, Czechoslovakia and the Soviet Union, giving rise to the appearance of different Schools, among which a special mention is due to those of Vienna, Prague and the Soviet Union, which belong to what is known as the "linguistic-terminological current".

In this historical context and in the field of engineering the figure of the Austrian Eugen Wüster (1898-1977) emerged and stood out. He is considered to be the founder of modern terminology and the main representative of the Vienna School. At the time, the Russian D. S. Lotte (1889-1950), founder of the Soviet School of Terminology, also came onto the scene. Thus, modern terminology as such arose during the 1930s and, in its early days at least, developed mainly thanks to Wüster's works in Vienna. In general terms, the grounding principles of modern terminology can be found in Wüster's PhD dissertation,[16] where the reasons for systematising the methodology of work in terminology

16 *Internationale Sprachnormung in der Technik, besonders in der Elektrotechnik.* [International Normalisation in the Technical Fields, especially in Electrotechnics].

are explained and the grounding principles for terminological works and the main features of a methodology for the management of terminological data are established. However, at that time, Wüster focused his interest mainly on methodological and normative issues, rather than theoretical ones (his interest in theory was to start later) and his first works were chiefly oriented towards eliminating ambiguities in technical and scientific communication.

In 1971, his most theoretical work appears, where the GTT[17] is described (see section 4.1.1). However, despite the important role played by himself in this field, in the opening session of the Infoterm symposium in 1975, Wüster attributed the intellectual "paternity" of terminology to four scientists: the German A. Schloman, the first to consider the systematic character of terms; the Swiss linguist F. de Saussure, the first to highlight the systematicity of languages; the Russian E. Dressen, the first to draw attention to the importance of normalisation and the driving force of the ISA organisation;[18] and the Englishman J. E. Holmstrom, who fostered (from the UNESCO) the international spread of terminologies and was the first to call for an international organism that dealt seriously with this discipline.

Personal considerations apart, what seems obvious is that terminology arises from the practice and from the necessity observed and experienced by scientists and technicians to standardise their disciplines from a conceptual and denominative perspective, with the ultimate aim of guaranteeing professional communication and effective knowledge transmission (Cabré, 1999 a).

Although the history of terminology is disclosed in more detail in subsequent sections (and since the origins of terminology as such have been outlined in previous paragraphs), I have included below a summary on the evolution of terminology in its more recent stages in order to provide a general panorama of its evolution as a whole. Following a

---

17 Also known as Classical Theory of Terminology or Traditional Theory of Terminology (Cabré, 1993).

18 ISA (International Standardisation Association), founded in 1926, was the first international standards organisation and was the foregoer of the ISO (International Organisation for Standardisation), the current international standardisation body.

chronological axis, Auger (1988 in Cabré, 1993: 28) structures modern terminology in four fundamental stages:

1 The origins (from 1930 to 1960). The first theoretical texts by Wüster and Lotte appeared in this stage, which was basically characterised by the preparation of terminological methods of work that took into account the systematic character of the terms.

2 The structuring stage (from 1960 to 1975). During this period, the most important advances in the field of terminology came from the development of macrocomputing and documentary techniques. At the same time, the first data banks appeared and the International Organisation of Terminology began to work.

3 The "flourishing/blooming" stage (from 1975 to 1985). In this stage, it became clear that terminology played a significant role in the process of modernising a language and the society in which it is used. Moreover, the expansion of microcomputing gave rise to a change in the conditions of terminological work and data treatment.

4 The widening stage (since 1985). This is where we are at the present moment. Computer science has become one of the most important elements fostering and enhancing the change. Apart from this, terminologists have access to both tools and work resources that are better adapted to their necessities, easier to use and more effective. In addition to this, the growth of the new market of language industries, in which terminology has a special place, is an element that must also be taken into consideration.

4.1.1. The General Theory of Terminology (GTT)

If a closer look is taken at the principles and mainstays of the General Theory of Terminology a series of aspects must necessarily be tackled, including its origins, defining traits and factors that lead to a necessary renewal with respect to this terminological conception.

a) Origins of the GTT

The Vienna School, founded on the grounds of the General Theory of Terminology, continued with the research started by Wüster in 1930. This research included a series of studies about specific problems in terminology and constituted the postulates of the GTT (Cabré, 1993): the production of normalised documents about the vocabulary of terminological work, the systematisation of the methods of working, data transfer and the presentation of terminological products.

At the time this classical theory saw the light, Wüster's worries were of a very practical nature, that is, mainly methodological and normative, rather than theoretical, since he considered terminology as a tool for disambiguating scientific and technical communication. However, the postulates of the GTT (represented by the School of Prague, the Soviet Union School and mainly by the Vienna School, with its highest exponent, Eugen Wüster) do not take into account the communicative dimension of terminology. The main postulates and the importance attributed to the concept by the Vienna School, and thus by the Classical Theory, can be easily appreciated in the words of Felber (1979), one of its members, who explains how Wüster established and developed the first principles for the management of specialised lexicon and emphasised the ruling position devoted to the conceptual dimension. Wüster's main objective was to normalise and set the relationship between term and concept with the final aim of constructing hierarchical systems of concepts. Hence, as Cabré (1993) states, the General Theory of Terminology is grounded on the view that the nature of the concept, conceptual relations, the relation term-concept and the attribution of terms to concepts occupy a key position. In addition to this, the method of working in terminology (onomasiological, that is, from the concept to the term) is, according to this theory, different to the one used in lexicography (semasiological, from the term to the concept).

Therefore, the first period of terminology as a proper discipline is mainly characterised, according to the GTT, by the consideration and use of methods of work that take into account the systematic nature of terms. Theoretical considerations, such as those regarding the nature of terms were to appear later on when terminological practice starts to be organised and structured in different subjects as a direct result of this practice.

In this way, the new proposals and new directions that terminology was to progressively and increasingly adopt appeared as a result of reactions against the proposals (principles and method) for the description of meaning that the traditional schools of terminology prescribed. These traditional schools, to which Wüster belonged, firmly believed in the need for standardisation with the clear objective of improving special language communication. In Temmerman's views (2000: 19), traditional terminology was based on a few premises which were considered to be unquestionable:

- concepts are clear-cut and can be defined on the basis of necessary and sufficient condition;
- univocity of terms is essential for unambiguous and therefore effective and efficient communication;
- and figurative language and change of meaning are linguistic subjects which are of no concern to Terminology, as Terminology restricts itself to the onomasiological perspective.

The following section offers an account of the factors that unleashed the thought that changes needed to be made in terminology.

b) The GTT: features of a theory to be revisited

Vargas (2005) contends that, in spite of being called a theory, the theoretical framework underlying classical terminology is more closely linked to the principles of a practical discipline whose main aim is to harmonise the terminological vocabularies at a world level to make specialised communication fluid and unambiguous. In this regard, the methodology of the GTT is of prescriptive and normalising nature, instead of acquiring theoretical postulates that explain the true functioning of the aforementioned vocabularies. Despite this, Wüster also recognised that terminology consists of a theoretical dimension when he referred to the concepts of monovalence and univocity (1979) but also when, with his theory, he was the first to lay the foundations that made it possible to develop theoretical postulates applied to terminology.

The main weakness of this classical theory is that the limits of the scope of action of the GTT do not take into account the communicative and pragmatic aspects inherent to the lexicon of the different specialised languages. In a way, the GTT can be considered a reductionist theory, since it reduces the terminological unit to its denominative condition and presents a lack of interest in the pragmatic and communicative aspects of terms, while failing to recognise their formal and conceptual variation. For the GTT, there are three main aspects that characterise terms:

1) Concepts exist independently of the term that designates them.
2) The biunivocal nature of terms: there is a single form for each concept and a concept for each form.
3) Terms are independent of context.

Hence, the two main shortcomings which have led to the questioning of Wüster's terminological theory can be summarised in two main points: the *reductionism* in the way of conceiving the subject and its applications, and the excessive *standardisation* the discipline was subjected to in the name of the universality of the principles that sustained it (Cabré, 1999 a).

However, before analysing in more depth the shortcomings of the GTT, it is perhaps worth pointing out here that its most outstanding characteristic is its focus on the concept, as well as its orienting terminological works towards the normalisation of terms and notions. Moreover, according to supporters of the GTT, it is the onomasiological approach (from the concept to the term) that distinguishes the method of working used in terminology from that employed in lexicography, as shown in figure 12.

Terminology	Lexicology
application	application
Terminography	Lexicography
from concept to term ⇩ Attributes denominations to concepts	from term to concept ⇩ It departs from denomination and establishes the functional and semantic features
ONOMASIOLOGICAL PROCESS	SEMASIOLOGICAL PROCESS

Figure 12. Onomasiological and semasiological approaches.

However, one of the main criticisms that can be made about the General Theory of Terminology is the fact that, from a communicative point of view, it does not "conceive reality in a realistic way". Thus, it assumes a uniformity in communication which is not so and which makes it ignore many communicative dimensions that are present in every interaction, whether specialised or not. Following Cabré (1999 a), the GTT alone is not enough to accurately and effectively explain and understand the complexity of real terminology. Basically, this is so because the number of communicative and informative necessities terminology has to fulfil is not successfully and fully covered by the postulates of the GTT, which are rather limited in their scope.

Hence, it is not so much that the Classical Theory of Terminology is not internally coherent but that it presents a rather reductionist-oriented view of terminology that has proved to be more social than Wüster and his followers acknowledged. This reductionism affecting the GTT makes it a theory that is unable to provide a complete account of the complexity of the terminological phenomenon in specialised communication. This is what has led the General Theory of Terminology to become a theory that works with rather unrealistic premises, whether consciously or unconsciously, since it seems to assume the existence of some sort of universal language that gives rise to a uniformity in specialised communication which in reality is not so. According to Cabré (1999 a), this view is what makes the GTT confuse *what terminology is* with *what we would like it to be* and consequently what has made this classical theory present and follow a methodology considered as being universally valid and uniform, whatever the specialised subject field, the aim pursued or the language used. Consequently, this conception makes it rather useless to resort to the notion and specificity of the context in which communication is always given.

This artificial, reductionist and non-realistic way of conceiving the specialised linguistic phenomenon has given way to prescriptions that are too tight and uniform and are more inspired in what language should be if it were completely logical, expectable, regular and controlled than in what it really is. The GTT does not contemplate, for instance, the possibility that language can be used in spontaneous situations and the fact that this spontaneity does not stop communication from being specialised.

Hence, the GTT has received various criticisms focused on certain aspects or on others, depending on the viewpoint or the perspective this criticism came from (Cabré, 1999 a):

a) From the social perspective, contrary to what the GTT proclaimed, the communicative character of terminology has been emphasised through the importance of its social role[19] as being a more decisive one than just its representational role or the standardisation of terms.

b) From a linguistic perspective, different critical voices have been raised against the weakness of some of the points that the GTT presents:

- Firstly, a great deal of criticism has supported the view that terminology is natural language and not artificial language so that, broadly speaking, it shares the characteristics of general language.

- Secondly, the fact that the Traditional Theory considered terms as units without syntactical interest and consequently irrelevant for the discourse has been criticised. This reductive view is, however, a logical consequence of considering that terminology must focus, methodologically speaking, on searching the denominations for already established concepts always with a standardising objective as a final goal.

- And thirdly, attention has also been drawn to the contradiction of defending the univocity and monosemy of terms on the part of the Classical Theory when the data directly extracted from reality present results that definitely contradict these conditions.

---

19 This study is a clear example of this perspective, as it is a specialised lexicographical work contextualised in a social reality that makes it relevant and socially pertinent (see section 6).

c) From a cognitive perspective, the basic criticism made about the General Theory of Terminology has been focused on the notion of concept, a deeply idealistic notion completely removed from the cognitive conception of social base that is predominant nowadays. Thus, the presumed universality of the concept and the belief that specialities – independently of subject fields and languages – are uniform, closed and static, have also been a motif of controversy mainly due to the impossibility of validating such concepts with empirical data. The conception of specialities as perfectly separated areas that lack any internal realism and offer the possibility of all of them being described by the same pattern, together with the plain character of the term (or, at least, of its identification), have been other main characteristics that have led this classical conception of terminology to be questioned. Thus, critical voices accused this theory of being unable to establish a corpus of true conditions that are capable of explaining the data of the specialised reality.

Hence, what has been explained up to now regarding the GTT may lead to the view that Wüster established a rather restrictive object of analysis and work functions in which most things were taken for granted. Wüster delimited the terminological object and its functions so much that, for him, terminological activity was limited to the compilation of concepts and terms for the standardisation of speciality terms. In other words, his aim was to set the standardised notions and denominations of speciality terms (understood as units integrated by the association of a concept and a denomination of symbolic character from science and/or technology) with the ultimate aim of ensuring the univocity of professional communication. Therefore, there are many aspects and features of Wüster's proposal that identify it as a rather reductionist one. Broadly speaking, many of the aspects of terminology proposed by this theory are presented without an empirical basis or justification, leaving to one side or even ignoring the real functioning of data in the reality of specialised communication. If we delve a little deeper into this reductionism, we can specifically notice the reductionist approach of Wüster's proposal in the following aspects signalled by Cabré (1999 a):

- The goals attributed to terminology are limited to ensuring the univocity of professional communication. This fact contradicts the complexity of the intrinsic interdisciplinary character of speciality areas and the wide range of socio-professional necessities that require an adequate terminological activity.

- The form of the terminological units is reduced to their denominative condition, disregarding the linguistic elements that form part of them and their internal morphological structures.

- As a logical consequence of the reductionist view of terms (such as merely having a denominative function), the syntactical aspects of the terminological units have not been taken into account. Consequently, research on the grammatical functioning of terminology has not advanced in parallel to the work undertaken on the lexical unit of the language and thus the terminological databases showed poor grammatical information.

- The fact it ignores the communicative and discursive aspects of terminological units (another consequence of the pre-eminence and even exclusivity assigned to the denominative function) has not allowed it to participate in the recently initiated investigation about the contribution of terminology to textual characterisation in its different types and levels of abstraction.

- The working method with a prescriptive basis is presented as valid for every kind of investigation, regardless of the topic or subject of the work, of its goals, of the contexts in which it is undertaken and of the linguistic typology. This method has been generated on the basis of the silence adopted with respect to the formal and conceptual variation of the specialised units (although it is something inherent to language and communication, whether general or specialised).

Consequently, these inadequacies of the GTT have been noted for several years and have become even more evident as terminology started to be extracted from running text (corpora) (Cabré, 1999 a).

c) *Shaping a renovation in terminology*

In accordance with what has been analysed hitherto, terminology was represented from the 1940s onwards almost exclusively by Wüster's General Theory of Terminology and only rather "recently" has its validity been questioned by different authors from different fields (linguistics or philosophy of science) on the basis of two main factors: the observation of terminological data in their real functioning and the experiments undertaken by psychology about how we (as human beings) categorise the objects of reality.

Thus, the restrictions and the reductionist view posed by the GTT have made it necessary to call for a renovation. Hence, worldwide, several people involved in terminological issues have manifested the need to revisit the Classical Theory of Terminology with a twofold fundamental objective, that is, to overcome the restrictive character of its grounding principles and to widen the limitations of its methodological proposals.

From the Vienna School itself, attention has been drawn to the need to provide the theory with greater flexibility and a more "open" character.

However, the voices that called for a renovation did not have a clear and common view regarding certain crucial aspects that had to be clearly established for the creation of a new alternative theory. As Picht (1996: 278) puts it:

> Una cuestión que se debe plantear es la formulación de una amplia (sic) teoría general de la terminología, capaz de adaptar los nuevos aspectos que han surgido durante los últimos 17 años, de manera que se incorporen a una estructura lógica completa.
>
> [A question that must be posed is the formulation of a wide (sic) general theory of terminology able to adapt the new aspects that have been arising during the last 17 years so that they are incorporated to a complete logical structure.]

Nonetheless, there is a fact that seems to be widely agreed upon and defended by both the followers of the Vienna School and those who defend alternative positions: terminology must be placed theoretically in the wide range of disciplines relative to knowledge. The main problem then becomes the diversity of opinions that come to the fore when questions regarding the delimitation of the field of study and the definition of the scientific object are posed. Hence, all these claims, together with the well-grounded belief that the complex nature of terminology cannot be accurately and completely accounted for by the GTT, have given rise to the appearance of a new basis for a novel theory that displays a more "sensitive" approach to terminology and its implications: the Communicative Theory of Terminology (Cabré, 1999 a). However, this theory is actually the result of a long process in which new postulates that have arisen as developments on and reactions to the GTT (without disregarding the important role played by Wüster's theory) finally gave rise to this new theory.

Nevertheless, this path towards a new, more comprehensive and more realistic theory of terminology has been long and hard, and has required huge amounts of observation on the failures and weaknesses of previous conceptions, especially the GTT. Thus, the CTT (the purely terminological theory which constitutes one of the pillars of the SLA) arose from the evident shortcomings of the GTT and from the real terminological necessities observed and experienced in speciality domains.

Hence, the state of the art towards the end of the times in which the GTT was still the ruling position in terminology was that more and more critical voices appeared calling for solutions to the shortcomings it presented. These critical voices claimed that terminology required a deep and determined revision of its grounding principles that was not limited, as had been done up to then, to denying the validity of every single postulate of the GTT or to strongly defending its relevance and adequacy.

It is in this light that the CTT started to be conceived as the alternative to the Classical Theory, one of its principal strengths consisting in the fact that it incorporated what was considered to be one of the main weaknesses of the GTT: the corroboration of its principles by contrasting them with empirical data that allowed them to be maintained, qualified or revoked. Hence, the following section describes the beginning of the process which led to the appearance of the Communicative Theory of Terminology and a complete account of it as one of the mainstays of the SLA.

4.1.2. A "new" theory of terminology: initial considerations for the CTT

Prior to the design of a new theory of terminology (or any other theory) an analysis of the state of the art must be conducted. In this case, this analysis was carried out by posing different questions that defined the lines of action of the new theory and its way of approaching terminology. Following Cabré (1999 a), author of the CTT, the first question to be clearly and sharply defined was: *What is [terminology] about?* – that is to say, a definition of what terminology is as a discipline. However, doing so required the formulation of other questions such as *What does terminology want to "describe" as a discipline or as a field of knowledge?* and *What is its "object of analysis"?* In Cabré's view (1999 a) this last issue can only be dealt with by acknowledging the existence of two different and possible objects: on the one hand, the communicative units belonging to the specialised disciplines (formal and content functional units) and, on the other hand, specialised knowledge in abstract. That is to say, two different perspectives can be managed to answer these questions: the first one would conceive the object of terminology as (specialised) knowledge in general, so that terminology would be placed in the field of cognitive sciences and only partially considered part of linguistics, whereas if the object of terminology is the units of (specialised) knowledge, terminology can be situated within linguistics or semiotics.

Another question that needs to be answered for the revision of the traditional theory and for the design of a new and more realistic one was *How are these units of analysis dealt with?* For this, Cabré's (1999 a) reflections on how to deal with the units of analysis of terminology start by posing the question of whether the object of terminology is knowledge or the units of knowledge, and her reflections are based on a series of further questions: if the object of terminology is knowledge, from which specific perspective is knowledge analysed? Which specific contribution does terminology offer in relation to other subjects which also analyse knowledge? Is it necessary to postulate different realities when we speak about science or the general world? Or would it be better to talk about different perceptions of the same reality? Does terminology analyse the relationship between knowledge and reality as language philosophy has already done? Must terminology study how language is acquired, systematised, categorised and how it becomes a concept, how it becomes thought? Should every kind of knowledge (emotive, relational, general and specialised) be included in the field of study of terminology? Must terminology establish a relationship between knowledge and the units of knowledge? What kind of units of knowledge must be included? And, if the object of study is the units of knowledge in general, what is the nature of these units? Are they language or not? And if so, are they natural language or not?

Another issue to be dealt with is the *functions* terminological units may have. Although it is generally assumed and agreed upon that terms accomplish two basic functions at the same time (representing specialised knowledge and being vehicles for the transmission of this knowledge), accepting such a double function does not necessarily imply that the notions of representation and transfer are necessarily univocal. Following Cabré again (1999 a), essentially *representational* terminology can be (although it does not necessarily have to be) artificial and arbitrary and can control variation perfectly well, thus preserving the principles of univocity and monosemy defended by the Classical Theory. However, essentially *communicational* natural terminology must necessarily be real, in the sense that it must be effectively, directly and fundamentally used and, consequently, because it is real, it presents variation. This distinction shapes the dichotomy between representational and communicational terminology of "*in vitro*" (standardised) knowledge or "*in vivo*" (natural, spontaneous) knowledge. This inevitably carries with it a first consequence: on the one hand, communicational, natural terminology must necessarily be descriptive and considerations as to whether it is adequate or not to intervene in order to reduce such variation will only be made in a stage that is subsequent to the process of compilation, that is to say, in a stage of analysis and problem resolution. On the other hand, terminology which is essentially representational of the standardised knowledge can be prescriptive so as to control variation. Moreover, both modalities of terminology are aimed at achieving different goals: the representational one is more oriented towards the standardising necessities of international communication, towards documentation and towards certain strict linguistic policies of intervention and knowledge engineering that seek to simplify and control expressive variations as much as possible. The essentially communicational terminology, however, turns out to be especially useful for translation, specialised expression and language standardisation in sociolinguistic contexts regulated by policies which allow variation.

Another issue that needs to be analysed in order to determine the status of terminology and to design a new theory that accounts for it is the question of *What is meant to be a "field" of interdisciplinary knowledge?* in contrast or in opposition to what is implied by being a *"discipline"*. If we depart from the observable fact that reality is so complex that no single discipline can provide or show knowledge as a whole, then it is necessary to consider that the study of knowledge is necessarily interdisciplinary, that is to say, it must be undertaken through the concurrence of various disciplines. For instance, taking an illustrative example from Cabré (1999 a), language is the object of study of linguistics and it is much more than just a grammar; nevertheless, linguistic theory has decided to study it firstly as a grammar, this being neither an impediment for later going deeper into other aspects of language as an object (such as language acquisition or language use) nor for leaving the analysis of other aspects such as cognitive, discursive or neurobiological features to other disciplines.

In this reflection, in which more questions have been posed than answers given, a series of initial features proposed by Cabré (1999 a) before definitely shaping her CTT have been presented. These considerations for the creation of a new theory of terminology (explained in the next section) comprise and include both representational and communicational functions as well as their materialisation at different levels of formality and for diverse specialised fields with very different and varied structures.

4.2. The Communicative Theory of Terminology (CTT)

In the following subsections, a comprehensive account of the different aspects shaping the Communicative Theory of Terminology has been provided.

4.2.1. The object of study of the CTT

It is commonplace and necessary in any research to establish and determine its object of study in order to act in a logical and coherent manner. Likewise, we must also rely on a well-established and precise theory that allows us to coherently deal with such an object. According to Cabré (1999 a), the *units called terminological*[20] are the first object of study of terminology as a discipline and these units must be analysed functionally, formally and semantically, including a description of their double systematicity, which is general with respect to the system of language they form part of, and specific with respect to the terminology of the area of speciality in which they are given and used. Such a description must lead to generalisations that allow for the construction of a wider theory which accounts for the terms as units of the natural language and which allows for the progressive integration of the theory of terms into increasingly wider theories that finally explain human knowledge in general. In this way, the importance and need to approach the terminological object from a precise and well-established theory does not prevent the analysis of such an object from progressively integrating aspects from other disciplinary views.

This initial proposal (which is the basis of the CTT) makes it possible, at a first stage, to focus on term study in natural language and to successfully delimit its field of study. In the same way, it opens up the possibility of explaining that the interest in terminology goes beyond the scientific space of linguistics and allows elements from other disciplines (or knowledge areas) to be incorporated into term analysis, as happens, for instance, with communication sciences. As Cabré (1999 a) puts it, within these communication sciences, terminology would figure among the group of communicative resources – including artificial and non-verbal ones – to be resorted to and, finally, the whole would be included in a wider theory that would account for knowledge in general.

Accordingly it seems that the most crystal-clear way of explaining this issue of the terminological object is to understand the area of study of terminology as an object which is organised in concentric circles

20 Terminological Units (TUs)

comprising an increasingly complex and wide series of phenomena. Consequently, in Cabré's (1999 a) proposals prior to the development of the CTT as such, the object which can be placed closer to terminology is the terminological unit understood as being a unit from natural language. At the same time, these units share alternative or complementary systems (artificial ones included) with the space of analysis of communication theory and shape or form a theory of communication which at the same time forms a theory of knowledge. Hence, as Cabré (1999 a) concedes, the linguistic, cognitive and ontological aspects of terminology would integrate in the first theory of the natural language as different aspects of the same object of study.

With her proposal, however, Cabré (1999 a) tries to make the possibility of focusing on homogeneous units of a linguistic basis for the study of terminology compatible with the viability of going beyond their linguistic aspects in order to account for the complexity of the TUs, a complexity which, on the other hand, could be reclaimed by all the other units of natural language. Since the dissatisfaction produced by previous theories which accounted exclusively for competence (not taking into account acquisition or performance) has been constantly emphasised, Cabré (1999 a) wanted to highlight the fact that the multifaceted linguistic-cognitive-social character of the terminological units is not exclusive of them, but also of all the units of language.

In order to better understand the CTT as a whole and its importance in the SLA, it is necessary to understand its integrating aspects and considerations. In the following subsections, the object of study of the CTT (together with other related aspects) is progressively introduced in order to provide a complete panorama of the way this object of study is dealt with in this theory and the reasons for constituting such an object.

4.2.1.1. Preliminary considerations

Generally speaking, there are two main positions regarding the similitude or divergence between terms (or terminological units – TUs) and words:

The first position (which is closely related to the view of those who consider that there is a perfectly limited boundary separating general and specialised knowledge) is the one adopted by those who maintain that term and word, even though they both belong to the lexical component, are different units. Terminological units have been traditionally dealt with as units that are different from lexical units (understood as words from general language). From the linguistic point of view, the aspects generally mentioned as being distinctive of TUs with respect to words, especially in the works immediately following the General Theory of Terminology, are the following:

- Monosemic and mononymic character;
- An essentially nominal character;
- A relationship of non-interdependence between meaning and form linked to the onomasiological approach of their treatment;
- Membership to a single thematic area of speciality.

If this first position is adopted, the first theoretical consequence derived from it is that words and terms would form different lexicons in the speakers' knowledge. Thus, speakers would develop differentiated lexicons: on the one hand, a lexicon as speakers of a language (integrated by the words of this language) and, on the other hand, a lexicon as experts in a given speciality or specialised field (integrated by the concepts of that speciality). In conclusion, the implication of this view is that terms would be units belonging to a system that is completely differentiated and identified with each specific field of speciality and would represent the conceptual structure of that speciality.

However, many experimental psychology studies have proved that specialised and non-specialised knowledge is organised in the human mind simultaneously and that the acquisition of new specialised knowledge is always carried out on the basis of some previous knowledge, be it general or specialised. Sometimes, a concept is learnt with no previous knowledge about it but on other occasions a new concept is learnt by associating it with another formal unit that has already been interiorised with another sense. In addition to this, in some other cases, the conceptual information that a speaker had already associated to a denominative unit is redistributed through the increase, loss or change of some traits of content and, in still other cases, new pragmatic conditions are associated to previously known units.

> Desde las ciencias cognitivas, se cuestiona la noción de conocimiento especializado tratado aisladamente y se pone en tela de juicio su uniformidad y su alejamiento del conocimiento general. Desde la lingüística, se objeta sobre todo la limitación impuesta por la TGT de interesarse sólo por los aspectos prescriptivos de los términos y de considerar a los términos como unidades diferentes a las unidades léxicas propias de la lengua general. Y desde la sociología, en cambio, se rechaza la concepción idealista de los términos, el carácter plano atribuido a la comunicación especializada, donde los términos pierden parcialmente su condición de unidades de la lengua natural y sus valores pragmáticos... (Cabré y Estopà, 2002: 143-144)
>
> [From cognitive sciences, the notion of specialised knowledge dealt with in isolation is questioned as well as its uniformity and separation from general knowledge. From linguistics, the main objection is the limitation established by the GTT when paying exclusive attention to the prescriptive aspects of terms as well as when considering terms as different units from the lexical units of general language. On the other hand, from sociology, the idealistic notion of term is rejected as well as the plain character attributed to specialised communication, where terms partially lose their condition of units from natural language and their pragmatic values...] (Cabré y Estopà, 2002: 143-144)

Moreover, if a close observation of TUs in their natural contexts – that is to say, in the texts produced in specific communicative situations – is performed, it can be seen that TUs present very similar characteristics to those of the words of general language.

Hence, if the cognitive simultaneity mentioned above exists, it seems logical and necessary to assume that words and terms share room within the same grammatical lexicon, that is to say, what in cognitive terms would be expressed as words and terms sharing common knowledge areas or spaces. This leads us directly to the second position.

The second position is the one adopted by those who, in spite of acknowledging their specific characteristics, consider terms and words to be the same kind of unit.

> De acuerdo con una visión lingüística de los términos, partimos de la hipótesis que las unidades terminológicas comparten muchas características con las unidades del lenguaje natural y que la comunicación especializada tiene un estatus que no es completamente ajeno al que tiene la comunicación general. Presuponemos también que el conocimiento especializado no es uniforme ni está completamente separado del general en todas las situaciones de comunicación. (Cabré, 2001 a: 130)

> [According to a linguistic view of terms, we depart from the hypothesis that terminological units share many features with natural language units and that specialised communication has a status which is not totally alien to the one of general communication. We do also assume that specialised knowledge is neither uniform nor separated from the general one in every communicative situation.] (Cabré, 2001 a: 130)

According to this position, terms are no longer isolated units constituting their own system but instead units that are incorporated into the lexicon of a speaker when (after a hard process of acquiring specialised knowledge) he/she reaches the role of specialist. Thus, these speakers would be at the same time speakers and professionals and will possess a huge amount of (formal, semantic, functional, pragmatic and encyclopaedic) knowledge about their area of speciality associated to lexical units.

Therefore, terminological units can be said to belong to natural language and to integrate or form part of the grammars of particular languages and to share many characteristics with the units of natural language. This fact entails three direct consequences, as pointed out by the IULA (2007 b):

- That specialised communication has a status which is not alien to that of general communication.
- That the speaker does not possess differentiated lexical competences.
- And that general and specialised linguistic knowledge are also integrated.

Consequently, with this threefold statement and with this position what is defended is that terms do not form part of a system that is independent from that of words or other methods of expression and communication, rather, they overlap with these systems.

> Considerados en su contexto natural, i. e. en los textos o discursos producidos en situaciones de comunicación especializada concretas, las UT y las palabras no parecen diferenciarse tanto. En todo caso, las diferencias entre estas entidades no parecen ser respecto de su estatuto semiótico, sino relativas a cierta especificidad en su funcionamiento. (Adelstein, 2004: 55)

> [If considered in their natural context, e.g. in the texts or discourses produced in specific specialised communicative situations, TU (terminological units) and words do not seem to differ so much. In any case, the differences between these entities do not seem to rest on their semiotic characteristics but on a certain specificity in their functioning.] (Adelstein, 2004: 55)

However, the differences between term and word are not limited to the use of the term in speciality domains and, although not so relevant, there are other distinctive aspects. The differences between term and word are structured, according to the IULA (2007 b), on five levels:

1. Cognitive level

On this level, a frontier between term and word can be highlighted. The knowledge that the specialist in a subject matter has allows him/her to establish a series of clear and precise limits of what is and what is not a term within their speciality. Hence, a term does always occupy a place inside the conceptual structure of this subject matter and the specialist is the person with the widest knowledge of this structure.

2. Semantic level

Terms have a series of clear semantic limits established by the specialists in each subject matter. This implies or means that every terminological unit is more precise than another unit of the lexicon of the language in which precision does not play such a fundamental role. This is so because, according to the IULA (2007 b), the semantic description of the lexical unit will have to contain:

- Un conjunto de rasgos generales en el que se incluyen todos aquellos rasgos sistemáticos asociados a la unidad léxica y constantes en todas sus realizaciones discursivas y un conjunto de rasgos generales casi-sistemáticos que aparecen automáticamente en aquellas situaciones que cumplen unos determinados requisitos pragmáticos: nivel de especialización, emisor, receptor, etc.
- Un conjunto de rasgos especializados entre los que están aquellos rasgos ligados a uno o más ámbitos temáticos y otra serie de rasgos especializados libres correspondientes a la unidad en cuestión. Estos últimos son rasgos exclusivos de las realizaciones de la unidad léxica como término.

- [A group of general traits in which all the systematic features associated with the lexical unit and constant in all its discursive performances are included, and a group of quasi systematic general traits that automatically appear in those situations that accomplish certain pragmatic requisites: specialisation level, addresser, addressee, etc.
- A group of specialised traits among which we find those traits linked to one or more thematic fields, and another series of "free" specialised traits belonging to the unit in question. The latter are exclusive features of the performance of the lexical unit as a term.]

3. Semantic-pragmatic level

The specification of the kinds of situation in which each group of features is updated constitutes the pragmatic characterisation of the lexical unit. The pragmatic parameters determining the selection or correct actualisation of the traits for the values of the term are the following: the field, the topic, the way of dealing with this topic, the kind of text, the kind of addresser and addressee, and the kind of communicative situation.

4. Semantic-syntactic level

Basically, the kind of lexical units that can be updated as terms belong to the noun category. This becomes apparent in the fact that the fundamental differences between specialised and non-specialised texts are based on the kind of referentiality. Hence, in specialised texts, there is an almost exclusive predominance of the referential function and, in fact, the terminological units from the adjective or verb category are usually morphologically related to a nominal unit.

5. Formal level

Terminological updatings can be monolexical and polylexical. However, depending on the domain of speciality, terminological units present structures that correspond to certain formation processes, for instance, cult or hybrid formation in medicine, certain kinds of suffixation in chemistry, etc.

4.2.1.2. The hypothesis of the lexical unit (LU) in the CTT

> Partimos, pues, de la hipótesis de la UL de la TCT de Cabré (Cabré 1999d, 2000; Cabré and Adelstein 2001; Adelstein and Cabré, 2000) que plantea que la unidad léxica no es PER SE palabra ni término, sino que se trata de una forma léxica que, de acuerdo con la situación comunicativa en la que se emplee, activa un valor especializado o no. La información semántica, según Cabré, está organizada en rasgos y módulos o paquetes de rasgos, que se activan de maneras diversas según cada situación, dando lugar a uno de los sentidos posibles de la UL. (Adelstein 2004, 90-91)
>
> [We depart then, from the hypothesis of the LU of the CTT (Cabré 1999d, 2000; Cabré and Adelstein 2001; Adelstein and Cabré, 2000) which sets out that the lexical unit PER SE is neither a word nor a term but a lexical form which, according to the communicative situation in which it is given, activates a specialised value or not. The semantic information, according to Cabré, is organised in traits and modules or packs of traits that are activated in different ways depending on the situation, giving way to one of the possible meanings of the LU.] (Adelstein 2004, 90-91)

Thus – and this is the conception of term adopted in this book in accordance with the principles of the CTT and the SLA – the term is the updating of certain traits or modules of traits according to specialised communicative situations. It is a unit in use and one of the possible ways of finding a lexical unit in discourse. In consequence, the features and the discursive-communicative situations are what determine the selective activation of information, be it through formally specialised units (units used exclusively and only in specialised contexts although with a potential general value) or through units that are specialised in meaning (lexical units used with a specific sense in specialised contexts and with an open sense in non-specialised ones).[21]

Hence, within this proposal it is assumed that in the lexical competence of a speaker neither words nor terms exist, but instead lexical units and semantic traits that may activate (or not) specialised values according to the contexts in which they are found. These traits that can be activated might be general morphosyntactic traits of the unit or specific semantic and pragmatic traits that would describe their specialised character within a given context.

21 What is normally known as sub-technical vocabulary.

Accordingly, the main objectives that a discipline like terminology should have are (IULA, 2006 a):

- describir formal, semántica y funcionalmente las unidades léxicas que pueden adquirir valor terminológico;
- dar cuenta de cómo se activa este valor terminológico, haciendo referencia a la estructuración en rasgos y módulos de rasgos semánticos;
- explicar los parámetros que activan la selección de rasgos especializados o, lo que es lo mismo, el paso de una unidad léxica sin valor especializado a una unidad léxica especializada; y finalmente,
- explicar las relaciones de las unidades terminológicas con otros tipos de signos del mismo o distinto sistema para hacer progresar el conocimiento sobre la comunicación especializada y las unidades que se usan en ella.

- [describe, formally, semantically and functionally, the lexical units that may acquire a terminological value;
- account for the way this terminological value is activated, making reference to the structuring in traits and modules of semantic traits;
- explain the parameters that activate the selection of specialised traits or, what is the same, the passing of a lexical unit without specialised value to a specialised lexical unit; and finally,
- explain the relations of the terminological units with other kinds of signs of the same or different system in order to make knowledge about specialised comunication evolve as well as the units used in it.]

Thus, as Adelstein states (2004), describing and explaining the functioning of specialised units may be done from different perspectives due to their polyhedral character. Consequently, and in order to progressively continue reasoning out the way of conceiving terms in the SLA, the next section attempts to provide a comprehensive account of other aspects that are crucial in this conception according to the CTT.

*4.2.1.3. Terms / terminological units (TUs) in the CTT and The Theory of Doors (*La Teoría de las Puerta*s)*

In Wüster's views, the object of terminology was to express concepts through denominations from natural or artificial languages. In this context, Wüster refers to terms to allude to the nominal units of natural language that denominate specialised concepts.

Vargas (2005) explains how the Classical Theory defends that the way of analysing and dealing with terms differs from that of dealing with words in three main senses:

1) Every terminological work has as its departure point a number of concepts which must be perfectly determined (Felber, 1987). Concepts exist independently from the terms that designate them because they are mental abstractions (representing features assigned to objects, facts, phenomena, etc.) to which we assign labels.

2) Wüster considers that the terminologist is only interested in terminologies or vocabularies and does not take into account morphology or syntax, from which it is implicit that grammatical rules only pertain to the general language. Wüster was not at all interested in the study of the terms in use but in establishing what they represented.

3) The terminologist is only interested in the synchronic study of terms.

Hence, traditionally, the word (understood as the unit of natural language) and the term (understood as the unit of specialised languages) have been distinguished. Nowadays, however, new proposals have been developed that conceive word and term as values of a same unit of the lexicon, depending on their context of use. Hence, as aforementioned, the notion of lexical unit would designate here an entity that is not identified with words or terms – a unit which is *per se* neither word nor term – but a form associated to, among other things, a great amount of semantic information. In this way, a lexical unit is potentially term and no term.

According to the CTT there are two "observation points" from which terminological units can be analysed:

> On the one hand, they can be analysed *in vitro*, that is to say, outside their natural context and in an isolated way by means of the units contained in dictionaries, databases or thesauruses. When we observe terminological units *in vitro*, these units possess a meaning and a form which could be described as stable and well-delimited.

> On the other hand, observation *in vivo* is also possible and this implies analysing units in their natural habitat in specialised communication, through the analysis of texts, whether oral or written, produced in real, natural situations. These units show a diversification that is produced without exception (although with different degrees) in any given specialised text.

In this sense, as Cabré and Estopà (2002) state, the analysis of terms in context opens the door to three important observations in the development of terminology as a field of study: firstly, it enables observing the formal, conceptual and functional diversification of terminological units. Secondly, it enables detecting other units of specialised knowledge beyond terminological ones; thirdly, it enables placing the units of specialised knowledge in a multirelational cognitive structure.

As has already been explained, formally and semantically terms do not seem to differ much from words, but if pragmatic or communicative criteria are adopted, the differences between the two become more acute (Cabré, 1993). The most outstanding peculiarity of terminology in contrast to the common lexicon is that the former is used to designate the concepts belonging to specialised disciplines and activities. Consequently, as may be deduced, terms are mainly known by specialists in each of these subjects and appear with a high frequency in the specialised documents of each discipline.

To proceed further into Cabré's (1993: 169) views on this topic, she states that terms, just like words from common language "son unidades sígnicas distintivas y significativas al mismo tiempo, que se presentan de forma natural en el discurso especializado."[22] Accordingly, they have a systematic side (formal, semantic and functional) and also show another pragmatic side, since they are units used in specialised communication to designate the objects of a pre-existent reality (see figure 13 below):

22 "Are distinctive and meaningful sign units that are given in a natural way in specialised discourse".

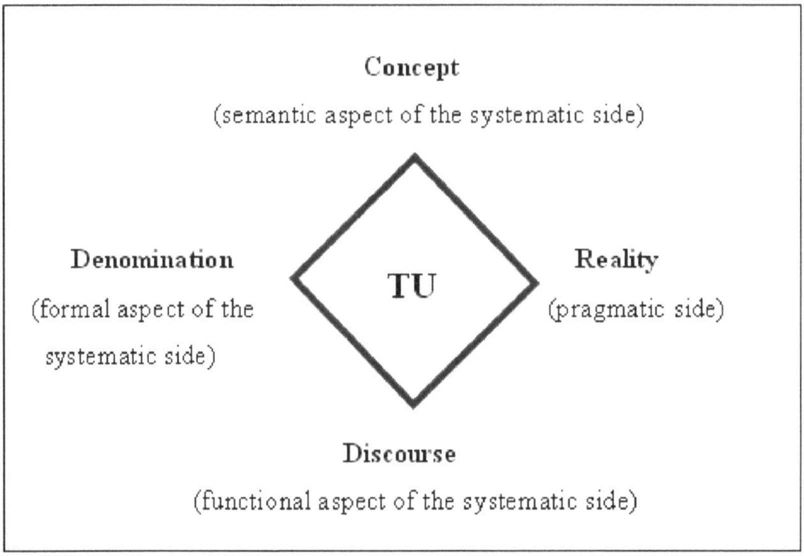

Figure 13. Adaptation of Cabré's (1993) representation of the terminological unit.

Cabré (1993) goes on to explain how terms, like any other significant unit of a linguistic system, form part of a structured system in which they occupy a particular level (the level of lexical units). They relate to the rest of the units on the same level and to the units on the other levels and, together, participate in the construction of discourse. Hence, the relationships established by terms, both with the lexicon in general and with the rest of the components of grammar, do not display any specificity that makes them systematically different from the relationships that words simultaneously maintain with their grammatical environment. However, as Cabré states (1993), it must be acknowledged that within the lexical component of a language, terms do relate far more closely with the other terms from the same discipline (with which they constitute specific structured subsystems) than with terms from other thematic areas. Hence, terms are units from a lexical system (including common lexicon and the different specialised lexicons) that form part of the general grammar system and, as such, they must share the same rules for sentence and discourse formation as the rest of lexical units from language (Cabré, 1993).

Therefore, if the proposal that terminology is an integral part of the lexical system of a "grammar" is accepted, terms are seen to be *signic* units which can be linguistically analysed from three different points of view (Cabré, 1993):

Formal (the denomination):

> Desde una perspectiva formal, los términos son conjuntos fonológicos susceptibles de ser articulados fonéticamente – y de ser representados gráficamente – con una estructura interna constituida por morfemas. (Cabré 1993: 171)
>
> [From a formal perspective, terms are phonological groups susceptible to be phonetically articulated – and to be graphically represented – with an internal structure made up by morphemes.] (Cabré 1993: 171)

Semantic (the concept):

> Desde un punto de vista semántico, los términos son unidades de referencia a una realidad, y por lo tanto están dotados de un significado que puede describirse como un conjunto de rasgos distintivos. (Cabré 1993: 171)
>
> [From a semantic point of view, terms are units making reference to a reality and therefore, they are provided with a meaning that can be described as a group of distinctive features.] (Cabré 1993: 171)

Functional (category and distribution):

> Desde una perspectiva funcional, los términos son unidades distribucionales que requieren un entorno lingüístico determinado, y que en el discurso se encuentran frecuentemente combinados con otros términos específicos (la fraseología). (Cabré 1993: 171)
>
> [From a functional perspective, terms are distributional units which require a specific linguistic environment and which are frequently combined with other specific terms in the discourse (phraseology).] (Cabré 1993: 171)

Although the word "term" is used to designate the complete terminological unit (formed by denomination and concept), it is also used as a synonym of denomination. This previous hint can be especially useful for attempting to explain certain aspects regarding denomination and to understand, first of all, Cabré's words (1993) when she concedes that the formal aspect of the terminological unit is known in terminology as "denomination" and also "term".

Linguistics, cognition and communication are three unavoidable aspects that must be considered in the study of terms as the elements that constitute its multifaceted nature.

Hence, bearing all these aspects in mind, it seems plausible to consider that terminological units can also be analysed from diverse perspectives. These different perspectives can be established according to different parameters, such as the dichotomies general/specialised, lexical/grammatical, expression/communication, synchronic/diachronic, grammatical/social, etc. Terminology is then, like a complex object, a discipline that can be analysed from different points of view. Each of these points of view, which are concentrated in a unit corresponding to each sphere, constitutes the principal object of a different discipline.

Accordingly, in Cabré's and Estopà's views (2002), the contributions made by linguistics, psychology and the philosophy of science to terminology in recent times have allowed such an object to be recovered, not as an exclusive object of linguistics, but also of other disciplines (Rey, 1979; Sager, 1990; Gambier, 1991; Gaudin, 1991; Slodzian, 1995; Condamines, 1994; Cabré, 1994, 1999 a; Temmerman, 1998; Ciapuscio, 2000).

Most of the criticism that the GTT has received over the years (the most significant part of which has been reproduced in this work) refers, basically, to the insufficiency that has arisen from the idealisation of reality, knowledge and communication, as well as to the limited scope of this proposal, which is reduced to standardisation. Such criticism comes from three different perspectives or approaches: cognitive, linguistic and social.

- Cognitive science grounds its critical views on the fact that the notion of specialised knowledge is dealt with by the GTT in an isolated way, which brings to the fore the question of its uniformity and its moving away from general knowledge.

- Linguistics basically questions the limitation imposed on the part of the GTT, this being translated as paying attention to and showing interest exclusively in the prescriptive aspects of terms, considering them as units that are completely and radically different to the lexical units that characterise general language.

- Sociology rejects the idealised conception of terms, the plain character attributed to specialised communication – where terms partially lose their condition of units from natural language and their pragmatic features – and the negation of discursive variation.

Hence, according to the CTT, the conception of terminology as a knowledge domain of a necessarily interdisciplinary nature that accounts for the terms and that integrates the cognitive, linguistic and communicative aspects of the terminological units is what has lead to the formulation of the Theory of Doors (*Teoría de las Puertas*) (Cabré, 1999 a, 2000 a). This theory accounts for the multidisciplinarity of the terminological object and states that the object *term* is a semiotic, linguistic, cognitive and social unit that can be dealt with by and from different perspectives,[23] the only condition being the fulfilment of the following three principles (Cabré, 2002):

- To start out from the principle that a discipline can never account for an object in its totality, but only contribute to the description and explanation of such an object.

- To conceive the units of specialised knowledge, as well as every unit of natural language, as multifaceted units that are cognitive, linguistic and social.

- To assume that, in order to properly and accurately deal with an object, a particular perspective must be adopted and made explicit. In terminology this positioning requires the selection of a single entrance door for the description of the units that convey specialised knowledge.

Hence, this theory of terms has been construed on the basis of different linguistic theories and includes different aspects of cognition and

---

23 These different perspectives are the "*puertas*" (doors) which we may go through to analyse terminological units. We can opt for analysing these units by going through the semiotic, linguistic, cognitive and social doors.

communication theory. According to the *Theory of Doors*, one may go into the terminological study through one of its doors, and later establish the necessary connections or links, that is to say, one may, for instance, "go in" from the knowledge until the linguistic and communicative matter is reached, or vice versa.

If we open the linguistic door, it must be noted that units that are considered to be terminological can be analysed at the same time from a formal, semantic and functional side; they are then considered to be similar to lexical units (which are not specialised) because, apart from sharing these three aspects, both kinds of units belong to a bigger lexical category. In the case of terminological units, there is no universal agreement on whether this bigger category is only and always the noun (Wüster, 1979; Sager, 1990) or the noun, the adjective and the verb (Cabré, 1994; Dubuc, 1985). It is precisely this condition the one that differentiates them from other units that are also semantic, formal and functional, such as morphological, phraseological or orational units. In consequence, functionally, both lexical and terminological units belong to one of the grammatical categories established. Also from the formal point of view, both the terminological and lexical units share the same structures and are explained by the same grammatical rules. From the semantic point of view they are not different either, since they are units with a meaning (and one or more senses) that can be represented through a definition. Finally, from the pragmatic point of view, both units participate in the communication scheme that is presupposed for any communicative interaction. Hence, one may wonder what the specificity of the terminological units is. According to Cabré (1999 a) and Lara (1999) it lies in the signification process: the processes used to categorise the same reality are what distinguish the specialist from the layman even though both of them use the same form. In an example proposed by Cabré (2002), the unit "salt" is, for the non-specialist, a "condiment used for cooking", but for the chemist it is "sodium chloride".

Moreover, as Gutiérrez (1998) points out, these categorisation procedures are different not only between the specialist and the layman. They can also be different between specialists, since not all of them analyse or understand reality in the same way: each topical area has its own objectives and references that make the perspective from which things are observed vary.

Therefore, if we assume that terminological units share the same characteristics as the lexical units of a natural language, it can be presupposed that the terminological and lexical units are not different grammatical units (Cabré, 2002). What is different, however, is the specialised/non-specialised value they acquire in a conversation. Hence, according to Cabré (2002) and her proposal, TUs are lexical units that are singularly activated by their pragmatic conditions, which make the terminological character of a unit a pragmatic value conferred by the discursive conditions in which a text is given within an area; that is to say, it depends on its use in a given and specific expressive and situational context. Consequently, a lexical unit is formed by a group of semantic parameters, some of which are activated, some of which are not, depending on their use in a specific domain (Cabré, 2002). Moreover, it is not true that the condition of specialised value is unique or static. The same unit may, on the one hand, activate different specialised values depending on the subject matter in which it is used (horizontal variation). On the other hand, the same lexical unit within the same specialised area may be more or less specialised, since the trait of specialised value carries with it gradual values of precision (accuracy), concision and scientific character (vertical variation). The examples that Cabré (2002) proposes to illustrate these two types of variation are, on the one hand, the lexical unit *consorcio* (consortium), which is an example of horizontal variation because it can be used in a non-specialised context or in specialised contexts that involve different topics. On the other hand, the example proposed to illustrate vertical variation is the lexical unit *hígado* (liver), which in texts about medicine is treated with different levels of specialisation.

To sum up, terms cannot be explained in an autonomous way independently from other denominative signs with which they share the "space" of specialised communication, nor isolated from the other signs of natural language made up of a form and a meaning (Cabré, 1999 a). Accordingly, terminology is presented as an interdisciplinary and multi-entry field of knowledge:

- Terminology is considered a field of knowledge and leaves apart the label "discipline". In this line, it is assumed that the structuring of knowledge around a well-delimited object shapes a field of knowledge;

- It is assumed that every object of study is interdisciplinary *per se* and as such it can be tackled or approached from different subject matters. This characteristic is embodied in the principle of the multifaceted nature of the object;

- It considers that every field of knowledge structured around an object facilitates a multiple entry to this object. The object is always the same but the "entrance door" to it may be different. This proposal is embodied in the "Theory of Doors/Doors Model" (Cabré 1999 a).

Consequently, if this view is followed, terminology is an interdisciplinary field of knowledge whose central object of study are terminological units, which, due to their multifaceted nature, can be approached as units of language, their conceptual condition or their socio-communicative function.

Thus, in order to completely understand the CTT it is necessary to be aware of the importance of the "Theory of Doors" (Cabré, 1999 a, 2000 a), which accounts for the already-mentioned interdisciplinary nature of terminology and the multidisciplinarity and multifaceted nature of the terminological object in a structured and coherent way.

4.2.2. Grounding principles of the CTT

On the basis of what has been mentioned hitherto, Cabré (1999 a) and her team introduced some of the grounding elements of their proposal for a new theory of terminology. These elements are presented in the form of principles (understood as the inherent conditions to be accomplished, or the alternative possibilities formulated in terms of whether a given feature is possessed or not) which facilitate or block the attribution of certain characteristics or the accomplishment of certain processes. Following Cabré (1999 a), the way of approaching and accounting for terminology is sustained upon six basic principles from which the CTT can be coherently explained:

a) Principle of the multifaceted nature of the term (see section 4.2.1.3)

According to this principle, terminological units are inherently multifaceted, that is to say, they are units that integrate three aspects in one, i.e. the linguistic, cognitive and social dimensions (see figure 14). This multifaceted nature is present, regardless of the fact that a study on terms may adopt an integrating position or, conversely, may be limited to examining a single phenomenon within just one aspect.

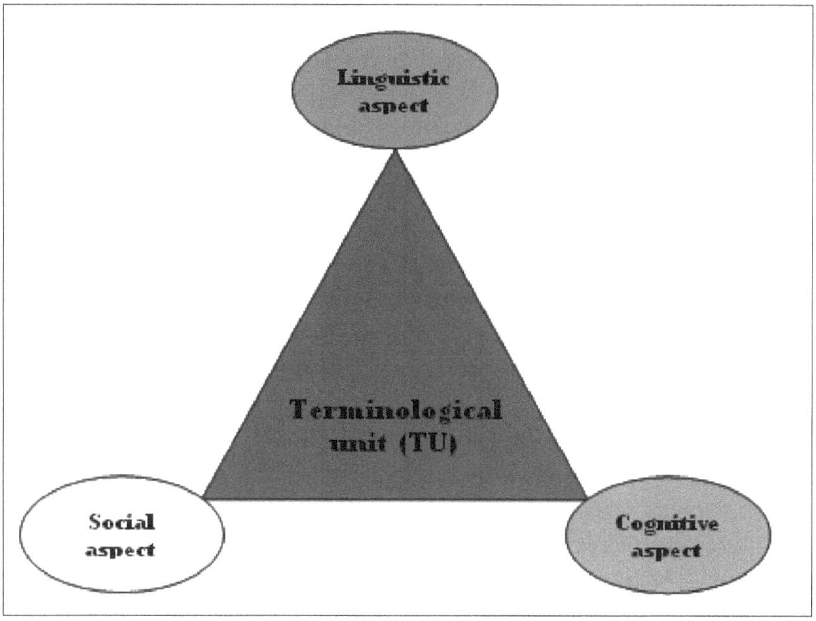

Figure 14. Illustration of the multifaceted nature of the terminological unit.

b) Principle of the communicative character of terminology

According to this principle (which is one of the most decisive and characteristic in the CTT, as its very name indicates), every terminological unit pursues a communicative goal, in either an immediate or a remote way. If this goal is immediate, it is materialised in the form of direct or indirect communication. Direct communication, on the one hand, takes place among experts, in didactic discourse or that used in the popularisation of science, among other possibilities. On the other hand, indirect communication can be understood as the communication via a process such as translation, interpretation or specialised journalism. In other cases, explains Cabré (1999 a), communication makes use of terminological units to represent knowledge, that is, to label the "knowledge knots" belonging to concepts of the specialised world. In these cases, the remote goal (in contrast to the aforementioned immediate goal) of such representation is to favour the univocity of communication among experts (international denominative standards) or among experts and expert systems (in documentation and in computational linguistics applied to knowledge engineering), thus creating a new conception of reality or conceptualising a new reality.

c) Principle of variation

According to the principle of variation, any process of communication inherently implies variation and such variation can be made explicit in alternative forms of denomination for the same concept (synonymy) or in the semantic openness of one form (polysemy). This principle applies to all terminological units, although it admits different degrees according to the conditions of each type of communicative situation. The greatest degrees of variation would be accomplished by the terms aimed for use in popularising science and technology, whereas the smallest degree of variation is the one corresponding to terminology standardised by groups of experts. The intermediate degree is represented by terminology used in natural, everyday communication between specialists.

d) The natural language condition. Following Cabré (2002), terminologies must be located within a specific area of knowledge where its object is defined. This statement implies the acceptance that an object of analysis is established only when it is defined within a field of knowledge. In this sense, the field of study of terminology is defined in terms of its location within a field of knowledge.

Consequently, as Cabré states, this is the only possible explanation for the wide range of interpretations given to the terminological unit up till now, and which can be summarised in the following perspectives:

- For linguistics, terminology is a part of the lexicon of a grammar specialised by topical, pragmatic and semantic criteria.

- For the different specialised subjects or areas, it is a means of professional expression and communication as well as a system for representing the structural knowledge of specialised areas.
- For translation, interpretation and technical writing, terminology is a group of communication units whose evaluation is measured in terms of equivalence, adequacy, precision and economy criteria.
- For linguistic planning, terminology is an area of language where intervention is needed in order to reaffirm the existence, utility and survival of a language understood as a means of expression.

Very significantly, in all the options or perspectives put forward above, terminological units have a tripartite character: linguistic, cognitive and social (see figure 14).

Despite this, terminology is viewed differently by those disciplines that are not interested in it from the communicative (and consequently linguistic) point of view but from the representational (and only indirectly from the communicative) point of view. Such a view would be the one adopted by terminology within knowledge engineering, documentation or international standardisation. In these cases, like any other communicative sign, units also accomplish the aforementioned principles since they are units with a tripartite (linguistic, social and communicative) character; but they may also present idiosyncratic aspects.

However, this condition of natural language attributed to terminology implies a series of consequences determined by the grammar that describes this natural language. Hence, the general morphological, syntactic and semantic properties of the words of a language also act on terms.

e) The special communication condition (attributed to terms)

It can be easily deduced from everyday evidence that general communication and specialised communication share common elements – such as the communicative scheme, the processes produced, the linguistic functions, the interchange conditions and so on – but they also present differences in certain aspects. If a deeper analysis is undertaken in this respect, specialised communication[24] is seen to differ from general communication in the selection of units, in the organisation of discourse, in the frequency of the linguistic functions that are selected, and so on.

In addition to this, there seems to be rather general agreement on the fact that scientific-technical communications elaborated on the basis of specialised languages – and in contrast to texts produced by general communication – are (overall) characterised by three main elements or aspects:

- The global semantic aspect: concise texts, which are usually hardly redundant, precise (this precision understood as the lack of ambiguity) and depersonalised (lacking the emotive function).
- The preponderance attributed to lexicon and, more specifically, within the lexicon, the quantitative and qualitative importance of nominalisations and nominal forms.
- The formal aspect of discourse: the high degree of elaboration of a text and, in certain areas or subjects, the integration of semiotic symbolic systems within the text.

Thus, there is fairly broad agreement upon the idea that specialised languages form a kind of subgroup within general language. In this sense, and after having analysed many scientific-technical communications, that is to say, the texts produced in such situations, Rondeau (1984) stated that the term "specialised language" can only be understood as a subgroup of the general language and differing from common language in the textual, lexical and pragmatic-functional dimension.

From the textual point of view, specialised texts are characterised by a specific global configuration.

From the pragmatic point of view, specialised languages are generally characterised by their easier intercomprehension beyond

24 The adjective "specialised" is understood here as that which accomplishes all the necessary semantic and pragmatic requisites, that is to say, it is topically marked, it is produced in a professional setting or situation, it belongs to a formal register and does not acquire its meaning directly from an object of reality but from a pre-established structure (Cabré, 1993).

the peculiarities of particular languages. In this sense and following Beaugrande (1987, in Cabré 2004: 7) "LSPs tend to share much of their resources not merely with LGPs, but also often have common cognate resources. LSP thus tends to be more 'international', or indeed 'universal', than does LGP".

Finally, from the lexical point of view, specialised texts are specific because of the terminologies they use. These terminologies can present various degrees of specialisation and levels of signification as well as different levels of peculiarity, depending on the kind of subject or knowledge area and the level of abstraction at which this is dealt.

To sum up, if Rondeau's (1984) views are accepted, it can be said that from a textual point of view general and specialised communication share the same "territory", make use of the same linguistic and textual rules and processes and, broadly speaking, their greatest discrepancy or difference lies in the selection of units and the frequency with which each resource is updated in the discourse.

f) The specialisation condition

Having a specialised character is a necessary condition that must be accomplished by the discourse in order to be considered special. However, what is not so clearly agreed is the definition of "specialised" and the different degrees it may present. Following Cabré (1999 a), what seems obvious is that if the adjective "specialised" is used exclusively to refer to discourse dealing with some strongly structured scientific-technical field, the notion of specialisation is stronger than if it is also applied to specialised activities. Whatever the case may be, within each speciality, discourse can be produced at different levels, thus also implying a different *terminological density*.

In Cabré's (1999 a) view, the condition of "specialised" is accomplished by those texts in which the conceptualisation they transmit has been achieved from the perspective of the speciality and the specialist, and not from the optic of the common speaker. Thus, the specialisation of a text is not so much based on the subject matter it acts as a vehicle for, but on the way this subject matter is conveyed.

If the degree of specialisation of communication is considered, Cabré (2000 a) states that it is not only dependent on the terminological density a text may present but also on the amount of expressive variation that can be resorted to when referring to a single concept. Hence, a highly specialised text tends to be precise, concise and systematic, its terminology tending towards monosemy and univocity. However, if the degree of specialisation decreases, the discourse shows features more akin to general expression. These features refer, for instance, to the fact that from a semantic point of view there will be more contextual variation, redundancy, ambiguity and a greater lack of precision; from a formal point of view, it will have greater variation as regards lexical synonymy, and it will show a greater use of paraphrastic formulae which contain analytical explanations of concepts. However, on a more specialised level, these concepts would be explained synthetically.

4.2.3. Characterisation of the CTT

Bearing in mind what has been explained so far and if we focus on the CTT as a whole, it can be said that from the 90s onwards, terminology has been undergoing a process of renewal. We have witnessed a deep critical revision of the theoretical and methodological postulates upholding the Classical Theory or GTT, leaving aside the idealised and normalising view of terms that characterised it. The appearance of other approaches, such as the sociolinguistic trend, made terminology go on with its development to a *descriptive* perspective in opposition to the *prescriptive* one that had prevailed up to that time. Rey (1979), for instance, proposes understanding of terminological production from a descriptive point of view because specialised lexical units are real linguistic issues and not homogeneous and ideal entities without conceptual ambiguities.

Therefore, new approaches to terminology have been developed which constitute a step forward with respect to the GTT. As has already been mentioned, terminology has progressively abandoned the main goal pursued by traditional postulates in the field, that is to say, to control and even eliminate linguistic variation. However, the modern conception of terminology does not imply rejecting terminological standardisation completely: it understands it as a means of intervention whose adoption will be considered positive or not depending on each situation and on each communicative context.

Following Vargas (2005), the new proposals of terminology are grounded in the principle according to which knowledge can only be produced and known through its materialisation in its different semiotic systems, among which the verbal one is the one that dominates in sciences and technology. Thus, contrary to what Wüster proclaimed, terminology deals with concepts and thus with knowledge structures only when they are represented in the language lexicon.

Consequently, a theory in which terms are conceived as linguistic and communicative units (CTT) will not have concept as a key point (GTT).

As has been progressively introduced in previous sections, Cabré was the first to provide an argued criticism of the GTT and to show the explanatory and descriptive shortcomings to be found in it. She does not question the whole GTT but criticises mainly the normalising and uniforming ideal it aims at, which ignores the communicative dimension of terms. In Cabré's (1999 a: 110) words, Wüster's theory:

> Establece un objeto de análisis y unas funciones de trabajo muy restrictivos, por cuanto limita el objeto a las unidades unívocas normalizadas propias de los ámbitos científico-técnicos, reduce la actividad terminológica a la recopilación de conceptos y de términos para la normalización (...) de los términos, circunscribe los ámbitos especializados a la ciencia y la técnica y limita sus objetivos a asegurar la univocidad de la comunicación profesional, fundamentalmente en el plano internacional.
>
> [Establishes an object of analysis and a series of working functions which are very restrictive since it confines the object to the univocal normalised units characteristic of scientific-technical fields, it reduces the terminological activity to the compilation of concepts and terms with normalisation as the final aim (...), it restricts specialised domains to science and technology, and its objectives are limited to assuring the univocity of professional communication, mainly in the international arena.]

Therefore, Cabré's work gathers a series of postulates in the form of a new theory of terminology grounded on the communicative aspects of specialised languages, leaving aside the normalising systematic conception that is characteristic of the Traditional Theory. Thus, this renewing effort was shaped into the already-mentioned CTT proposed by Cabré (1999 a and 2000 c among other works).

Throughout the previous sections most of the features that constitute the mainstays of the CTT have been progressively introduced.

Hence, in accordance with what has been discussed above, the CTT is a theory of a linguistic basis that explains terminology as a group of denominative-conceptual units from natural language representing specialised knowledge within a precise thematic area and hence acting as a vehicle to convey professional natural communication.

Hence, the pillars of the CTT are mainly grounded on seven basic assumptions that have made linguistic reflection advance and evolve (Cabré, 2000 a) and which characterise the CTT as follows:

- It considers reality to be only one and assumes that just the ways of approaching, conceptualising and categorising it give way to two kinds of knowledge: general and specialised.

- It understands that general and specialised knowledge, which share the field of study of cognitive science, can manifest themselves formally through the units of articulated natural language or through units of other symbolic languages.

- It assumes that, placed in articulated natural language, knowledge of the world is materialised in referential units that are integrated within the grammar of the speaker and that, within this grammar, they form part of the lexical component.

- It considers that the speakers' knowledge, if materialised in linguistic units, is included in their grammar-based linguistic competence and the knowledge of the units of reference in the pragmatic module of their grammar.

- It postulates that referential language units included in a speaker's grammar are neither words nor terms – neither in the first instance nor in the abstract. Instead, they are believed to be units of the lexicon of which, according to the features of the communicative situation, only a specific set of characteristics is selected from the totality which describe them. Consequently, any unit having a reference can potentially be a term or a word. However, it is also possible that some highly specialised units in special subjects may become only terms, as they are always used to denominate special concepts. In spite of this, this does not mean either that they are unable or cannot eventually become part of the general language due to the spread of special knowledge.

- It maintains that the fact that all referential units have the possibility of becoming both terms or words (when expressing special or general knowledge respectively) does not mean or imply that they function as both in all cases. In consequence, the lexical component of grammar would contain only the real information and not the potential information for every unit.

- It maintains that a model like the one suggested can only be sustained if it sets out from a strong lexical theory that contemplates a lexical component in a grammar model that includes, apart from grammatical data, pragmatic and encyclopaedic information about the units of grammar. Moreover, it must possess a mechanism that accounts for the selection of traits (not marked / marked) undertaken by the speaker in a given situation. This selection process could be designed as a mechanism of activation of the marked thematic features when the communicative characteristics so require.

Hence, the CTT (which was already constituted as a proper theory after a deep reflection on the shortcomings of former theories of the sort) pays attention in all its dimensions to the linguistic variation that so annoyed Wüster and takes into account the conceptual, textual and discursive features of terms. Cabré (1999 a) thus conceives a new theoretical framework applied to terms and observes them *in vivo*, that is to say, as they appear in different communicative situations and, therefore, subject to change. At the same time she takes into consideration the different degrees of specialisation a text, a term or some given knowledge may present:

> Tanto el conocimiento especializado como los textos especializados, como las unidades terminológicas pueden darse a diferentes niveles de especialización y describirse en distintos niveles de representación. Sólo así, los términos pueden explicarse en toda su realidad comunicativa y representacional. (Cabré, 1999 a: 126)

> [Both specialised knowledge and specialised texts and terminological units may be given at different levels of specialisation and be described in different representation levels. This is the only way terms may be explained in all their communicative and representational reality.] (Cabré, 1999 a: 126)

According to what has been mentioned so far, the main features on which the CTT is built can be summarised as follows (Vargas, 2005):

- Terminology is an autonomous interdisciplinary subject, not simply an autonomous one, something which must be clearly stated within a theory of language which is at the same time inserted within a theory of communication and knowledge. This linguistic theory includes linguistic, as well as cognitive and pragmatic, aspects.

- The resemblances and differences between general and specialised knowledge are explained by this theory within the competence of the speaker-specialist without dissociating them, although at the same time the singularities of each of them are maintained.

- It explains the interdisciplinarity of terminological units and accounts for the diversity of views that the different specialists involved have of them. Therefore, it conceives terminological units as multifaceted units made up of the three disciplinary aspects that describe them, i.e. linguistic, cognitive and pragmatic.

- It provides an explanation for the fact that a concept may form part of the conceptual structure of different disciplines, assuming, however, that a term may be used in the field of a speciality area and transferred from one speciality to another or from the general language to a specialised language.

- It assumes the polysemic character of terms, so that it also takes into account the possibility of specialised units becoming "trivialised" in some particular moment, of the continuous "terminologising" of units from the general language, as well as the possibility of there being a constant entrance of terms from one speciality field to another (pluri-terminologising).

- It admits synonymy as a real phenomenon within natural specialised communication.

- It must take into account that terminological units are processed in a natural way in the discourse and that, consequently, they have a syntactic projection that goes beyond the denominative limits and varies depending on the discourse being dealt with.

- It considers the variation of the discourse and establishes the variables that describe this variation in the field of communication in general, and in specialised communication in particular.

To sum up, terminology has experienced a qualitative "leap forward" in the sense that the former privileged position of the conceptual schemata in scientific-technological fields has given way to the privileged role of the text or discourse, which accounts for the important role played by corpus linguistics in this work. This change, undertaken mainly thanks to the efforts of Rey (1975), Sager (1993) and, of course, Cabré (1999 a), among others, has made it possible to develop a theory of terminology that takes into account the different aspects of languages within their pragmatic scope and that, therefore, fits the SLA. In Vargas' (2005: 196) words:

> La TCT ha abierto nuevos caminos más apropiados y adecuados para la tarea terminográfica pues asume la diversificación discursiva en razón del tipo de situación, del destinatario, de la temática, del nivel de especialización de los textos, del grado de formalidad, de la finalidad del discurso, entre otros aspectos.
>
> [The CTT has opened up news paths, more appropriate and adequate to the terminographical task since it assumes discursive diversification depending on the kind of situation, the addresser, the subject matter, the level of specialisation of the texts, the degree of formality, and the final aim of the discourse among other aspects.]

Therefore, the CTT not only takes into account the linguistic, pragmatic and communicative aspects of the specialised lexical units, but also designates the specialised text as the base unit for its analysis. In this way, terminological research acquires a textual dimension that allows the terminologist to observe texts in context, which at the same time leads to the adoption of a phraseological dimension. Thanks to this, not only single terms have been studied in this research, but also other kinds of combinations of terms that work within the specialised text and which are crucial to the SLA.

This communicative theory of terminology leaves aside the more restrictive views of the classical one, based on a systematic normalising conception. Throughout these sections I have tried to account for the main postulates of this Communicative Theory and its different views about the essence and aims of terminology. In a way, I have attempted to show how the GTT was developed to fulfil a specific necessity and how many of its contributions have been and still are vital for terminology, so that terminologists will always be in debt to it; no-one can deny the importance of the GTT in the process of establishing terminology as a field of knowledge by determining its object of study. However, its shortcomings and failures (namely and mainly the fact it ignores the communicative dimension of terminology) cannot be forgotten and, consequently, the step forward represented by the CTT has been thought to constitute the best alternative to account for terminology in general and to frame this study, as well as being the most realistic way to do it.

4.3. Terminology as a field of knowledge and its relationship with lexicology, lexicography and terminography

For the correct characterisation of the SLA in this first part of the book, we are progressively disclosing the great number of aspects that, from a theoretical perspective, shape this approach. With this aim, it is also necessary to take a closer look at terminology, terminography, lexicology and lexicography and their fields of work. All too frequently, the boundaries between disciplines or fields of knowledge are too blurred due to the proximity, similarity, merging nature and subtleties of their functions, topics and goals. In this particular case this is so because of the interdisciplinarity of linguistic activity in general and, more specifically, of terminological practice. Therefore, in order to clarify the scope of action of these highly related "disciplines", one must be aware of the ways in which they are interrelated and cooperate with each other, as well as know the most significant and even opposing views regarding their scopes and roles that have been put forward by different authors.

When it comes to distinguishing between terminology/terminography and lexicology/lexicography, most authors usually establish a parallel correspondence between lexicology and terminology and lexicography and terminography. On the one hand, lexicology is understood as the discipline focused on the study and description of the lexicon of a language and lexicography is conceived as the applied branch of lexicology and focuses on the elaboration of dictionaries. On the other hand, and correspondingly, terminology is considered an area of theoretical and methodological study, terminography being the applied, practical aspect of terminology responsible for the elaboration of specialised dictionaries. Accordingly, lexicology is to terminology what lexicography is to terminography (Pérez, 2002).

But why, then, are terminology, terminography, lexicology and lexicography disciplines which may present blurred boundaries that need to be clarified? Alcaraz and Martínez Linares' (1997) definition of lexicography and lexicology may contribute to start forming an idea about these issues. In its second and more modern sense, in the quotes below, the word lexicography refers to both a theoretical and a practical dimension (in a way, the same as what happens with the use of the label "terminology" to refer also to its applied dimension, which is also known as terminography). Lexicography thus in a way absorbs the more theoretical field of action of what has been traditionally known as lexicology (meaning 1 in the quotation below).

> LEXICOGRAFÍA **1)** Atendiendo a su cometido estrictamente práctico, la "lexicografía" se ha venido definiendo como el arte o la técnica de componer léxicos o diccionarios (Casares, 1950; Lázaro Carreter, 1968; DRAE), siendo su contrapartida, en el plano teórico, la LEXICOLOGÍA, disciplina encargada del estudio científico del léxico y, en consecuencia, de los principios que rigen la elaboración de todo tipo de obras lexicográficas (Fernández Sevilla, 1974).
> **2)** Actualmente, el término "lexicografía" designa tanto a la técnica científica de componer diccionarios, léxicos, etc., como la disciplina lingüística que proporciona las bases teóricas y metodológicas de la praxis lexicográfica. (DRAE, 1992; Alvar, 1993, Azorín, 1994)

> [LEXICOGRAPHY **1)** Paying attention to its strictly practical aim, "lexicography" has normally been defined as the art or technique of compiling lexicons or dictionaries (Casares, 1950; Lázaro Carreter, 1968; DRAE), whereas in the theoretical aspect, LEXICOLOGY is the discipline in charge of the scientific study of lexicon and, consequently, of the principles that rule the elaboration of every kind of lexicographical work. (Fernández Sevilla, 1974).
> **2)** Currently, the term "lexicography" refers both to the scientific technique of making dictionaries, lexicons, etc. and to the linguistic discipline that provides the theoretical and methodological bases for the lexicographical praxis.] (DRAE, 1992; Alvar, 1993, Azorín, 1994)

However, Fernández-Sevilla (1974, in Martínez de Sousa 1995: 254) tries to assign to lexicology the importance he thinks it deserves. In Fernández-Sevilla's words (1974: 17):

> "No existe acuerdo acerca de qué deba ser la lexicología, cuáles sus límites y alcance. Ni siquiera existe unanimidad en relación con la legitimidad de su propia existencia"

> ["There is no agreement about what lexicology should be, which limits it should have and its scope. There is not even unanimity regarding the legitimity of its own existence".]

In addition, he concedes that:

> "No pocos opinan que la lexicología ni siquiera tiene razón de ser en el marco de la lingüística de nuestro tiempo. Su presunto cometido deberían repartírselo la semántica, la fonología, la morfología y hasta la lexicografía. Sin embargo, parece lícito y necesario postular su existencia y desarrollo, entendiéndola como disciplina lingüística que se ocupa del vocabulario global de una lengua como conjunto estructurado (…), es decir, de los problemas generales relativos al sistema o conjuntos estructurados de palabras". (Fernández-Sevilla, 1974: 18-19)

> [More than a few believe that lexicology has not even sense in the framework of nowadays linguistics. Its supposed task should be shared out by semantics, phonology, morphology and even lexicography. Nonetheless, it seems reasonable and necessary to postulate its existence and development understanding it as a linguistic discipline in charge of the global vocabulary of a language as a structured group (…), that is, of the general problems regarding the system or structured collection of words".] (Fernández-Sevilla, 1974: 18-19)

Sager's (1990) considerations on this topic go a step further and establish a rather delimited boundary between terminology (in its wider sense including terminography) and lexicography that is coherent with Sager's separate, independent vision of LSP and general language (see section 2.1):

> Terminology is the study and the field of activity concerned with the collection, description, processing and presentation of terms, i.e. lexical items belonging to specialised areas of usage of one or more languages. In its objectives it is akin to lexicography which combines the double aim of generally collecting data about the lexicon of a language with providing information, and sometimes even an advisory, service to language users. The justification of considering it a separate activity from lexicography lies in the different nature of the data traditionally assembled, the different background of the people involved in this work, and to some extent in the different methods used. (Sager, 1990: 2)

I do not totally agree with this view since he traces a too abrupt line between general and specialised languages, between terms and words, between onomasiological and semasiological methods. According to the SLA, language is a *continuum* that is better defined by inclusive relationships which contemplate language as a whole, with different degrees of specialisation that range from general language to the more specific or specialised instances of it – these specialised instances also being able to constitute a somehow independent phenomenon with its own particularities (see section 2). In this sense, all the words in a language, regardless of their degree of specialisation, form the lexicon of this language and consequently lexicology is the wider discipline in which this study or any study dealing with terminology can be contextualised.

According to Cabré (1993: 80), theoretical lexicology is responsible for describing the words in a language. Its goal is to explain as accurately as possible the functioning of the speaker's lexicon. However, even though descriptive lexicology aims at no applicative objective for the lexicon, this does not prevent applied linguistics from having a more practical interest for the subject. Lexicography is one of the disciplines responsible for this topic and in charge of the principles of dictionary elaboration. To establish the same parallelism as the one established with terminology and terminography, it can be said that, for Cabré (1993), lexicography is an applied branch of lexicology that deals with the elaboration of dictionaries, a dictionary being, in Cabré's (1993) view, a linguistic product that gathers a selected group of words (or other language units) and illustrates them with a series of information. The group of dictionary entries constitutes its macrostructure and the information about the entries, its microstructure.

For some other authors, one of them is part of the other (terminology is part of lexicology) while for some others they are differentiated subjects. Although I tend to consider that terminology can, in general, be regarded as part of lexicology, in 1993, before the CTT emerged, Cabré (1993) pointed out certain diverging traits that made it more advisable to treat them individually and some others that did not. These factors are specified below, although highlighting the fact that some of these views have been changed over time owing to the new considerations introduced by the CTT some years later.

- Regarding the field of work, lexicology deals with the whole group of words that the speaker of a language knows, that is to say, it deals with the analysis and description of the lexical competence of the speaker, whereas terminology only focuses on the words belonging to a speciality field (like ceramics) or a professional area (like commerce or industry). Therefore, their fields of work participate in a relationship of inclusion, i.e. the field of lexicology is wider and includes terminology (indeed, in the case of specialists, their lexical competence as speakers includes terminology). Therefore, according to the criterion of the field of work, terminology is part of lexicology.

- Moreover, although the focus of the work is different, one being more general (lexicology) and the other more specific or specialised (terminology), in this study and according to the CTT, terms have been considered first as lexical units, components of the whole lexicon of the speaker. In other words, terms are primarily considered to be lexical units which, depending on certain factors of different natures, may or may not activate the specialised traits necessary to become terms. However, no-one can deny their specialised nature or the specific pragmatic and contextual features they present, which make them lexical units with different levels of specialisation appearing in specific contexts. Therefore, they are also terms. This leads us directly to the next point.

- Regarding the base unit, lexicology deals with the study of words whereas terminology is responsible for the study of terms. A word is a unit described by a group of systematic linguistic characteristics with the property of referring to an element from reality. From the linguistic point of view, a word is a unit characterised by having a phonic and graphic form, a simple or complex morphological structure, a grammatical characterisation and a meaning that describes the class to which a given element belongs, the same as a term. The difference lies in the fact that a term is a unit of similar linguistic characteristics used in a speciality domain. Accordingly, a word belonging to a specialised domain would be a term. However, especially from a pragmatic point of view, there are certain features that allow a distinction to be made, as has already been mentioned in the previous point. Pragmatically, terms and words are distinguished by their users, the situation in which they are normally used, the subject matter they deal with, and the kind of discourse in which they normally appear. All these features act as the "activators" of the specialised character of terms but in their origin, the lexical unit is the base unit both in lexicology and in terminology.

- From the point of view of the applied objectives, terminology and lexicology can also be distinguished by the objectives they have. Lexicology, if considered from the point of view of theoretical linguistics, deals with words with the objective of showing the linguistic competence of speakers, whereas terminology deals with terms with the aim of fixing a reference form (Cabré, 1993). However, I do not wholly agree with this since, as has already been discussed, terminology may have prescriptive but also descriptive objectives (the ones pursued in this study). Even Cabré (1999 a), some years later, acknowledges that this distinction is not valid nowadays, since terminology always needs to be descriptive in the beginning and may have a final descriptive objective as well.

- With respect to the method of working, lexicological works set out from a theoretical hypothesis that will be rejected or validated through the analysis of samples of the speakers' productions; terminology does not explain any behaviour, but looks for the denominations of concepts which have been previously established. Over time, however, this distinction regarding the method of working has also become relative and not so clear; semasiology has also proved to be widely used and useful for terminological works like the one presented here.

Thus, although in 1993 the comparison between the pragmatic aspects and prospective goals of terminology (denomination and normalisation) and lexicology (description) led Cabré to differentiate between the two subjects, their comparison nowadays gives rise to a more confusing situation. It can be argued that the work process of both lexicography and terminography is materialised in compilations of lexical or terminological units in the form of dictionaries. Moreover, description has become an essential step in any work involving the creation of dictionaries, whether they are specialised or not.

Before reconsidering some of these aspects by means of the CTT, Cabré (1993) goes on to explain how lexicography and terminography are differentiated by other aspects that make a common language dictionary a different product from a specialised terminology dictionary:

- The linguistic aspects of dictionaries: the elaboration of a dictionary goes through several stages, and in each of these stages, the author(s) make(s) a series of choices that will result in dictionaries of different kinds. It is at this point that terminological and lexicological works are mainly differentiated, because in terminological projects, in some stages of the elaboration process, certain possibilities are selected while others are rejected because they are deemed to be more suitable for general language dictionaries or, at least, not appropriate for a specialised one. Terminologists make use of specialised documentation, whether oral or written, as their only material source; they select the entries according to the topic of work and they preserve only the information that can be considered relevant (according to relevance criteria) in terminology. In this respect, I agree with Cabré's considerations, but one must consider as well that general language dictionaries also make a selection, excluding those lexical units that are considered to be too specialised.

- The function of the terminographical work: if the aforementioned linguistic aspects of dictionaries already allow us to establish differences between terminography and lexicography, the main goal to be reached by both subjects makes this distinction even clearer. Following Cabré (1993), in terminology, the elaboration of dictionaries leads to normalisation (in the sense of standardisation) of the terms belonging to a given speciality domain. Terminological work is not usually limited to compiling the denominations of a given area with an informative or descriptive function. Apart from this, the intention is to fix certain terminological units as normalised forms with the aim of achieving professional, precise, modern and univocal communication. Accordingly, in lexicography, the only dictionaries that, at least partially, coincide with terminology due to their function are normative ones. In this case, the words they contain are correct according to an academic institution that supports them, whereas in terminology, normalised forms are preferred because users (specialists) have agreed on them (Cabré 1993). With the CTT, however, Cabré (1999 b) started to consider the need for description in terminology, at least in its initial stages, and this reconsideration is what allowed the creation of descriptive specialised dictionaries like the one presented here. Thus, the dictionary entries presented in section II are aimed at contributing to the achievement of professional, precise, modern and univocal communication, but not at fixing certain terminological units as normalised forms because, among other reasons, I lack the authority to do so.

- The work process in terminography: the orientation of the process of work in terminography does not coincide with that of lexicography either; in this case the elaboration of a general lexicon dictionary starts out from a list of words that constitutes the inventory of the entries of a dictionary. The lexicographer then proceeds to semantically describe them by means of the definition. The process is then semasiological – we go from the form to the meaning (Cabré, 1993).

- The process of work in terminology goes the other way round. The terminologist establishes first a list of concepts that form part of a notional structure. The concepts belonging to this structure are interrelated logically and ontologically and their group constitutes the conceptual system of a discipline or specialised activity. The terminologist then attributes to each conceptual square a denomination that corresponds to the form that the specialists effectively use when referring to the concept of a notional structure. This process, which goes from the concept to the denomination in terminology, is called an onomasiological process (Cabré 1993) and is illustrated, together with the semasiological one, in figure 15:

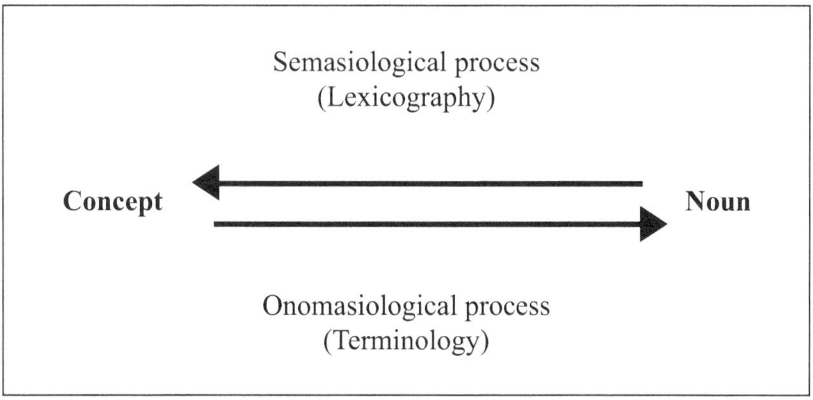

Figure 15. Cabré's (1993) views on semasiological and onomasiological processes.

Nowadays, with the CTT, Cabré's (1999 b) views have also changed in this respect and a less abrupt line has been traced, since reality constantly shows that semasiology is also used in terminology, especially when a corpus is used, as in this case.

In spite of the apparent distinction that can be made between both the object of study of the terminological and lexicographical approach (words from the general lexicon and terms, respectively) and the approach to this object (from the word to its designation in one case and from the concept to the term that designates it in the other), for Sager, in 1991, the reality of the terminographical practice placed both disciplines much closer:

> Traditional terminological theory identifies its approach as "onomasiological", i.e. a "naming" approach, because, in principle, it starts from concepts and looks for the names of these concepts. By contrast, the lexicographical approach is called "semasiological", i.e. a "meaning" approach, because it starts from words and looks for their meaning. In reality, the onomasiological approach only characterises the scientist who has to find a name for a new concept (an invention, a new tool, measurement, etc.); the terminologist, like the lexicographer, usually starts from an existing body of terms to start with. (Sager, 1990: 27)

Cabré (1993) considers that the fundamental aspect that separates terminology from lexicology is the conception that both disciplines have of the language: lexicology grounds its study in lexical units and does not conceive meaning if it is not linked to a word. In contrast, terminology, and especially the GTT, focuses its attention on the concepts, which are considered to be previous to lexical expression, and can be conceived independently of the terminological denomination assigned in each language (Pérez, 2002).

Another feature in order to distinguish between terminological and lexicological studies may be the interest in the grammatical and contextual behaviour of their units of study. In the lexicological and lexicographical field, increasing importance is granted to the study of word behaviour, both in their grammatical co-text and in their sociolinguistic context, and they are considered to be basic elements for discourse construction. In contrast, on terminology, terms have traditionally been studied in an isolated way, with a minimal interest in the study of their morphology or syntax (Pérez, 2002), although this tendency seems to have been overcome nowadays, especially if a corpus linguistics approach is followed.

In this sense, one of the objectives of this study is to show the importance of giving the contextual and co-textual study of terms the importance they deserve, because the sociolinguistic situation in which they are used is decisive in order to obtain and reflect all the shades of meaning a term may have and consequently to try to obtain an effective tool for accurate specialised communication. Thus, taking this fact as our starting point, the importance of creating an active dictionary like the one proposed and under development here becomes more easily understandable.

Another characteristic that makes terminological studies different from lexicological and lexicographical ones is, as has already been mentioned, the kind of product offered to their users, i.e. the kind of dictionary or terminological lexicon. The difference arises in the starting point traditionally assigned to each discipline. Terminology has been thought to depart from the concept, whereas lexicography departs from lexical units (Pérez, 2002). However, in this study, even when dealing with terms, the lexical units (prospective terms) provided by the corpus have been taken as the starting point.

After these initial reflections on these disciplines, in subsequent sections (and with the objective of clarifying the blurred boundaries that terminology, terminography, lexicology and lexicography may present nowadays) some of these aspects have been examined in greater depth. In section 4.2.1 a basic aspect for understanding the CTT has already been dealt with, namely, the definition of the nature of the objects of study of terminology and lexicology, which has made it necessary to elaborate on the notions of word, term and lexical unit.

To go on with this aspect, the next section (4.3.1) has tried to establish the "limits" (if any) of terminology with respect to linguistics and more specifically to lexicology.

Finally, in order to coherently conclude how this study has been approached from specialised lexicography, a key question has been posed and answered through section 5: is terminography specialised lexicography? Or even more significantly, why does this book call "specialised lexicography" what most authors would call, at first sight, "terminography"?

4.3.1. Terminology and lexicology: independent disciplines?

Apart from the reflections in this respect made in the previous section, there are two main viewpoints when posing the question of whether lexicology and terminology are independent disciplines:

- On the one hand, we find those defending the idea that terminology and lexicology are two disciplines with nothing in common and so they are completely differentiated. They view terminology as an autonomous discipline.

- On the other hand, we find those who argue that terminology can also be explained from linguistics, since specialised lexical units can be described from a language theory. They conceive terminology as part of lexicology (and hence as part of linguistics).

If we delve further into this topic, we will observe that grammar has traditionally been considered to be made up of four basic modules: the phonological, syntactic, semantic and lexical modules. Lexicology is the linguistic discipline responsible for describing the lexical module of a language. That is to say, it is the module in charge of the description of the group of lexical units a language is made up of, together with the rules that allow their formation, the use speakers make of them and the mechanisms that allow the lexical component to be related to the other components of the grammar of this language.

As a discipline,[25] terminology must have a series of well-established theoretical bases together with a specific object of study. However, as has been introduced above, there is no universal agreement regarding this object of study: for some people the object of study of terminology are the concepts of each speciality field (GTT). For others, however, the object of study are the lexical units that denominate these concepts, and which are made up of form and meaning, thus constituting a special kind of lexical units called specialised lexical units or TUs (CTT). This dichotomy regarding lexicology and terminology is the origin of the current panorama in terminology and has also favoured the appearance of questions like: are lexicology and terminology independent disciplines? Is terminology part of lexicology? or Is terminology (part of) linguistics? These questions (already indirectly

25 The term "field of knowledge" has been preferred to that of "discipline" to refer to terminology as a whole in this study, in spite of the wide acceptance of the latter.

answered in previous sections), which arise from the aforementioned dichotomy, have resulted in the two contradictory views just mentioned and which we will now attempt to explain in more detail.

On the one hand, those who defend that terminology is an autonomous discipline are mainly supporters of the views and ideas of Wüster's General Theory of Terminology, proposed in the 50s. Consequently, following Wüster and his GTT, terminology is an autonomous discipline, completely independent from linguistics because:

1) Terminology departs from concepts with the final aim of establishing delimitations among them and, in consequence, it presupposes the independence of these concepts with respect to linguistic forms.[26] In this way and according to this view, for terminology, concepts are prior to and independent from the denominations or terms that designate them, whereas lexicology is always based on words and cannot conceive meaning without them.

2) Given the ruling position of concepts, terminology studies only the lexicon of a language, leaving aside its syntactical projections or its morphology. However, lexicology never ignores grammar, and words are described taking into account their possible contexts of use.

3) Terminology focuses its analysis from a synchronic point of view, without considering the diachronic aspects of terms. However, for lexicology, both approaches are interesting.

---

26 In this respect, as Cabré (1993: 48) remarks: "*una prueba de ello es que los conceptos no siempre se representan mediante unidades de caràcter lingüístico (unidades morfológicas, léxicas o fraseológicas), sino también por medio de símbolos, fórmulas, o iconografías que no pertenecen al sistema de la lengua.*" [*a sign of this is that concepts are not always represented by linguistic units (morphological, lexical or phraseological units but also by means of symbols, formulae or iconographies that do not belong to the language system.*]

4) Terminology only takes into consideration the conscious and generally agreed formation of language (what is called the prescriptive norm), whereas lexicology generally accepts the study of language as an object of natural evolution and the norm is the result of use.

5) Terminology prioritises the written form of terms and not their phonetic form, which is the one favoured by linguistics.

Thus, in spite of the fact that from a historical point of view terminology has developed, up to now, "hand by hand" with other disciplines such as linguistics and conceptology, those who support and maintain that it is an autonomous discipline ground their views on the belief that it possesses a series of specific theoretical principles. The reason for this is based on the assumption that two different objects of study are dealt with, i.e. words, in the case of linguistics, and concepts, in the case of terminology. Thus, this view originated in the belief that two different objects of study were enough to justify that a discipline such as terminology could be dealt with and developed while leaving linguistics completely out of the picture. In this sense, Cabré (1993: 83-84) points out that:

> Si partimos del principio de que la terminología es una aproximación a las palabras distinta de la que hace la lingüística, la materia que se ocupa de los términos debe tener elementos que muestren claramente esta especificidad. Wüster señala dos que son fundamentales: la aproximación al objeto de estudio y las características de los diccionarios que se elaboran en una y otra perspectiva
>
> [If we depart from the principie that terminology is an approach to words different to the linguistic one, the subject field in charge of terms must have elements that clearly show this specificity. Wüster signals two of them that are fundamental: the approach to the object of study and the features of the dictionaries that are elaborated in one perspective and the other.]

And Adelstein (2004: 13) adds:

> Dado que una disciplina, en principio, se distingue de otras por tener un objeto de estudio discreto, para constituirse como disciplina la terminología necesitó distinguir su objeto del de la lingüística: opuso el término a la palabra.

> [Given that a discipline is, in principle, distinguished from others by the fact of having a discrete object of study, in order to be constituted as a discipline terminology needed to distinguish its object from that of linguistics: it then opposed term to word.]

On the other hand, those who maintain that terminology is an integrated part of lexicology sustain their views in the following points:

1) The object of study of terminology are the terms that appear in the oral and written texts created by professionals.
2) These terms, framed within the text, are the lexical units through which specialised knowledge is accessed.
3) Terminology is understood as a "theory of terms", understood as units of the lexicon and not as a "theory of concepts".

Accordingly, terminology *is* linguistics provided that terms (that constitute its object) form part of language. In this sense, and since this book is based on the Communicative Theory of Terminology, it is interesting to note that this second viewpoint has been regarded as the most plausible one for the study of terminology (understood as an integrated part of lexicology and, hence, of linguistics). This is therefore the conception adopted by the SLA:

> La terminología, en nuestra opinión, no puede explicarse autónomamente, al margen de otros signos denominativos dotados de capacidad referencial con los que comparte el espacio de la comunicación especializada, ni aisladamente de los signos del lenguaje natural compuestos de forma y significado. […] Así pues, en contraste con las suposiciones de la TGT, en nuestra propuesta teórica, que denominamos Teoría Comunicativa de la Terminología (TCT), partimos del supuesto que los términos no son unidades aisladas que constituyen un sistema propio, sino unidades que se incorporan en el léxico de un hablante en cuanto adquiere el rol de especialista por el aprendizaje de conocimientos especializados. (Cabré, 2001 a: 130- 131)
>
> [In our opinion, terminology can be explained neither in an autonomous way, leaving apart other denominative signs with referential capacity with which it shares the room of specialised communication, nor in an isolated way with respect to the signs of natural language made up by form and meaning. […] Therefore, in contrast to the assumptions of the GTT, in our terminological proposal, that we call Communicative Theory of Terminology (CTT), we

depart from the assumption that terms are not isolated units that constitute their own system but units that are incorporated into the lexicon of a speaker when he/she acquires the role of specialist through learning specialised knowledge.] (Cabré, 2001 a: 130- 131).

However, whereas linguistics deals with the study of language conceived or understood as a grammatical and/or social system made up of components on different levels (phonology, morphology, lexicon, syntax and discourse), terminology, as a matter of study and application, would only deal with language from one of these components, i.e. the lexical one. Consequently, when the question of whether terminology is linguistics is posed, one could answer that terms, as an integral part of the lexical component, form part of language and may be studied by linguistics and, more specifically, by lexicology and terminology. Nevertheless, this does not necessarily imply that terminological units cannot be tackled from other speciality fields.

If this interdisciplinary character of terminology is considered together with the fact that terminology is the result of the intersection between linguistics and other disciplines (of a very different nature in most cases), the result is that terminology is a subject that forms part of the language sciences, due to the fact that language is its grounding element, that is, its substance. Terminology is language. However, as an intersection discipline, it can be considered both from the linguistic perspective and from the perspective of the other disciplines that form part of it, namely (Cabré, 1993: 83):

- Desde la lingüística, la terminología es una parte del léxico especializada por criterios temáticos y pragmáticos;
- Desde las disciplina científico-técnicas, la terminología es el reflejo formal de su organización conceptual y, en consecuencia, un medio inevitable de expresión y comunicación;
- Desde la perspectiva del usuario (…), la terminología es un conjunto de unidades de comunicación, útiles y prácticas, que deben evaluarse en función de criterios de economía, de precisión y de adecuación a su expresión.

- [From Linguistics, terminology is a part of the lexicon which is specialised by means of subject matter and pragmatic criteria;
- From scientific-technical disciplines, terminology is the formal reflection of their conceptual organization and, consequently, an unavoidable means of expression and communication;

- From the user's perspective (...), terminology is a group of communication units, useful and practical, that must be evaluated according to economy, precision and adequacy criteria with respect to expression.]

Accordingly, for Cabré (1993: 37) there are four different approaches regarding the study and practice of terminology:

- Para los lingüistas, la terminología es una parte del léxico especializada por criterios temáticos y pragmáticos.
- Para los especialistas, la terminología es el reflejo formal de la organización conceptual de una especialidad, y un medio inevitable de expresión y de comunicación profesional.
- Para los usuarios (directos e intermediarios) la terminología es un conjunto de unidades de comunicación, útiles y prácticas cuyo valor se mide en función de criterios de economía, de adecuación y de precisión.
- Para los planificadores lingüísticos, la terminología es un ámbito del lenguaje donde se debe intervenir para reafirmar la existencia, la utilidad y la pervivencia de una lengua, y para garantizar, mediante su modernización, su continuidad como medio de expresión.

- [For linguists, terminology is a part of the lexicon specialised by topic and pragmatic criteria;
- For specialists, terminology is a formal reflection of the organization of a speciality as well as an unavoidable means of expression and professional communication;
- For users (whether direct or indirect) terminology is a group of communication units, useful and practical , whose value is measured according to economy, adequacy and precision criteria;
- For linguistic planners, terminology is an area of language in which intervention is necessary in order to reaffirm its existence, utility and the survival of a language, and in order to guarantee, through its modernization, its continuity as a means of expression.]

Bearing in mind these four approaches, which comprehend and clarify the scope of terminology, two broad perspectives of this discipline could be stated: the first one involves all those people using it for communication, whether directly or through intermediaries, and the second one is the perspective of those who work on it, either with the goal of producing glossaries, making communication easier, or with other information-related objectives. Therefore, it could be argued that terminology presents two different dimensions that are related to each other, i.e. the linguistic and the communicative. Therefore, for Cabré (1993), the word 'terminology' designates at least three different concepts:

1) Referring to the discipline, terminology is the conceptual basis and the group of principles that govern the study of terms;
2) Regarding methodology, it comprehends the guidelines used during the terminographical work;
3) When it comes to the designation of the group of terms of each specific thematic area, terminology is the group of terms of a given speciality area.

In order to deal in depth with this topic and better define terminology as such, Vargas' (2005) views on the topic are also very useful. For her, terminology as a discipline has received increasing attention from theoreticians and linguists because it is the field of knowledge responsible for the study of the lexical elements that form part of a structured system of concepts in which terms are the main elements that lead the knowledge of a given scientific, technical or professional community. The international norm ISO 1087-1 (in Vargas 2005: 169) defines terminology as: "el conjunto de designaciones que pertenecen a un lenguaje especial y como ciencia que estudia la estructura, formación, desarrollo, uso y gestión de terminologías en varios ámbitos".[27] For Cabré (1993), for specialists, terminology is a formal reflection of the conceptual organisation of a speciality field and an unavoidable means by which professionals express and communicate with each other. In an attempt to pay attention to all the aforementioned aspects, the *Asociación Internacional de Terminología* defines it as "el estudio y uso de sistemas de símbolos y signos lingüísticos empleados en la comunicación humana en áreas especializadas del conocimiento"[28] (Sager 1993: 23). This definition, which contemplates the interdisciplinary aspect of terminology, again highlights the fact that, as an applied discipline, terminology is related to lexicography and uses techniques from science and information technologies.

27 "The group of designations that belong to a special language and science that studies the structure, formation, development, usage and management of terminologies in various fields"

28 "The study and use of linguistic symbols and signs employed in human communication in specialised areas of knowledge"

Terminology is also used to refer to the structured group of terms used within a given field of knowledge (medical terminology, ceramics terminology, etc.). These terms, when appearing in texts used by specialists, acquire a clearly defined and even restricted meaning.

In order to complete and clarify these issues regarding terminology, I have included a series of brief definitions on the topic:

In Frawley's (2003: 225) words:

> Terminology is an interdisciplinary study of the principles and theoretical bases of concepts, concept systems, and the designation of concepts in scientific, technical and other professional fields. Its origin lies in the efforts made in order to solve professional communication problems resulting from the internationalisation of commerce, technology, and science in the 20th century (…).

For Lewandowski (1982: 352), terminology is conceived as "el vocabulario técnico, el léxico específico de una ciencia; el conjunto de los términos de una especialidad, que forma un terreno especial en el léxico de una lengua."[29]

In this study, however, the way of understanding terminology as a field of knowledge is in line with Alcaraz and Martínez Linares' (1997: 503) views, which in turn fully coincide with Cabré's (1993) (mentioned above). According to this viewpoint the word 'terminology' is defined and used in three situations:

1) Conjunto de términos especializados de una disciplina; en este sentido es sinónimo de metalenguaje. [Group of specialised terms from a discipline; in this sense it is synonymous with metalanguage].
2) Ciencia interdisciplinar (lingüistas, especialistas de la materia) que estudia la confección y el análisis de términos especializados. [Interdisciplinary science (linguists, specialists in the field) that studies the elaboration and analysis of specialised terms].
3) La teoría especializada en el análisis de los términos. [The theory specialised in the analysis of terms].

To sum up, as has already been explained in section 4.1, during the 18th and 19th centuries, scientists were mainly concerned with the proliferation of denominations in different and varied fields of knowledge or speciality

29 "The technical vocabulary, the specific lexicon of a science; the group of terms from a speciality that make up a special field in the lexicon of a language"

areas which, consequently, led to the need to "put them in order". Their main aim, then, was to "clear up" the mess of forms and relationships between forms and concepts that made communication more difficult. Thus, terminology arose from the explicit necessity specialists have always had (and still have) of ordering the denominations of their conceptual systems with the aim of achieving a more reliable professional communication.

However, these scientists concerned with the proliferation of denominations were not interested in knowing the nature of the concept or the theoretical grounds governing the creation of new terms. The theoretical questions about the nature of a term were posed later, when terminological practice started to become, at least minimally, organised in certain fields. This was the approach Wüster first adopted: he paid special interest to terminological compilation and normalisation methods and, afterwards, he began to look into the theoretical aspects of the terms themselves.

Nowadays, terminological theory develops almost hand-in-hand with practice, with the intention of solving communicative linguistic problems. In addition to this, terminology is continuously developing, fostered by the evolution of science and technology, the changes produced in international relationships and the importance acquired by information and communication technologies, among other reasons.

Terminology, as a subject that is concerned with the compilation, description, management and presentation of the terms that belong to the speciality fields of one or more languages, is not a practical activity that can be justified by itself, but must be considered within a wider scope. It has to be aimed at solving social needs linked to the optimisation of the communication between specialists and professionals (whether directly or through translation) or related to the process of normalising the language. This pragmatic and applied conception of terminology fits better into the spirit of current society (Cabré, 1993) and the CTT.

The interdisciplinarity of terminology is determined by the characteristics of the terminological units that are, at the same time, language units (linguistics), cognition elements (cognitive science) and communication "vehicles" (communication theory). Terms appear in specialised communication (documentation) and are usually processed by computers in the terminographical activity (computer science).

To conclude, it can be said that, in the conception of terminology as a discipline there also exist diverging opinions and trends. Cabré (1993, in Vargas, 2005) differentiates three positions: in the first, certain authors who feel close to the GTT defend the autonomy and self-sufficiency of terminology as a discipline with its own grounds, although they acknowledge the close historical relationship it has had throughout history with other disciplines. In the second one, it is considered as part of other disciplines (such as linguistics or philosophy) and therefore lacking any kind of autonomy. In the third view, authors like Cabré (1999 a) defend, as has already been explained, the autonomy of terminology but at the same time highlighting its interdisciplinary character because of its adoption of concepts and methods from other disciplines. Thus, it is influenced by the scientific-technical areas to which it renders service. According to Cabré (1999 a), terminology is a discipline that benefits from the grounds of other disciplines, selects elements from them and builds its own original space, and in this sense it is different from other scientific fields. For other authors within this position, like Loening and Sonnenveld (1993), terminology results in a multidisciplinary field of study (with knowledge coming from different sciences such as computer science, linguistics, and so on) but with methods and principles of its own.

4.3.2. Descriptive versus prescriptive terminology

Despite the fact that the specialised lexicographical tool (the specialised dictionary of the ceramic industry) developed throughout this study has a descriptive character, I thought it would be a good idea to close this reflection on terminology as a field of knowledge by presenting some of the most significant aspects of terminology as regards its most paradigmatic and internationally relevant function, i.e. prescription or normalisation. In addition to this, even descriptive terminology is benefited and influenced by certain aspects of normalisation, such as normalised documents (which can be compiled for the creation of a working corpus) or the bodies and associations of terminology, as explained in subsequent sections.

But, what is really meant by normalisation?

> La normalización, en su sentido más general, es "una actividad que consiste en establecer, con respecto a problemas reales o potenciales, disposiciones para uso común y repetido, encaminadas al logro del grado óptimo de orden

> en un contexto dado. La normalización consta de tres procesos: formulación, publicación e implementación de las normas". (ICONTEC, 2003)
>
> [Normalisation, in its widest sense, is "an activity dealing with establishing, with respect to real or potential problems, conditions for common and repeated use, directed at achieving the optimum degree of order in a given context. Normalisation involves three processes: formualtion, publication and implementation of the norms".] (ICONTEC, 2003)

When referring to languages, the term "normalisation" refers to two different concepts which have been used in terminology:

- Giving priority to certain linguistic forms that become "norms". This first sense of normalisation, which is synonymous to standardisation, is used to create a hierarchy of the different denominative possibilities for a concept, one of them being considered the reference form (however, more than one possibility may be accepted). This reference form or denomination is the one that is called the *normalised term*, a concept prototypically used within the context of international communication.

- The extension or area of use of a language for which a normal situation of use (that is regular and without restrictions) is desired. This second way of conceiving terminology is used in situations of linguistic planning and refers to the process that turns a language into usual (it is used by its speakers in every communicative situation). In this case, the normalisation of terminology deals with the implantation of terms in real use.

Following Cabré (1993), in its first sense, normalisation is the result of a decision reached by consensus by a representative commission which is gathered and kept in a document called a *norm*, in which the different aspects agreed upon among the parts are specified and where their contexts of application are used. Among the different aspects suitable for being the object of a norm, one may find: the products and/ or processes of industrial and service sectors, units of measurement, terminology, and so forth.

Terminological normalisation can be applied in two different fields:

- The normalisation of terms.
- The normalisation of the principles and methods of theoretical and applied methodology.

With respect to the way terminology is organised, there are six different parameters taking part in it with respect to a specific social, political and linguistic context:

1. Planning, coordination and management of the terminological resources.
2. Terminological work.
3. Normalisation of the terms; this implies the fixing of forms that are considered to be standard, as well as the assessment of those repeatedly used to designate the very same concept.
4. Diffusion of the normalised terms and resolution of terminological queries.
5. Implantation of the terminology in the different areas of work and activity.
6. Formation of terminology; this entails the training of specialists for the elaboration of, or participation in, terminological projects.

Focusing on point 3, the normalisation of terms, the IULA (2006 b) describes it as:

> Un proceso complejo que comprende distintas operaciones: la unificación de conceptos y sistemas de conceptos, la definición de términos, la reducción de homonimia, la eliminación de sinonimia, la fijación de denominaciones, la creación de nuevos términos, etc.
>
> [A complex process comprehending different operations: the unification of concepts and systems of concepts, the definition of terms, the reduction of homonymy, the elimination of synonymy, the fixation of denominations, the creation of new terms, etc.]

If point 6 in the list above – the one dealing with the formation of terminology (terminological neology) – is considered in depth, this neology may be understood as an activity of creating new denominations, which is considered necessary in domains of speciality due to the constant appearance of new concepts (the ceramic industry is a clear example of this phenomenon since it is in constant evolution.) Neologisms are then a special kind of term that appear in fields such as:

- Lexicography (since general language dictionaries must be updated).
- Terminology (since the denominations of specialised languages must be created or adapted).
- Linguistic planning (since criteria for orienting lexical creation must be established).

The decisions adopted by normalising committees about new denominative proposals aimed at filling "gaps" in a specialised lexicon make up an array of possibilities that are interrelated with one another and are normally oriented by a series of preferential political criteria. Following the IULA (2006 b), according to these criteria, normalisation bodies can make different decisions about a neologism: accept it (both if it is a loan or a lexical creation), reject it, and accept it but adapting it to the linguistic system if it is a loan. In the same way, the IULA (2006 b) proceeds, the terminological normalisation bodies usually accept neologisms if:

- They are necessary.
- They are widely used.
- They have been spread in the professional field or area in question.
- They have been gathered by general lexicography.
- They have been spread by a linguistic body.
- They show a parallelism with other languages of similar culture.

Looking at this topic in more detail, Estopà (2003) divides the criteria for the acceptability of a neologism into three different kinds:

a) Linguistic criteria:

- Phonetic and orthographic adequacy.
- Morphological adequacy.

- Semantic adequacy (precision, transparency and a motivated form).
- Syntactic adequacy.

b) Terminological criteria:

- Relation between notion and denomination.
- Term included in an array of notions and denominations, not an isolated unit.
- Formal analogy with other related terms of the same field.
- Analogy with other languages.
- Respect for the terminological trends of each field.
- Preference for Greek-Latin forms.
- Adequacy to the recommendations of the international normalising committees.

c) Pragmatic and sociolinguistic criteria:

- Level of formation of the users and degree of linguistic sensibility.
- Current trends.
- Social and professional prestige in means of diffusion and dissemination.
- Real necessity of creation.
- Belonging to a formal register.
- No pejorative connotations.
- Euphony and ease of pronunciation.
- Brevity, simplicity and synthetic character of the term.
- Mnemotechnic ease.
- Frequency of use.
- Dissemination of the form.
- Consensus by specialists.
- Viability, feasibility of the proposal (analysed or determined through polls).

4.3.2.1. The normalisation of principles and methods of theoretical and applied terminology

Terminology as a discipline and terminography as a practice have also been the object of international normalisation on the part of ISO Technical Committee 37.

Among the main terminological norms created by this Technical Committee, it is worth mentioning:

- ISO 704:2000 "Terminology work - Principles and methods".
  ISO 860:1996 "Terminology work - Harmonization of concepts and terms" (norm currently under review).
- ISO 1087-1:2000 "Terminology work - Vocabulary - Part 1: Theory and application".
- ISO 1087-2:2000 "Terminology work - Vocabulary - Part 2: Computer applications".
- ISO 12620:1999 "Computer applications in terminology - Data categories" (norm currently under review).
- ISO 12616:2002 "Translation-oriented terminography".
- ISO/TR 12618:1994 "Computer aids in terminology - Creation and use of terminological databases and text corpora".

The dissemination of normalised terminology is usually done through norms or recommendations.

4.3.2.2. The role of the specialist and the terminologist in terminological normalisation

Specialists play an important role in basically two moments of the process of terminological normalisation:

- In term fixation; specialists are the main source when it comes to confirming all the possible variants of a term, indicating the "use", proposing neologisms, deciding about cases of synonymy, choosing the equivalents of terms in other languages and disseminating the normalised terms.
- In concept fixation. The specialist is the person in charge of "delimiting" the concept belonging to the term that is being

normalised, that is to say, the person who places the concept within the field and subfield to which it belongs within the conceptual system.

Hence, and following the IULA (2006 b), specialists play an important role in terminological normalisation because they are the real users of terminology. Thus, the establishment of nomenclatures has its basis in the consensus about concepts, systems of concepts and the use of terms. Accordingly, for the normalisation process to succeed, a consensus must be achieved among specialists of the different areas of knowledge and among terminologists.

Regarding the role of the terminologist "la normalización de los términos es un trabajo de equipo en el que deben participar especialistas y terminólogos"[30] (Cabré 1993: 437).

In this very same sense, Rondeau (1984) states that the terminologist intervenes in three stages of the process:

- In the preparation of materials (in the elaboration of the normalisation dossier).
- In the discussions about the terms proposed for normalisation, contributing to them with his/her knowledge on morphology, etymology, lexicology, stylistics and methodology of the definition.
- In the dissemination of the normalised terms through glossaries or norms.

What seems beyond question, thus, is the important role played by terminologists in terminological normalisation, a process that is also determined by the existence and work of bodies devoted to this aim.

30. "The normalisation of terms is a team work in which specialists and terminologists must participate"

If language is not correct,
then what is said is not what is meant:
If what is said is not what is meant,
then what must be done remains undone;
If this remains undone,
morals and art will deteriorate;
If justice goes astray,
the people will stand about in helpless confusion.
Hence there must be no arbitrariness in what is said.
This matters above everything.
Confucius

5. Specialised lexicography

Once the theoretical aspects that shape and originate the SLA have been progressively presented to characterise this approach, it is necessary to put forward what is specialised lexicography as such, what differentiates it from other similar disciplines and what it implies from an applied perspective that makes it go "a step further" in specialised dictionary-making. We are aware of the fact that most linguists would, at first sight, identify the kind of work here presented as terminography and thus the approach adopted as terminographical but the considerations put forward so far, this last theoretical section, the method proposed for specialised dictionary-making and the final results obtained try, as a whole, to show the step-further the SLA implies with respect to "plain" terminography.

5.1. The applications of lexicology and terminology: lexicography and terminography

As has already been explained, in general, in this study the way of conceiving terminology corresponds to the definition put forward by

Cabré (1993), Sager (1993) and Alcaraz and Martínez Linares (1997, 2000):

1) "*El conjunto de principios y de bases conceptuales que rigen el estudio de los términos*" ("the group of principles and conceptual bases ruling the study of terms") (Cabré, 1993:82), that is to say, the theory or theoretical groundings.

2) "*El conjunto de directrices que se utilizan en el trabajo terminográfico*" ("the group of guidelines used in terminographical works") (Cabré, 1993:82), that is to say, the practice of this discipline: the study and field of work related to the compilation, description and presentation of terms in one or more languages. It is for this second sense of terminology that Rey (1975) suggested the aforementioned name of "terminography".

3) "*El conjunto de términos de una determinada actividad*" "the group of terms from a given activity") (Cabré, 1993:82), that is to say, the vocabulary of a specialised thematic field.

Hence, for the second sense of terminology Rey (1975) proposed the name "terminography". Cabré (1993) corroborates this view by considering the stages of compilation, systematisation and presentation of the terms characteristic of a specific domain or speciality as being part of the terminographical activity. In this respect Sager (1994) also comments on the coherence of the denomination since the practical work within terminology, that is to say, terminography, is very similar to that undertaken within lexicography. Therefore, the term "terminography" is semantically appropriate given that it follows the same logic as analogous formations, such as the already-mentioned disciplines of lexicography or even bibliography. In the same line, Vargas (2005) uses the term "terminography" to refer to the practical activity of terminology that is responsible for the elaboration of dictionaries, vocabularies, glossaries, databases and any other kind of terminological application in a given specialised field. In Lorente's (2001) view, terminography is the group of activities leading to the design and production of all those terminological applications based on the idea of a lexical inventory with associated pieces of information.

However, as Pérez (2002) points out, there is an issue that must be taken into account within this framework: the relative newness of the term "terminography" in comparison to the well-established lexicographic tradition. This term, "terminography", was first used in 1975 when the *International Organisation for Standardisation* (ISO 1087) introduced the term to refer to that part of terminology devoted to the production of terminological dictionaries (Bergenholtz and Tarp, 1995: 10). It is also quite usual to find that, with the exception of certain publications (Sager, 1994 and Meyer and Mackintosh, 1996, among others), the terms "terminology" and "terminography" are very often used without distinction, including only occasional references to terminography or using other denominations such as terminology processing (Wright and Budin, 1997) or terminology management (Sager, 1990) in order to cover the applied aspects of terminology. As has been explained earlier, in this book the word terminology has been used on many occasions as entailing both a theoretical (terminology) and a practical/applied (terminography) dimension – as suggested by the definitions proposed by Cabré (1993), Sager (1993) and Alcaraz and Martínez Linares (1997). Terminology in its wider sense and scope therefore includes the terminographical practice, since without the terms forming part of a domain and without the principles and conceptual bases that govern the study of terms, that is to say, without terminology in its purest sense, terminography would not exist and would make no sense.

Nowadays, closely linked to terminology and its practice (terminography), that is to say, to terminology in its wider sense, we can also find "Terminotics" (see section 5.2) and all the benefits and advantages it entails for studies like the one presented here, so dependent on computer-aided tools. The SLA is deeply and unavoidably linked to terminotics in the dictionary-making process as the method described shows but, what is meant by terminotics?

5.2. Terminotics: terminology, linguistic engineering and computational linguistics

In order to understand what is meant by terminotics and its importance for terminological research in general and for this study in particular, it is crucial to take up again what is meant by terminology and to introduce the concepts of linguistic engineering and computational linguistics.

As has already been explained, terminology is conceived as the discipline that deals with the study of terms, understood as both the group of principles underlying term compilation and the group of terms from a specialised field and their codification in the form of dictionaries, databases, vocabularies, thesauruses, etc.

Computational linguistics, on the other hand, is focused on the study of language with models that can be implemented with computer technology. When it started, computational linguistics aimed at establishing systems of automatic translation. However, in the 80s, when it became clear that the expectations created could not easily be accomplished, a more applied approach of computational linguistics appeared, i.e. natural language engineering or linguistic engineering. Hence, linguistic engineering is described by the IULA (2007 d) as the application of the knowledge about a language for the development of computer systems able to recognise, understand, interpret and generate human language in all its forms. Accordingly, computational linguistics and linguistic engineering can be said to complement each other, the former representing the research approach and the latter the applied approach.

Terminology uses computational linguistics and linguistic engineering in order to constitute its own object of work, in order to improve its applications or to better organise the terminographical process. Accordingly, the convergence between computational linguistics (investigation), linguistic engineering (application) and terminology (understood both as the group of principles governing the compilation of terms and as the group of terms as such) is materialised in the branch of terminology called terminotics – represented by T in figure 16.

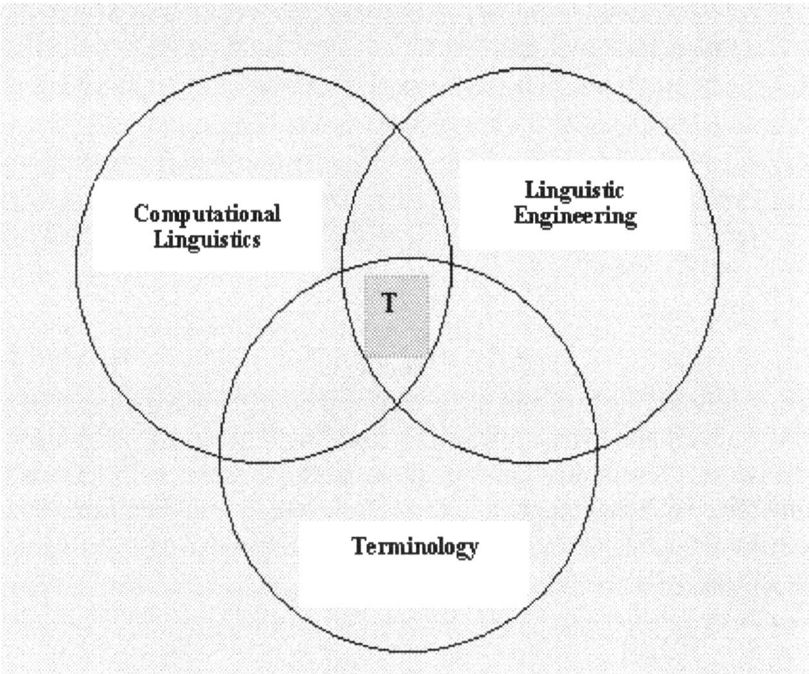

Figure 16. Graphic representation of Terminotics (T) as the convergence point between computational linguistics, linguistic engineering and terminology (IULA, 2007 d).

Consequently, terminotics stands at a mid-way point between computational linguistics (computer science applied to the treatment of language data), linguistic engineering (development of resources and tools) and terminology. It thus becomes a research object in applied linguistics and a pragmatic object linked to the industrialisation of linguistic products.

In general, the crucial role terminotics and its tools play nowadays in terminographical tasks – and, consequently, in this study in particular – can be summarised in the following contributions (IULA, 2007 d):

- The automatic selection of the corpus and the information regarding a given topic.
- The selection and extraction of the terms of a field of work from a corpus.

- The morphological analysis of terms with the object of offering neological proposals.
- The attribution of terms to one or more speciality fields depending on their frequency of appearance in the texts.
- The automatic elaboration of definitions starting out from the analysis of the text the term has been extracted from.
- The automatic elaboration of the conceptual structure of a speciality field.

As is analysed in more detail in subsequent sections dealing with the method of work, the contributions of terminotics have been especially useful for some activities in this methodology, especially those regarding the compilation of terminology and in organising the work. Terminotics makes it possible to work on previously automated textual corpora and extract relevant information from them (also automatically). Likewise, it allows textual and terminological databanks to be exploited.

To conclude with this section, it is important to highlight that there are at least five activities that are carried out in the course of the terminographical process in which terminotics becomes especially important (for a more detailed explanation of the way in which these activities have been undertaken in this specific work with the help of terminotic tools, see section 8). These activities are:

- Documentary research prior to the work, since this facilitates access to the information given about a speciality field through terminological, documentary and textual databanks.

- Elaboration of the working corpus and extraction of terminological data: if these documents are in an electronic or digital format, terminotics facilitates their automatic incorporation into the textual database. If they are in a printed format, terminotics allows them to be digitised through optical character recognition (OCR) software using a scanner and the keyboard. This allows the text to be analysed in order to extract prospective terms, contexts and so on.

- Elaboration of card indexes, that is to say, the terminologist may use terminotics for the elaboration of terminological cards by transferring some data directly from their reference text, for instance, the entry, the source, the context, etc.
- Verification and completion of information.
- Edition of the terminology. The information can be offered in electronic (CD-ROM, Internet) or paper format.

5.3. Lexicography and terminography: blurred boundaries to be clarified

As happens with lexicology and terminology (see section 4.3), their applied branches (lexicography and terminography) also present aspects that nowadays, and given the communicative approach adopted in this study, make the boundary between them somewhat blurred or fuzzy. In the following sections, an account of some of the most significant factors involved in distinguishing (or not) between terminography and specialised lexicography, and thus in choosing the most adequate "label" for the approach explained and used in this work have been provided.

5.3.1. Lexicographical methodology versus terminographical methodology

The different working methods adopted in lexicographical and terminographical works are another argument used by the supporters of the notion of considering lexicography and terminography as different disciplines, since, for them, the two kinds of practice are distinguished by the method they use, i.e. the semasiological one (lexicology/lexicograhy) and the onomasiological one (terminology/terminography).

Traditionally it has been postulated that terminography works with an onomasiological methodology. In this kind of methodology the terminographer "denominates" concepts, that is to say, he/she attributes to each concept of the speciality a given form or denomination that represents it (the term). However, one may wonder whether the working method of terminography is always an onomasiological one, which raises two further questions: Who plays the role of terminographer? and, Who is the user (the consumer) of terminographical products?

On the one hand, and regarding the first question, given the interdisciplinary character of terminology, there are different people or collectives that can play the role of terminographers: the terminographer may be a specialist in a subject matter who adopts the role of terminographer in order to contribute to the development of his/her speciality area, or a translator undertaking a terminological work linked to his/her translational task or perhaps a professional terminographer who compiles and illustrates the terminological units that will form part of terminographical products as a routine part of his/her daily work. On the other hand, and regarding the second question posed, in the same way as occurs with the professional profile of the terminographer, there are also many different kinds of prospective or potential users of terminographical products.

According to all the factors mentioned up to the moment, once it is admitted that the role of the terminographer is not always played by the same kind of professional, the question of whether the method used in terminography is always the same one presents multiple shades of meaning. In fact, two different answers or options can be provided, each of them with its own methodological consequences:

If the person responsible for (undertaking) the terminographical work is a specialist-expert in the domain/subject matter, he/she controls the conceptual scheme of the field in which he/she works on a daily basis. Consequently, he/she already has prior knowledge of the concepts of his/her speciality domain and they are taken as the starting point in the terminographical work. The terminographer later looks for the linguistic forms responsible for their representation, thus using an onomasiological method of working.

However, if the terminologist is not a specialist (as in my case), but a linguistic professional who progressively acquires (and does not possess beforehand) the information related with the speciality field on which the work is being carried out, the terminographer will have to document himself/herself in order to acquire the necessary cognitive competence. At the same time, this documentation (translated into texts) will be useful as a source (corpus) for the extraction of the terms that are to be included in the terminographical work itself. Hence, the method of work used here is partially different because the point of departure are the linguistic forms and the target is to reach or discover the corresponding concepts or meanings, which thus makes it a semasiological method.

In spite of this, in current conceptions of terminology this distinction between the lexicographical and terminographical methods of work is not so widely used, since in the descriptive work aimed at the compilation of terms (be it lexicographical or terminographical) the working method normally used is semasiological: the starting point is the identification of the term in the texts in which it is used (normally through the compilation and exploitation of a corpus). As has been explained, only in those specialised terminographical works undertaken by the specialists within a field with a normalising orientation (for fixing a term) is the usual method onomasiological.

In the specific case of this research, the method is clearly semasiological since the corpus was the tool used for term extraction (I set out from the identification of terms in those texts in which they are naturally used), so that the traditional and presumably clear distinction between terminography and lexicography is not so clear if the method of work is considered.

5.3.2. Is terminography specialised lexicography?

At this point and in accordance with all the aspects mentioned so far, the final question to be posed is whether terminography can be considered a synonym of "not plain" lexicography but what has been called "specialised lexicography". For Bergenholtz and Tarp (1995), some of the features that are accepted within the more traditional framework, such as trying to differentiate terminology and lexicography by identifying experts as the target group for terminology and having laymen as the target group for lexicography, are a mistake. In the same way, they are against the view that states that lexicography deals with the description of general-language words, whereas terminology focuses on the description of LSP terms, because this would therefore establish a too clear-out boundary between the language used in the transmission of specialised knowledge and general language, and hence between term and word. Neither do they agree with the belief that terminology is prescriptive whereas lexicography is descriptive, since this conception places terminography within the classical prescriptive model adopted by the GTT. What they propose, then, is to use the term *specialised lexicography* (Bergenholtz and Tarp, 1995) instead of terminography.

So what is specialised lexicography for these two authors? "Specialised lexicography is the branch of lexicography which is practised by LSP lexicographers who prepare specialised dictionaries" (Bergenholtz and Tarp, 1995: 28). For them, starting out from a specialised knowledge domain with its corresponding specialised language, terminographical/terminological research is undertaken in order to compile and describe its terminology (understood here as the terms that characterise a given specialised activity). Terminology is thus the "mere" study of terms (which is made possible thanks to the activity of compiling and describing them, called terminography) which, at the same time, may be complemented by the wider projection of specialised lexicography for the compilation and elaboration of LSP, user-oriented dictionaries.

Following Bergenholtz and Tarp (1995), terminology and lexicography are disciplines that must cooperate with each other when it comes to compiling specialised dictionaries and, in fact, these authors consider terminology as an integrating part of specialised lexicography:

> [...] In our opinion LSP lexicography and terminology/terminography have a great deal in common.
> [...]We consider serious terminological work an absolute prerequisite for high-quality specialised dictionaries. In this respect, specialised lexicography may benefit from terminology, and it is in this light that we view terminology, or at least areas of terminology, as an integral part of specialised lexicography in a wider sense. Correspondingly, terminography has much to learn from the long lexicographical tradition in terms of preparing user-friendly quality products. (Bergenholtz and Tarp, 1995: 11)

Bergenholtz and Tarp (1995) understand specialised lexicography (in a wider sense) as being part of general lexicographical theory and practice. According to these authors, specialised lexicography may benefit from terminology as an integrating part of it. Terminography would then be used to designate that part of terminology concerned with the production of terminological dictionaries in their most basic, purely linguistic sense, but again "terminography has much to learn from the long lexicographical tradition in terms of preparing user-friendly quality products" (Bergenholtz and Tarp, 1995: 11).

For them, there is a close relation between terminology and lexicography because specialised lexicography (or *Language for Special Purposes – LSP – Lexicography*), or what most linguists would call terminography, is characterised as:

- A special part of lexicography in general, LSP lexicography certainly does work with LSP terms.
- LSP lexicography works with both systematic and alphabetic macrostructures, deciding in each individual case which is the more appropriate.
- LSP lexicography must necessarily, to a greater or lesser degree, be both descriptive and prescriptive.
- LSP lexicography addresses itself to laypeople and experts alike.
- LSP lexicography prepares dictionaries for both encoding and decoding purposes.

(Bergenholtz and Tarp, 1995: 11)

According to Bergenholtz and Tarp (1995) specialised lexicography conceives terminography as a special part of lexicography in general. In this sense, Knowles (in Martínez de Sousa, 1995) defines terminography as "*parte de la lexicología que estudia la actividad lexicográfica de la terminología*",[31] so that the inclusive terminology-terminography relationship also extends to lexicology-lexicography. In this same trend, Martínez de Sousa (1995) also proposes the term "terminological lexicography" (*lexicografía terminológica*) as a synonym for terminography. Martínez de Sousa (1995) also proposes the term "applied lexicology" (*lexicología aplicada*) to refer to lexicography, thereby again showing the close interconnection of all these disciplines and how the names of some of them may be used to name others, thus supporting the inclusion criteria.

Therefore, in accordance with Bergenholtz and Tarp (1995), all these disciplines present an inclusive relationship which makes each of them a conforming dimension of another, which progressively increases their general character, as shown in figure 17:

31 "Part of lexicology which studies the lexicographical activity of terminology."

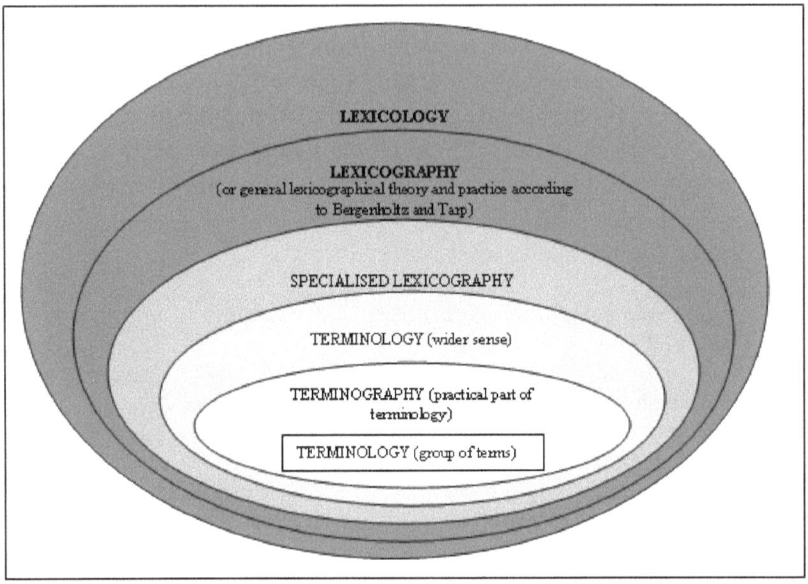

Figure 17. Schematic representation of Bergenholtz and Tarp's (1995) conception of specialised lexicography and terminography.

Another possible way of dealing with this issue is the one proposed by the IULA (2007 c). As they explain, initially the label "specialised lexicography" was proposed as an alternative to the label "terminography", which was exclusively associated by many scholars to the methodology and practice of the prescriptive classical model, that is to say, Wüster's GTT. However, although this label of specialised lexicography, as a synonym for terminography, has been adopted to describe the kind of work presented here, this alternative also presents a series of problems directly related with the polysemic character of the term "specialised lexicography", since in many meta-lexicographical studies, the denomination "specialised lexicography" is used without distinction to refer to different realities:

1) Specialised lexicography is the kind of lexicography which contributes to the elaboration of thematically specialised works with its methodology and techniques. Hence, it would be a specialisation of lexicographical work in terms of content.

2) Specialised lexicography deals with those inventories that are differentiated for some reason from the most prototypical of all lexicographical works, i.e. monolingual dictionaries of general language. The kinds of specialised works that could be included within this kind of lexicography would be the following:

- dictionaries of verbs, idioms, formants, etc. The reason would be the kind of linguistic units they introduce;
- visual dictionaries, encyclopaedic dictionaries, etc. because of the way in which contents are represented;
- learning dictionaries, children's dictionaries, etc. because of the kind of users.

3) Specialised lexicography is that part of lexicography which studies the thematically specialised units (the terms) that can be found in dictionaries of the general language.

To sum up and following again the IULA (2007 c), the fact that this denomination has been used before with other meanings seems to be a strong reason to support the idea that the practical part of terminology (responsible for the elaboration of lexical inventories) is called terminography. However, the label "terminography" may also carry connotations which, in spite of not being valid nowadays, may suggest that terminography makes exclusive reference to works with a prescriptive character – although currently it can also be used for all those works conceived from other terminological orientations.

5.4. The specific case of this study: why specialised lexicography?

To sum up the different views regarding specialised lexicography and terminography and to justify our clear preference for the former in a study like this, it should be contended that there are different attitudes towards the question of whether terminography is specialised lexicography, depending on the field of application in which the question is posed (terminography and lexicography), on other aspects related to the theoretical disciplines (terminology and lexicology) and on the different objects of study (term and word). Therefore, as the IULA (2007 c) advises, the best way to answer this question is in the form of trends that account for two possible options:

- Terminography is not specialised lexicography if terminology is conceived as an independent discipline differentiated from lexicology and with a particular object of study (the concepts of a speciality). For those defending this option, the two disciplines would not relate at a theoretical level or at a practical or methodological one.
- However, terminography is specialised lexicography if we consider that:

• Terminology can be explained from linguistics, and more specifically from lexicology.

• The condition of term can be explained starting out from the activation of a series of semantic features or traits of the lexical units when these are used in speciality contexts. In this sense, as Cabré points out and still following the CTT:

> El carácter de término se activa en función de su uso en un contexto y situación adecuados. Esta activación consiste en una selección de los módulos de rasgos apropiados, que incluyen los rasgos morfosintácticos generales de la unidad y una serie de semánticos y pragmáticos específicos que describen su carácter de término de un determinado ámbito. (Cabré, 2001 a: 132)
>
> [The terminological character is activated according to its use in an adequate context and situation. This activation consists of a selection of the modules of appropriate traits, these including the morphosytactic traits of the unit and a series of specific semantic and pragmatic features that describe its terminological character in a given field.] (Cabré, 2001 a: 132)

• The methodology used in the elaboration of different terminographical and lexicographical works does not allow a clear, perfectly delimited boundary to be traced between the two disciplines.

In its primary essence and according to the theoretical positioning adopted, specialised lexicography is at its base terminography. We acknowledge that the more generalised denomination "terminography" could also be used to name the dictionary-making process and approach here described because of its wide social acceptance to refer, in general, to works of this kind. Thus, this would make this term also acceptable – although not accurate – in the context of this work. Nonetheless and to sum up, throughout this book, specialised lexicography has been undestood as "the branch of lexicography which is practised by LSP lexicographers who prepare specialised dictionaries" but which transcends the "mere" study of terms (possibly thanks to the activity of compiling and describing them, called terminography) by complementing it with the wider projection of specialised lexicography for the compilation and elaboration of LSP, user-oriented and user-friendly quality products in the form of dictionaries.

Language is only in part an individual instrument. It is in the main a community instrument used for community purposes. As such it tends to launch out on a career of its own, to which individuals contribute very much as the coral insect contributes to the growth of a coral reef or island.
L.S. Amery

6. Socio-economic context for the research

Language and reality go hand in hand. Specialised lexicographical works are normally (and advisably) created with a series of objectives in mind, to meet specific needs arisen in real, professional/specialised contexts. These works should then be developed according to the domain they aim to characterise from a linguistic point of view, which necessarily implies understanding this domain as a whole. Contextualising a research is always essential and in the specialised lexicographical approach this contextualisation acquires a new dimension because of the applied nature of the works it develops. In the specific case of this study, I have analysed the socio-economic context for the research of the industrial ceramics domain in Spain, which is the origin and target of this research.

6.1. An economic overview of the ceramic industrial district in Spain

The concept of "industrial district", originally developed by A. Marshall (1925), is traditionally defined as a "socio-economic entity which is characterised by the active presence of both a community of people and a population of firms in one naturally and historically bounded area" (Becattini, 1990: 39). The concept of industrial district has also reinforced its position thanks to the success observed in economic activities that are geographically concentrated (Foss and Eriksen, 1995). In broad terms, these views have been the grounding principle for considering that it is preferable to adopt the term "industrial district" to refer to the socio-economic reality of the tile industry in Spain than that of the more widely used denomination of "industrial sector". In Molina Morales' (2005: 74) words, "territorial agglomerations of firms, such as the industrial district, can be identified as dense strong-tie networks and are thus suitable for exploiting activities." This organisational structure fits into the traditional perspective of social capital (Coleman, 1990), which stressed the positive effect of the cohesive structure of networks on the production of social norms and sanctions that facilitate trust and cooperative exchanges, something also closely related to the concept of discourse community put forward by Swales (1990).

The role played by the ceramic tile industry in the Valencian Region,[32] and especially in the province of Castellón (where this study originates), is so significant for the economy of the region that the figures speak for themselves: in an area of 800 km^2 (district boundaries are within a 20km radius of the town of Castellón de la Plana), 90% of the Spanish ceramic industry is concentrated in Castellón. In the industrial area that is limited to the north by Alcora, to the south by Nules, to the west by Onda and to the east by Castellón de la Plana, one may find 80% of the Spanish companies working in this district, which results in more than 265 companies devoted to this industrial field. These 265 companies are called "final firms", that is to say, they undertake the last phase of the ceramic process and obtain the final ceramic product. However, altogether there are about 700 firms in the province related in one way or another to the ceramic tile industry; in addition to "final firms", there are also glaze and frit firms, machinery, special pieces and atomised clay firms. These figures therefore show the high concentration and importance of the ceramics industry and ceramic-related activities in the province of Castellón. This situation is illustrated in figure 18, representing both final firms and the aforementioned related companies in the region.

32 The Valencian region is formed by three provinces (from North to South): Castellón, Valencia and Alicante. This region is on the Eastern (Mediterranean) coast of Spain, to the South of Catalonia.

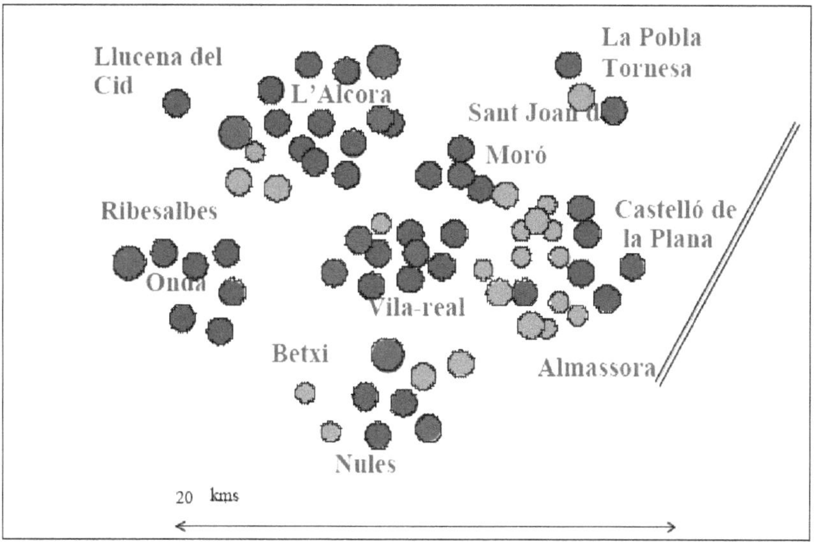

Figure 18. Map of the ceramic industrial district in the province of Castellón (Molina-Morales, 2002).

In spite of the difficult moments global economy is currently going through, the ceramic industry in Spain represents millions of euros in investments, production and profits both in national and international markets. Around 80% of this production is generated and concentrated in the province of Castellón. The reasons that make Castellón the most important industrial area in terms of the ceramic industry are manifold. First of all, it must be pointed out that Castellón is a region that is limited to the east by the Mediterranean Sea. This proximity to the sea constitutes a great competitive advantage because transport is one of the most important strategic elements for this industry given the fact that more than 50% of the total production is exported. Although 40% of the distribution is done by sea and the rest by plane or by road, the costs of the former are notably lower, and this increases competitiveness. These reasons support the claim made by the ASCER, an institution which, in an attempt to guarantee the competitiveness of the industry, strives to improve both the infrastructures of the commercial ports and railway connections in Castellón and Valencia and the accesses to the province. In addition to this, the industrial area devoted to the ceramic industry in Castellón can be said to constitute a dense and strong network, thus reinforcing its "district values". This network is characterised by redundant and frequent relationships, and common values and norms which give rise to competitive leverage, high quality information and tacit knowledge transmission, all of which is translated into an exploiting advantage for firms. The main industry of the province of Castellón is, thus, the ceramic one, along with furniture and chemical industries, tourism and agriculture.

At the beginning of June 2002, Náger (2002) highlighted that more than 100 firms work at an international level. In this way, both the firms that produce ceramic floor and wall tiles and the ones producing glazes, frits and ceramic colours are the companies that are most widely and firmly established abroad with subsidiaries, warehouses, warehouse centres and shops. In the same way, some firms in Castellón obtain investments from large multinationals. The data published by the *Instituto Valenciano de la Exportación* (IVEX) on its web site reflect how the province of Castellón represented 22% of the foreign sales of the Valencian Region in 2001-2002. More specific data offered by the *Cámara de Comercio de Castellón* in 2001 show how, in that year, the ceramic district (ceramic floor and wall tiles companies mainly) was the leading source of export activities in the economy of Castellón (51.72% of the total).

According to the data provided by ASCER and as shown in figures 19 and 20, the Spanish ceramic industry is very productive, although it has undergone some uncertainty in recent years due to the increasing competition mainly from Asian countries. This decreasing but not alarming trend started, as can be seen in figures 19 and 20, in 2002-2003; in 2004, 2005 and 2006 it seemed to be slowly changing towards increasingly positive figures again and recovering – although with greater difficulty than desired – its former tendency towards growth; nowadays (2009), and as almost any other industrial activity, ceramics is going through a difficult period because of the global economic situation. Predictions, however, are rather optimistic about the recovery of the industry even though it will be difficult to reach again the economic data achieved during the "golden" era of industrial ceramics.

Production and sales of the ceramic tile industry in 2001 and 2002		
	2000	2001
Production	621	638
Sales national market	1428.9	1484.6
Exports	1872.1	1987.8
Total sales	3301.0	3472.4
Sales in millions of EUR and production in millions m^2		

Figure 19. Basic economic data of the Spanish ceramic tile industry in the period between 2000 and 2001 (ASCER, 2005).

Production and sales of the ceramic tile industry (2002-2006)					
	2002	2003	2004	2005	2006
Production	605.7	583.4	595.5	609.2	608.4
Domestic sales	1361	1379	1500	1609	1802
Exports	2059	1939	1977	2041	2183
Total sales	3420	3318	3477	3650	3985

Figure 20. Basic economic data of the Spanish ceramic tile industry in the period between 2002 and 2006 (ASCER, 2007).

In addition to the current global economic situation, it is a fact that many countries, some of which are still not fully developed, have become new ceramic producers constituting a serious menace to European production. Although Europe is still the main ceramic-producing area, it is losing the battle against Asian countries in terms of amounts produced. However, even if we agree with the experts that it will be difficult for the Spanish ceramic industry to maintain the impressive rate of growth obtained over the last few years, an important growth is still foreseen due to the tendency towards technological innovation, both in processes (from the single to the double firing process) and products (porcelain stoneware, larger sizes, more variety, greater resistance, and so forth). In addition to this, the quality of the Spanish and Italian products is, generally, higher than that of the emerging countries, although the competition is becoming increasingly harder because these producers from developing countries are acquiring the new technologies offered, paradoxically, by Italian manufacturers and the products and designs offered by manufacturers of glazes and colours.

Thus, one of the main challenges of the district is to increase internationalisation, both in production and commercialisation. This fierce competition and struggle to maintain the leadership of the district is forcing countries like Spain to enhance its competitiveness by fostering all the areas involved in the production and commercialisation of the ceramic industry products. The international ceramic fair CEVISAMA, a yearly event that takes place in Valencia and which attracts thousands of people involved in the ceramic industry and particularly prospective clients, is a good example of the initiatives that the Spanish ceramic tile district undertakes in order to enhance its potential, become aware of the latest advances and trends in the sector, advertise its products and, what seems even more significant to me, open up new markets and consolidate those that are already established. CEVISAMA 2005, for instance, increased the number of visitors, of firms exhibiting their products, and the metres devoted to the exhibition, which is a clear sign of the importance assigned to the worldwide diffusion of the novelties in the district and a successful attempt to establish commercial relations between professionals and their companies. The number of display stands in the fair held in 2005 was 1,124, apart from more than 86,000 net square metres of exhibition space and over 140 foreign firms also exhibiting their products. Just to refer to data of another nature, in the fair held in 2004, CEVISAMA received a total of 86,566 visitors and the number of foreign prospective buyers/visitors exceeded 10,000.

What can be deduced from this data is that the importance of the district in Spain and especially in the Valencian Region is undeniable, that this industry generates huge amounts of profits and mobilises people from all over the world. It is also clear that the tendency is to continue to grow and to extend internationalisation in spite of the difficulties. This expectation of progressively reaching more international markets is reflected in the specific objective of placing the generic brand name "Azulejos de España" (*"Tile of Spain"*) in other markets with the aim of achieving the recognition of the Spanish product among importers and distributors. ASCER and ICEX (Instituto Español de Comercio

Exterior – Spanish Institute of Foreign Trade) are working hard in this respect and that is the main reason why the number of professionals from foreign countries invited to CEVISAMA increases every year.

However, the Spanish ceramic industry has to innovate and raise its level of competitiveness because the situation does not offer any security and is being seriously threatened, especially by China. As has been already mentioned, the main potential of the Spanish ceramic industry to maintain its profitable situation is to reinforce and strengthen internationalisation, while China supplies its own needs – a situation that will, however, not last forever.

All these data and this overview of the situation that the industrial ceramic district is going through can give us a hint to the importance of being as competitive and efficient as possible in every single aspect or process involved in the ceramic industrial activity. As mentioned before, the importance of a good, solid distribution net all over the world that allows good sales results to be obtained is undeniable. Especially at this point, once the production chain is closed and the product must be distributed and sold, a convincing and well-constructed sales discourse and marketing strategy on the part of the people in charge of commercialising the product becomes fundamental. A perfect and accurate knowledge of the terms involved in a specific area such as ceramics, both in Spanish (mainly because of the importance of this district in Spain and more specifically in this region where a dense and strong network is established) and in English (basically because of the importance of English as a *Lingua Franca* world-wide), will make the dictionary on ceramics terminology a tool that meets and fits the terminological needs of this ceramic industry and its professionals.

6.2. The need for this study

The specialised lexicographical approach has its origin in studies similar to the one here presented regarding other industrial activities that are important for the Valencian Region. Dr. Enrique Alcaraz Varó

(Universidad de Alicante, Spain) was the pioneer in promoting and directing the elaboration of different specialised dictionaries related with different industrial sectors in the province of Alicante. He was the first one in acknowledging the need of this kind of works in specific socio-economic contexts. Consequently, he and his team undertook, for instance, the English-Spanish dictionary on stone and allied industries and the English-Spanish dictionary on the shoe industry and developed the basis of the methodology which is presented here.

However, the fact of developing a dictionary on industrial ceramics is not a novelty in itself. What makes the research here presented a "breath of fresh air" in the terminological arena is the approach adopted (both from a theoretical and methodological perspective) and the kind of work to be obtained with this approach.

Although several dictionaries and glossaries on the suggested topic already exist, the years and the lexicographical framework in which they were undertaken (the 80s and early 90s) must be taken into account in order to understand how necessary a renewal in the approach of specialised dictionaries applied to the ceramic industry is. Some of these dictionaries published during the 80s and 90s are: *Dictionary of Ceramics* by Arthur Dodd, revised and edited by David Murfin (1994); *Porcelana, cerámica y cristal* by Ángel Escárzaga (1986); *Ceramic Glosssary*, edited by Walter W. Perkins (1984) and *Ceramic Dictionary* (Schmid, 1997). These works lack, in general, examples, collocations, technical and grammatical information, thus constituting what I have called *passive* dictionaries, as opposed to the active one under development here. This concept of active dictionary, which will be explained in detail in section 7.3, is fundamental when it comes to understanding or completely grasping the meaning of a word, and the same is true of the semantic shades of meaning of a term or collocation.

Several industrial sectors in Spain and, more specifically, within the Valencian Region, demand extensive work in specialised lexicography and in-depth linguistic research on many specific fields or areas of knowledge that are not directly related with linguistic issues. Like every discipline, they need to use language and, more specifically, accurate terminology to be able to develop and maximise their potential. These linguistic needs give rise to the emergence of specialised dictionaries aimed at fulfilling the terminological shortcomings, pressures and innovations posed on these industrial sectors, and the ceramic tile industry is no exception.

The importance of language in every stage and dimension of our lives is undeniable, and even when the subject matter has nothing directly to do with linguistic issues, there is an intrinsic need to make use of language in order to refer to the concepts of that field. In this specific case I have dealt and will be dealing with very specialised terms that only experts in these areas of knowledge are usually aware of, but these terms constitute a reality and a necessity in communication for those people, who may find it very hard to express these concepts in a language other than their mother tongue without the help of a "terminological aid". These communicative needs are fulfilled by the referential function of language and a hard terminological research in order to successfully establish the relationship concept-term in the different languages under study and can then be materialised in the form of specialised dictionaries, such as the one introduced in this study. In this specific case, the final dictionary has been a bilingual one (English-Spanish, Spanish-English) since it intends to organise the lexical units of the ceramic tile industry systematically in both languages so that it will be easier to manage for both the Spanish and English (whether native or not) ceramic specialists/professionals, as well as translators.

As has been mentioned already, the main ceramic exporting countries in the world are Italy and Spain, although on an international level the presence of countries like Turkey, Brazil and Mexico is becoming increasingly more significant and it is foreseen that soon other countries will start to have an important production surplus. Accordingly, the Valencian Region and more specifically Castellón, whose economy is deeply grounded on the ceramic tile industry, has to improve and develop in every aspect involved in this industrial activity so that it can successfully withstand the threats from other countries.

Hence, the reason for undertaking this research is quite easily understandable if the economic overview in section 6.1 is taken into account: in view of the huge profits and production obtained by this district in Spain, and especially in the area of Castellón, the aim of the dictionary is to respond to the linguistic requirements stemming from the socio-economic demands of this activity. And such needs make it necessary to establish a perfectly organised and systematic inventory of all the terms involved in the ceramic industrial district. Sometimes, it is also difficult for specialists in a given field to be aware of all the terminology (especially neologisms) used in their speciality areas of knowledge even in their own mother tongue. For this reason, this dictionary is not merely intended at providing a translation into Spanish or English of the different terms but at explaining and clarifying them by means of examples, collocates, quotations and technical explanations. This information will make this dictionary an active one – a relatively new and practical approach to understanding terminography and lexicography in the area of ceramics – as is explained in section 7.3.

In general terms, the analyses performed in the ceramic industry seem to indicate that this is a business in which the high level of cost-effectiveness obtained in former periods may tend to decrease, although this business will remain profitable for the companies that are able to adapt better to the new market conditions, which includes internationalisation, among other factors. Within this internationalisation, especially in commercial terms, English is the key language. However, the need to know the English language is not just limited to its oral component. The world of mass media we live in, the technological advances that our society is undergoing, and the increasing use of computers and the Internet all make it essential to be efficient in written as well as spoken competence.

Marketing is another basic aspect to be developed in order to increase competitiveness. The large number of possibilities offered by the new digital genres in the form of websites for advertising the different companies must be taken into account and the possibility of reaching markets anywhere in the world must be exploited by including versions of websites in as many languages as possible. Among these versions in different languages what is becoming a constant feature is the inclusion of an English one, and if just one version can be offered in a foreign language (due to the reasons that I explain below and as experience shows), then the chosen language would most likely be English. Opening up to new markets is necessary in order to raise competitiveness.

In this respect, Cabré's (1993: 43) words summarise the importance of this kind of lexicographical and terminological studies as follows:

> (...) No podemos olvidar que la terminología nace de la necesidad manifestada por los especialistas de ordenar las denominaciones de sus sistemas de conceptos, con la finalidad de conseguir una comunicación profesional más fiable.
>
> [(...) It cannot be forgotten that terminology arises from the necessity expressed by specialists of ordering the denominations of their conceptual systems with the aim of achieving a more reliable professional communication.]

Therefore, there are many reasons that explain the benefits that a bilingual specialised dictionary on this topic both in Spanish and in English may offer: the importance of this industrial district in Spain and, more particularly, in Castellón; the need to expand to other markets and adapt to current trends in international commerce and transactions, marketing, specialised professional translation and business written communication; and the terminological pressures stemming from rapid technological and scientific developments.

To sum up, the reasons for undertaking the development of a dictionary like the one here described according to the SLA have been:

- The need to renew the conception of specialised language dictionaries applied to the ceramic industry (resulting in an active dictionary).
- The need to enhance competitiveness in terms of linguistic competence both in Spanish and English ceramic terminology by responding to the linguistic pressures originated by the socio-economic demands of the ceramic industrial district.
- The need to adapt to linguistic demands at both a national and an international level.
- And the need to create an ordered and systematic repertoire of ceramic terms and equivalences in Spanish and English in order to clarify concepts, become aware of neologisms and help both professionals from the ceramic district and translators.

II. How to compile a specialised dictionary

Though this be madness, yet there is method.
William Shakespeare

According to the SLA, the method used in the development of the dictionary of industrial ceramics terminology has comprised seven broad stages (see section 8) based on Auger and Rosseau's (1987) study *Méthodologie de la recherche terminologique* and the adaptation made of it by Gómez and Vargas (2002, 2003 a, b) so that it fits into current methodological trends and technological innovation in the field of corpus linguistics applied to specialised lexicographical research. However, before disclosing the method as such, there are a series of previous methodological reflections that must be put forward to understand the SLA and its dictionary-making process.

Methods and means cannot be separated from the ultimate aim.
Emma Goldman

7. Preliminary methodological reflection: Why "a step-further in dictionary-making"

As the title of this book says, the specialised lexicographical approach is considered here as a "step further in specialised dictionary-making". The purely theoretical aspects of this approach have already been disclosed but obviously "dictionary-making" implies a method. This second section of the book presents this method but a preliminary methodological reflection is put forward to introduce it so that the reader may more easily understand what a dictionary like the one developed here and a thesaurus have in common, why description has been preferred over prescription and what is really meant by an active dictionary.

7.1. Methods in lexicology: dictionaries vs. thesauruses

Halliday (2004) mentions two principal methods for describing words (understood in the sense of lexical items), which can, in addition, be combined in different ways. These two methods are writing a dictionary and/or writing a thesaurus. But what are the differences between a dictionary and a thesaurus? What may a dictionary like the one presented here and a thesaurus have in common? Why is a dictionary a more suitable tool for specialised lexicography?

The main difference is that in a thesaurus words that are similar in meaning are grouped together (as would be the case, for instance, with all the words referring to farming, emotions or species of insects). In contrast, in a dictionary, words are arranged in such a way – usually in alphabetical order – that the place in which a word is found tells you nothing about its meaning. This meaningful placing of words which is a clear potential of a thesaurus is, however, "compensated" in the SLA by the inclusion of a piece of data, the semantic field, in the entries (see section 8.3). This semantic field, presented in the entry immediately after the entry term or the subentries, does also allow the user to meaningfully place the term in the reality of the domain. Hence, in a dictionary, each entry stands by itself as an independent piece of work (Halliday, 2004: 4) but with the SLA this does not imply loosing the "placing potential" offered by thesauruses.

Regarding the format of the entries as such, in Halliday's (2004) views entries are organised, in general, with the following structure, variations in the kind of data included in each type of lexicographical work being common and perfectly acceptable:

1. Headword or lemma, often in bold or some other special font. The lemma is the base form under which the word is entered and assigned its place, that is to say, the stem or simplest form. For instance, the lemma of the chain *take*, *takes*, *took*, *taking* or *taken* would be the infinitive form take. In the same way and due to reasons concerning space (economy principle), certain forms may not be entered if predictable, which is normally the case of, for instance, plural forms. However, the irregular past form of the verbs is given and some irregular phenomena, such as the doubling of certain letters in the spelling of some inflected forms, may be made explicit. In this sense, an irregular form may also appear as a separate lemma with a cross-reference.
2. Pronunciation (in some sort of alphabetic notation).
3. Word class ('part of speech'). With respect to word class, in the case of English words we may find verbs, nouns, adjectives, pronouns, prepositions, conjunctions and determiners/articles. At the same time, some indication of a subclass – such as count or mass noun, transitive or intransitive verb – can also be added to class specification.
4. Etymology (historical origin and derivation).
5. Definition, which, broadly speaking may take one of two forms, description and synonymy:

   > The description may obviously need to include words that are 'harder' (less frequently used) than the lemmatised word [...] With synonymy, a word or little set of words of similar meaning is brought in, often giving slightly more

specific senses. All definition is ultimately circular; but compilers try to avoid very small circles, such as defining *sad* as *sorrowful*, and then *sorrowful as sad.* (Halliday, 2004: 7)

6. Citations (examples of use). With respect to citations, Halliday defines them as numbers referring back to definitions or senses which show how the word is used in context. Such citations may illustrate the earliest recorded instances of the word, a typical usage and/or more "special" usage in well-known literary texts. In the same way, there might also be "set expressions" (idioms and clichés), where the expression functions like a single, composite lexical item (e.g. *bear in mind*).

In the cases of common words, like *bear* or the verb *cut*, there is a good chance of finding subdivisions in the entry corresponding to different meanings of the word. With respect to compound words and derivatives, these are often entered under the same lemma – compounds appearing under the first word (*cutthroat* under *cut*) and derivatives under the stem (*cutting* under *cut*). This is the case of the dictionary here presented – as may be observed in final entries. However, this is not a hard and fast rule and in certain dictionaries compounds are given separate lemmata and even in certain instances a derivational affix (such as *anti-*) is used as a lemma under which derivatives are grouped (*antibody*, *anticlimax*, *antidote*, etc.).

Thesauruses, which, as stated above, constitute the other method used in lexicology mentioned by Halliday, do not contain separate entries for each word. As has been mentioned in previous paragraphs, in a thesaurus a word is placed and occurs as part of a list and it is precisely the place occupied by this word in the whole construction of the book that gives its meaning to the user. Thus, as Halliday (2004) states, if we look for *cut* in Roget's *Thesaurus of English Words and Phrases*, we will find it – among other places – in the middle of paragraphs such as the one below, in which, although not much organisation seems to have been applied, it is the final layer in a comprehensive lexical taxonomy:

v. cultivate; till (the soil); farm, garden; sow, plant; reap, mow, cut; manure, dress the ground, dig, delve, dibble, hoe, plough, harrow, rake, weed, lap and top, force, transplant, thin out, bed out, prune, graft.

Thus, a thesaurus takes all the lexical items it contains and arranges them in a single comprehensive taxonomy, a lexical taxonomy, which is an organisation of words into classes and sub-classes and sub-sub-classes on the basis of meaning, that is, semantic classes rather than grammatical ones. In a taxonomy, the main semantic relationships involved are those of hyponymy ('*x* is a kind of *y*') and meronymy ('is a part of'), this latter being used mainly for classification purposes. Thesauruses constitute a truly interesting choice in lexicography but in the case of speciality domains they lack pieces of information which are necessary from the user's point of view, especially from a communicative perspective.

It is interesting at this point to introduce the concept of collocation, a key element in the SLA and a necessary reference for Halliday (2004: 11) when proceeding with analysis/reflection on thesauruses:

> Another way of thinking about this shared privilege of occurrence that unites the words in one paragraph of the thesaurus is in terms of collocation. Collocation is the tendency of words to keep company with each other: like *fork* goes with *knife*, *lend* goes with *money*, *theatre* goes with *play*. Of course, if words do regularly collocate in this way, we shall expect to find some semantic relationship among them; but this may be quite complex and indirect. Collocation is a purely lexical relationship; that is, it is an association between one word and another, irrespective of what they mean. It can be defined quantitatively as the degree to which the probability of a word *y* occurring is increased by the presence of another word *x*.

To illustrate this, Halliday gives the word *injure* as an example, explaining that when it appears the probability of the word *pain* also occurring is much higher than that determined by its overall, general frequency in the English language as a whole. Hence, those words that appear grouped together inside the same paragraph in a thesaurus usually have a strong collocational bond, either with each other or, even more powerfully, each of them with a third party. However, as final entries show, dictionaries created under the SLA do also include collocational information, this being one of the mainstays of this approach. The very same subentries of the dictionary are collocations and additionally the contexts of use provided try to show the terms accompanied by words with which they tend to appear in habitual company more frequently than with others. In this sense, specialised dictionary-making according to the SLA is intended to provide comprehensive information on how terms collocate in real linguistic contexts of use. Specialised lexicographical works may thus have a more marked collocational behaviour than thesauruses if pertinent and adequate information is included.

A dictionary is a linguistic product within which words (or other units of language) are compiled and illustrated with the corresponding information necessary for their characterisation. Thesauruses do not (cannot) include all the information contained in a dictionary; they cannot either arrange it in the same way or provide bilingual information in the straightforward way a dictionary does (so necessary from the user's point of view). It is not that dictionaries are better than thesauruses They are simply different, but for the aims of specialised lexicography a dictionary presents a bigger potential and allows the inclusion of more useful linguistic data without losing the essence of a thesaurus.

7.2. Description versus prescription in the specialised dictionary of the ceramic industry

As is explained in detail in the section devoted to considerations involving the definition of the work (8.1), it is important to establish the thematic delimitation of a dictionary from the very beginning. In this sense, two types of terminological activity should be considered: the prescriptive or normalising terminology and the descriptive one. In the same way, the prescriptive and descriptive interests of the GTT and CTT have already been introduced in sections 4.1.1 and 4.2, respectively.

On the one hand, descriptive terminology (terminography) is mainly undertaken by translation professionals, editors of technical texts and researchers in social sciences because it is their job to document and compile terminologies, but they are not in charge of determining the use to be made of a term in a specialised domain (Wright and Budin, 1997). On the other hand, and according to these same authors, the normalisation bodies (both national and international), the governmental regulating bodies, the specialists in the creation of nomenclatures and the bodies devoted to linguistic planning will be the ones in charge of normalising terminology (Wright and Budin, ibid.), and thus of undertaking prescriptive terminology (terminography).

According to the definition of descriptive terminology proposed by Wright and Budin (1997), translation professionals, editors of technical texts and researchers in social sciences who undertake such work are only responsible for documenting and compiling new terminological data and, therefore, their decisions or opinions are not decisive in the specialised context of their work. Therefore, one may consider that "the most authorised terminological activity, so to speak (prescriptive terminology), can only be undertaken within a normalising body and that other kinds of terminological activity are consigned to solutions ad hoc" (Wright and Budin, 1997).

However, other authors, like Sager (1990: 3), do not explicitly refer to the normalising activity in their definition of terminology and, like Cabré (1993: 35-36), emphasise the determining task undertaken by terminology as a vehicle of communication between specialists and professionals. Indeed, mention is only made of those cases in which terminology resolves communicative needs quickly and effectively (for example in the translation of technical texts).

The theoretical conception of this book and of the dictionary here presented and elaborated under the SLA is grounded in a more recent text by Cabré (1999 a) in which she states that every terminological work has to be, at least initially, descriptive because this kind of work implies the compilation of terms used in the specialised community. Only after description does it become possible to reduce the possible variants to just one, which must be considered as preferable or recommendable (Pérez, 2002). In the same way, Sager (1990: 212 in Pérez, 2002) also considers descriptive work as a preliminary work that is compulsory for normalisation:

> Earlier terminologists attempted to record only accepted or approved usage, thereby establishing something like a recommended form of a term. It is increasingly being recognised that fixation of usage, e.g. by means of prescription or standardisation, follows established usage and does not precede it. This attitude points to a more realistic appreciation of the uses of language whereby the communicative use is given the primary position before the classificatory and ideational uses which we observe in action during term formation. This fundamental shift in emphasis places considerable stress on the observation and recording of usage which in turn can positively influence term formation. (Sager, 1990: 212)

Taking up again the controversial distinction between terminology/terminography and lexicology/lexicography regarding description and prescription, another important aspect is the traditional normative character of the former as opposed to the descriptive character of the latter. Although this distinction is true in terms of theory (at least according to GTT), it is a fact that in lexicography there is also a long tradition of normative dictionaries (Diccionario de Autoridades de la Real Academia de la Lengua Española, Dictionary of the English Language, and many others). Currently, most of the dictionaries that are published, whether they are specialised or not, have a descriptive character (like the one presented here), and are merely intended to describe a linguistic use. In spite of this, no-one can deny that depending on their scope and dissemination, they can exert an indirect fixing or normative influence upon language and its use, what could be called the "dictionary effect". This is due to the fact that, although they were designed with a descriptive intention, almost any dictionary user tends to regard a word or a meaning as normative simply because it is included in a dictionary. The SLA, so deeply grounded on the linguistic reality offered, is merely aimed at describing.

7.3. Specialised lexicography in the elaboration of an active bilingual specialised dictionary

To coherently conclude this previous methodological reflection and given the objectives posed in this book, this section introduces the specific aspects relative to the creation of an **active** specialised dictionary, a notion inherently linked to the SLA. Firstly, however, some brief hints on the creation of a bilingual specialised dictionary instead of a monolingual one have been put forward in order to explain the convenience of the former in cases that are similar to the one here illustrated. In general, leaving aside the specialised character of the dictionary under development here, although "monolingual dictionaries for foreign-language learners tend to be unquestioningly regarded as better than bilingual dictionaries" (Thompson, 1987: 283) it is also true that "compared with monolingual dictionaries, bilingual ones have clear (and acknowledged) advantages from the point of view of the translator" (Kromann, Riiber and Rosbach, 1991: 2117). If we bear in mind the fact that the dictionary on ceramics terminology is intended to become a translational tool, is being created from a user-friendly perspective that takes very much into consideration the prospective user of the specialised lexicographical (or terminographical) tool, and given that its prospective users are, in this case, specialists and translators, it seems logical and sensible to produce a bilingual work.

Kromann, Riiber and Rosbach (1991) go further into this topic and present the reasons that, in their opinion, make a bilingual dictionary a more useful tool for the translator. They mention the possibility of having direct access to equivalents that are immediately insertable. In the same way, they also consider the orientation towards a specific language pair, the scope for an adequate meta-language and the non-inclusion of superfluous material in the form of etymology, lexical definitions and encyclopaedic information to be advantages.

Likewise, Kromann, Riiber and Rosbach (1991) put forward the major objections they observe from the point of view of the user who translates with just a monolingual dictionary. The following are all considered to be handicaps: the fact of not having direct access to equivalents, the fact (also mentioned by Thompson (1987)) of being presented with explanations of the unfamiliar in a foreign language as well as the inclusion of irrelevant etymological information or superfluous lexical definitions and encyclopaedic information. In spite of this, it is also acknowledged the considerable progress that has been made regarding information about patterns of use, collocational behaviour or phraseology "aimed precisely at fostering the active use of language, and specifically at helping the foreign learner to construct sentences..." (Cowie, 1981: 227). In this sense, Desmet (1994) points out that the necessity to study the phraseological component in speciality languages carries with it two theoretical-methodological consequences: firstly, the need to take context as the basis for the analysis, that is, to extract phraseological data from professional and academic discourse; secondly, the need to define the very same concept of phraseology, and analyse the relations occurring in specialised statements between terms and their co-occurrents.

However, there are also voices pointing out the lacks and inferiority of bilingual dictionaries with respect to monolingual ones: Harrell (1967: 51), for instance, states that "it is clearly impossible to pay equal attention to both X-speakers and Y-speakers in one and the same work", so that the deficiencies of these bilingual dictionaries have also been highlighted and discussed by many authors.

In spite of his acknowledgment of the several advantages that monolingual dictionaries present, Thompson (1987: 284) also draws attention to a series of disadvantages that, in spite of being focused on language teaching situations, can be extrapolated to any dictionary-related context. This author talks about the difficulty in knowing which word to look up and in understanding the definitions in the foreign language when conducting a search in a monolingual dictionary. In this sense, Thompson (1987: 284) claims "that bilingual dictionaries are potentially more efficient and more motivating sources of information for language learners. However, new kinds of bilingual dictionaries are needed [...]" and this is what an active dictionary aims at becoming, i.e. the missing part required to turn bilingual dictionaries into completely effective lexicographical tools.

Specialised lexicography is based on the development of user-friendly technical dictionaries like the one presented here. Looking back a few years into the history of this field, it is significant to mention that the dictionaries written four thousand years ago to explain religions in the Middle East can be considered the very first instances of specialised lexicography. Nowadays, the latest trend for these lexicographical undertakings, as detected by Nida (1997), especially among the work of terminologists within the European Union, is to pay more attention to context, a view that fully coincides with the principles of the CTT. Longman's *Language Activator* (1993), the *Word Selector* (1995) by Cambridge University Press or the *Collins Cobuild Series* are examples of this new tendency in lexicography. More specifically, Alcaraz and Hughes' (2004) English-Spanish, Spanish-English *Diccionario de términos económicos, financieros y comerciales*, and other similar specialised dictionaries which Alcaraz, Vargas and other relevant authors at the Universidad de Alicante have compiled are also good representatives of this trend in the area of specialised lexicography.

However, this pragmatic perspective is not to be considered a specific novelty in translation or lexicographical work. The importance of context, supported by pragmatic linguists (Alcaraz, 1990) in the description of language, had already been emphasised by Malinowski in 1935 for the specific task of translating in his article on "The translation of untranslatable words":

> Words do not live in a sort of super-dictionary, nor in the ethnographer's notebook. They are used in free speech, they are linked into utterances and these utterances are linked up with the other human activities and the social and material environment. The whole manner which I have adopted for the presentation of my linguistic and ethnographic material brings the concept of context to the fore. Not only have I tried in the definition of technical terms to show how these terms form groups of kindred entities, not only have I tried, by placing the linguistic account against an outline of real activities, to give them life and body; but the division of the linguistic material under headings which closely correspond to the chapters of the descriptive account keeps every word, every phrase and every text within its proper context of culture. (Malinowski, 1935: 154)

In spite of this, the general feeling was that Malinowski's words had been forgotten until pragmatists and specialised lexicographers brought them back to life in the last decades. When terminographers and linguists started to check specialised dictionaries, they noticed a lack of entries dealing with categories other than nouns, as well as a lack of contexts that helped to illustrate the use of terms.

As Nida (1997: 265) puts it, nowadays, in all these general or specialised dictionaries "more attention is paid to words in phrases" than to words by themselves, this being also one of the grounding principles of corpus linguistics and explaining its close and even necessary connection with lexicography.

The SLA in general and the terminological perspective defined by Cabré (1999 a) in the CTT in particular foster this view as well, emphasising the need to provide the field of terminology with materials that satisfy the communicative necessities that arise in speciality areas and that are the result of studying terms *in vivo*. These materials should respond to the expectations of a society in constant evolution that calls (often out of pure necessity) for approaches that are more pragmatic and applicable than theoretical. This is so because terminology is not an activity that can be justified by itself; it is an activity aimed at solving social needs linked to the optimisation of communication between specialists and professionals or at fostering different aspects related to language normalisation.

Hence, the public image offered by dictionaries has been changing from a more authoritarian position on the part of lexicographers to the elaboration of dictionaries that are more aware of the prospective user of the product. Accordingly, Welte (1985) defines lexicography as a research domain with a strong pragmatic orientation because it must always consider and take into account the needs and expectations of the potential group of users of the lexicographical work.

Therefore, nowadays a comprehensive needs study, which includes a typology of the users to whom the dictionary may be addressed (Hartmann, 1987, 1989) is necessary. In the same way, it becomes necessary to analyse the specific needs of each type of user (Cowie, 1987).

Another issue that must be taken into account is the fact that the adequate and effective use of a dictionary depends on the capacity to use it both at a macrostructural and microstructural level (Hatherall, 1984) and that the format of the dictionary is crucial to determine its satisfactory use.

Having taken all these factors that define modern specialised lexicography into consideration for the elaboration of the English/Spanish-Spanish/English technical dictionary on ceramics terminology, a pragmatic, user-oriented perspective that is far more context-centred and aimed at solving communicative needs has been adopted. All these features will be shaped in the form of an active dictionary capable of making up for the shortcomings posed by passive dictionaries. In this sense, figure 21 shows the differences in content and structure per entry between *active* and *passive* dictionaries, as remarked by Posteguillo and Piqué-Angordans (2005: 460-461).

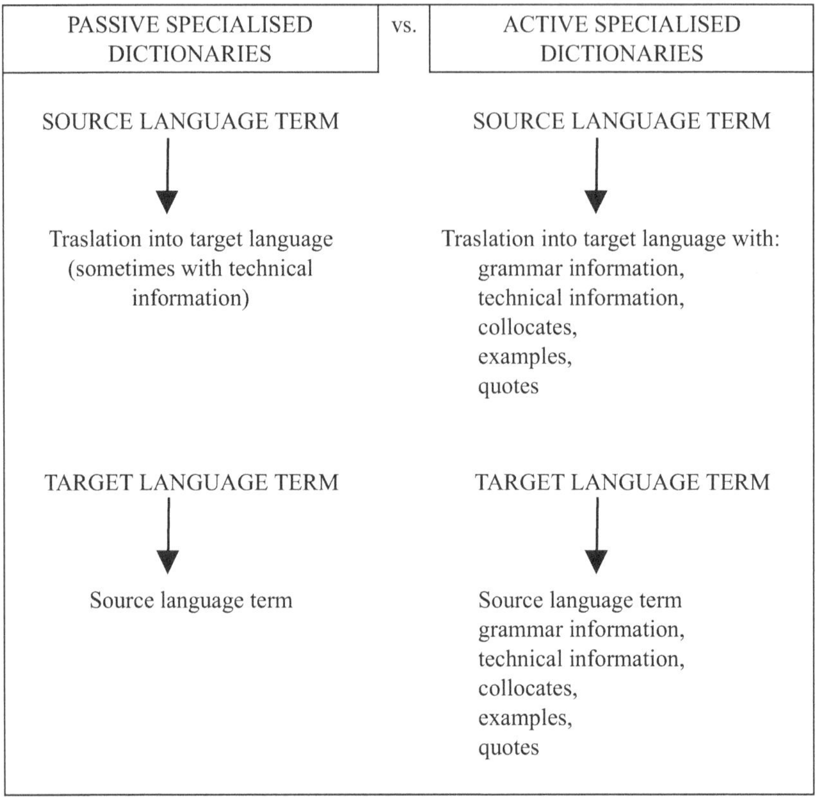

Figure 21. *Passive* versus *active* dictionaries in specialised contexts (Posteguillo and Piqué-Angordans, 2005: 460).

Accordingly, in the entries from the active specialised dictionary presented here, each entry may include up to eight distinct items of technical, grammatical or pragmatic information, namely, part of speech (adj., adv., n., v., etc.), gender (m/f), translation, semantic field, collocations/collocates, acronyms, examples, quotations and definitions/technical information.

It has thus been a central issue throughout the development of the dictionary to bear in mind considerations like Picht's (1991: 103), who again refers to the need to incorporate phraseology that shows the use of terms in context, because the terminological unit activates a specific knowledge depending on the context in which it is found: "El lenguaje para fines específicos no puede reducirse en modo alguno a los denominados *tecnicismos* que aparecen en los diccionarios, una idea que está muy extendida."[33]

Thus, an active dictionary takes into account the fact that every term is always accompanied by other words or terms with which it may appear more frequently than with others. In this way and considering all the factors above, I have tried to somehow complement and reorient previous lexicographical work in the area of specialised industrial ceramic terminology in English and Spanish (see an illustrative sample of final dictionary entries in the section devoted to results (number 9)). Our proposal has aimed at improving and complementing previous lexicographical undertakings and at obtaining a linguistic tool that fits the perspectives of modern specialised lexicography, thus showing the grounding principles of the SLA and the aspects that make its dictionary-making method and final dictionaries in itself go a step further.

33 "Language for specific purposes cannot be reduced in any way to the so called 'technicisms' (technical terms) that appear in dictionaries, a highly widespread idea."

When it comes to getting things done,
We need fewer architects and more bricklayers.
Colleen C. Barrett

8. General-theorical considerations and working stages in the compilation of a specialised dictionary of industrial ceramics terminology

The subsections included in this chapter try to provide, first of all, a reflection on the different theoretical aspects related with and considered for the different stages involved in the compilation of a dictionary on industrial ceramics. Likewise, after the theoretical considerations, the method of working (strictly speaking) used in the SLA is also described from a practical, applied point of view throughout the subsections entitled "stage of…".

Regardless of the way terminology is conceived from a theoretical point of view, its practice in every case follows a process which can be subdivided into stages. As has already been explained in previous sections, specialised lexicographical work is the applied version of a field of knowledge (terminology) that we have characterised as interdisciplinary and communicative in nature, but which accepts and has accepted many different conceptions throughout history.

However, before presenting the working method adopted throughout this work for the compilation of the dictionary entries, Cabré's (1993) classification of the kinds of terminological work may be useful:

There are basically two general criteria for characterising the work in terminology: the number of languages of/at work (in which the work is undertaken) and the systematic character of the work. As regards the first criterion, the terminological work can be monolingual or plurilingual and the second one means it can be systematic or restricted (what Cabré calls *puntual*). On the one hand, a work is said to be monolingual if it is based on a single language, whereas it is plurilingual if it comprises more than one language. On the other hand, a given terminological work is systematic if it intends to deal with every single term of an area, or if a group of terms from the same area or sub-area is wide enough to make it necessary to establish the conceptual system of this area. A work is restricted, however, if it only affects a single term or a small group of terms of a given area, or if it is about a group of terms that belong to different terminological fields.[34] Hence, as has already been explained, a work is considered to be systematic if it comprises all the terms from a thematic area or sub-area or if a group of terms (from the same area or sub-area) is wide enough to make it advisable to construct the conceptual system of the area beforehand. Although the working methodology of the monolingual systematic work constitutes the basis of plurilingual systematic work, I have focused on the second as the one this work represents. These classificatory criteria (number of languages and systematic character of the work) are combined with each other to produce four kinds of terminological work, each with their own methodology, process and working criteria, but methodologically coherent with one another:

- Monolingual systematic work
- Plurilingual systematic work
- Monolingual restricted work
- Plurilingual restricted work

Accordingly, the kind of work presented here would correspond to the second category, that is to say, a plurilingual (more specifically bilingual: English and Spanish) systematic work.

What follows is a detailed account on the most important theoretical aspects to be considered regarding the seven stages of the method of work as well as the explanation of these stages of the method as such, which are:

34 As Cabré (1993: 290) points out: *A título sólo indicativo (y basándonos en los criterios que utilizan algunos organismos) esta frontera se situaría en torno a los 60 términos de la misma área.*
[Just for informational purposes (and based on the criteria used by some organizations) the boundary could be placed at around 60 terms of the same area.]

1. Definition of the work
2. Work preparation and corpus compilation
3. Elaboration of the field diagram
4. Documentary corpus management
5. Term extraction
6. Data processing
7. Revision, normalisation and edition

8.1. Considerations for definition of the work

The launch of a systematic terminological work like the one presented here has involved, first of all, the consideration of four previous basic determining factors that condition the rigour of the work once it is finished and the accomplishment of the goals that were initially set:

1. The topic of the work
2. The addressees of the work
3. The function the work is aimed at accomplishing
4. The work dimensions/scope

1) A crucial issue to be considered before starting to create a terminology (understood as the group of terms characteristic of a speciality area) is the subject matter of the work, which must be clearly and neatly delimited by its authors since, as reality reveals, many works start without taking into account and hence without solving such an elemental question. As Cabré (1999 a: 293) indicates:

> Los autores de un trabajo, en efecto, suelen definir previamente y de forma global el tema que quieren estudiar. Pero muy a menudo no valoran suficientemente el alcance conceptual y terminológico que la obra debe tener, ni la diversidad de perspectivas con que una misma temática puede enfocarse. En consecuencia, muchos trabajos deben reorientarse durante su realización, limitando su alcance conceptual o redefiniendo la perspectiva de análisis, con los costes añadidos que suponen todos esos cambios.

[Tha authors of a work tend, in fact, to define previously and in a global way the subject matter they want to study. However, very often they assess neither the conceptual and terminological scope a work must have nor the diversity of perspectives from which the same field may be approached. Consequently, many works must be reoriented during their carrying out, limiting their conceptual scope or redefining the analysis perspective with the added costs all these changes imply.]

2) Secondly, it is fundamental that every terminological work about a given topic takes into account the public to whom it is addressed (Cabré, 1993). Although it is obvious that the group of terms of a specialised discipline is basically the same regardless of the terminological work, it is also true that the precise selection of terms, the corpus to be prioritised as a source for term extraction, the way of presenting the data and even the kind of work that must be edited will differ depending on the features of each situation and its addressees. A semi-expert tenor usually demands an agile work which allows easy reading and searching or consultation whereas, on the contrary, a highly specialised public would reject a work containing information which is too basic or redundant (Cabré, 1993).

3) Thirdly, Cabré (1993) highlights the fact that the functions aimed at by terminological works do not always coincide. Hence, a distinction can be made between descriptive and prescriptive works (see section 4.3.2, among others): descriptive works compile the terms of a speciality field with no normalising aspiration whereas the goal of the latter, that is to say, prescriptive ones, is to prioritise the use of the terms they consider recommendable (that is, normative or normalised) in opposition to those marked as rejectable. The final aim of this prescriptive work is to orient the speakers about the correct use of terminology. As this author goes on to explain, within prescriptive works we can make a further distinction between those works which prescribe directly on the form of the term and those which prescribe directly on the concept (and also indirectly on the denomination).

4) Finally, once the topic and the addressees and functions of the work have been established, the people responsible for a

terminology will have to consider the reach or scope of a work, not only according to the factors put forward but also taking into consideration other more pragmatic reasons such as the material and economic resources available, the deadlines established for finishing the work, the number of authors to take part in the work, the terminological necessities of the working area and so on.

8.1.1. Stage of definition of the work

According to what has been just mentioned in the previous section, the first stage in the compilation process of a specialised dictionary is that of definition of the work. In this initial stage, the main aspects to be defined before the development of the terminological work as such have had to be established, these comprising, in the specific case of the industrial ceramics dictionary:

- The addressees of the specialised lexicographical tool, in this case translators and specialists in the ceramic industrial field.
- The delimitation of the linguistic functions, which in this case has been a descriptive one.
- The thematic delimitation of the specialised lexicographical work with the aim of excluding a priori all those aspects non-relevant for the purposes of the work.
- The selection of a work team and advisors or consultants in order to supervise the work and balance and guarantee the quality of the linguistic and technical knowledge.
- The definition of the resources available, among which we find computer equipment and programs which in this case have been: *OmniPage Pro 12.0*, *WordSmith Tools 4.0*, *TermStar XV*, *Gendic*, *Excel* and *Word*.

Figure 22 below summarises all the aspects to be considered in work definition for the specific case of the work presented here:

BILINGUAL DICTIONARY OF THE CERAMICS INDUSTRY		
TOPIC OF THE WORK	Subject matter	The specialised language of the ceramic industrial district (focus on its terminology).
	Languages	English-Spanish, Spanish-English.
	Data included	Mainly, entry, equivalent, grammatical category, synonym(s), cross reference(s), context of use, phraseology, quotations, data source, semantic field and definition.
ADDRESSEES OF THE WORK	Addressees	Translators and specialists in the ceramic industrial field.
FUNCTIONS OF THE WORK	Aim/objective	• To become a useful specialised lexicographical tool for those professionals working in the area. • To analyse, describe and present the terminology characteristic of the specialised language of the ceramic industrial district systematically and coherently from a communicative, pragmatic and corpus-based approach.
WORK DIMENSIONS	Dimensions	A prospective total of 22,000-25,000 terms

Figure 22. Considerations for definition of the work in the specific case of the bilingual dictionary of the ceramics industry.

8.2. Considerations for work preparation and corpus compilation

Once all the considerations regarding the definition of the work have been posed and discussed from a theoretical point of view, the reflection on the preparation of the work has comprised, broadly speaking, five main activities, in accordance with Cabré (1993):

1. The acquisition of the necessary information about all the aspects of the work and about the material, professional, conceptual and scientific framework of the topic.

2. The selection of work assessors.
3. The conceptual structuring of the field.
4. The proposal of a definitive working plan.
5. The selection of the information and the fixation of the corpus for subsequent term extraction and analysis.

1) Prior to the compilation of the corpus as such there are a series of preliminary questions to be posed and considered, that is, the acquisition of the necessary information about all the aspects of the work and about the material, professional, conceptual and scientific framework of the topic. In this respect and in Cabré's (1993) opinion, any specialist or linguist who is about to start a systematic terminological work must have certain knowledge about four aspects of the topic of his/her work:

a) The contents of the topic/subject matter.
b) The documentation available.
c) The professional setting in which the topic is developed.
d) The sociolinguistic situation of the domain.

a) Regarding the first item from the list, as has already been mentioned, the reference bibliography constitutes the best means to acquire a general idea about the contents of the topic/subject matter dealt with for a terminologist who is not a specialist in a scientific-technical topic (or any other specific/specialised activity). If the terminological work is undertaken directly by a specialist, this first step is obviously much simpler since this knowledge about his/her speciality field has already been acquired as a basic requisite to become such a specialist. However, this training is absolutely crucial for the terminologist-linguist who is not an expert (as in this case), since it allows greater agility, adequacy and rigour when structuring the speciality domain, when selecting the most adequate material and in the term extraction stage.

A thorough knowledge of the contents of the subject matter to work with and of its conceptual system then makes it possible to structure the notional field of the discipline. This conceptual system can be schematically represented with a field diagram (see section 8.3), which, in this case was tentatively initiated in the stage of "definition of the work" and completed in the stage of "elaboration of the field diagram"), thus allowing the complex conceptual system of relationships shaping the subject matter to be visualised in a simple way.

b) However, this information about the content of the field of work is not enough to make up the previous knowledge a terminologist should have in order to undertake a specific work about the terms of a speciality area. He/she must also have information about the documentation available for use. This documentation refers to other terminological works edited in the same or related fields, to representative works that can be used (and have in fact been used) as information sources of the contents to be dealt with and to the documentation considered appropriate for term extraction.

In spite of this, as has been the case in this study, a linguistic terminologist must rely on a specialist in the discipline in order to obtain useful and reliable information about the documentation available for his/her purposes, as well as being able to count on the help of specialists in documentation who are aware of how to gain access to and consult the information sources. In this sense, a good previous documentary work has greatly facilitated the tasks to be undertaken in subsequent stages.

Moreover, apart from the information on the topic area as such and adequate documentary research, the authors of a systematic terminological work must also have pragmatic data about the organisational and linguistic reality of the professional setting in which this topic area is created, developed and used.

It was thus necessary to be aware of the "poles" around which the structures of work of the professional or speciality area of industrial ceramics are organised. The knowledge of these poles and the detection of the most significant diffusion points facilitated the terminological work a lot since they made it possible to gather the information with the greatest prestige or authority in each field and may also help to organise the subsequent implantation of the elaborated terminology in a more effective way in future stages (Cabré, 1993).

2) The selection of work assessors, which is important because of the aforementioned reliability of their contributions regarding the validation of results, suggestions and their global understanding of the domain, is highly enlightening for the non-specialist, especially in the early stages of the work.

3) The conceptual structuring of the field. In this stage, "the conceptual structuring of the field" refers to the consideration of the more theoretical preliminary steps for the actual "elaboration of a field diagram" in the next stage. Generally speaking, with all the information gathered so far, the specialised lexicograher (preferably with the help of a specialist) can start to create a conceptual structure of the field he/she is working in and to represent it graphically. In this work, this representation of the conceptual structure of a thematic domain has been illustrated in the form of a "field diagram" which, in spite of not being exactly a conceptual map, allows every concept to be placed within an ordered, coherent structure of the different areas forming part of a domain. In this way, this coherent and significant placing of every concept of a speciality domain within a general structure representing the structure of the whole domain, can be said to share many features with pure conceptual systems.

As Cabré (1993) points out, every speciality area transmits a determined view of reality that is represented in the form of a system of concepts. A conceptual system is formed by a structured group of concepts organised in conceptual classes. The big conceptual classes and the subclasses, as well as the concepts of the same class, are related to each other by the features they share or in the way they are used in the real world. In this sense, as Cabré goes on explaining, specialised thesauri and subject matter classifications are highly useful tools in order to orient the structuring of a field, a task which deals with representing the big branches or sections in which each speciality is organised.

Although structuring a specialised field is no easy task because of the different factors involved in it, a well-elaborated conceptual structuring must have the following characteristics, according to Cabré (1993):

- It must cover all the field of work (and, if possible, it must frame it within the field that is immediately above it so that the specific field of work is one of the components of the more general field).
- It must contain or include all the structured branches of the sector dealt with.
- It must present or represent the relationships given between the different branches and inside them.
- It must not include non-pertinent conceptual blocks.
- It must be structured in such a way that the same concept is not repeated in different branches.
- It must not include non-productive conceptual blocks, that is to say, those which do not lead to a group of concepts (and denominations referring to them).

These conceptual structurings are usually represented by means of diagrams that are very often (although not necessarily) tree-like (like the one used and presented here).

In conclusion, it is important for the specialised lexicographer to devote the time and effort necessary to establish the notional field of a thematic area, since the more detailed and rigorous this conceptual structure is, the easier the subsequent work about terms will be; at the same, other aspects regarding the conceptual aspect of the work will automatically be improved too (Cabré, 1993), for example:

- The delimitation of the subject matter and its scope.
- The control of term extraction.
- The selection of terms.
- The attribution of a thematic sub-area to the terms.
- The formulation of definitions.
- The control of key descriptors.
- The incorporation of the terms into a database.
- The subsequent automatic retrieval of information.
- The establishment of new related conceptual fields.

4) The proposal of a definitive working plan: the data and the information gathered up to the moment make it possible to

reorganise (when necessary) the working process that was broadly designed during the work preparation, as well as to design a definitive execution plan. A working plan like the one used here normally includes all the features mentioned up till now (also in the stage of "definition of the work") apart from other aspects concerning subsequent stages. According to Cabré (1993: 301: 302) these are:

- El título del trabajo.
- La delimitación del campo de trabajo.
- Los objetivos que se propone cubrir.
- Los destinatarios de la obra.
- La información sobre la situación terminológica y bibliográfica del área.
- La información sobre la organización profesional del medio.
- La información sobre la situación lingüística del medio.
- La estructuración del área de trabajo.
- El establecimiento del corpus de vaciado.
- La propuesta de organización del trabajo:
  - Los agentes del trabajo: autores, colaboradores, informadores: nombres y distribución de responsabilidades.
  - La metodología: fases generales, operaciones específicas para cada fase
  - El calendario.
  - Los recursos: presupuesto, material, infraestructura.

- [The title of the work.
- The delimitation of the field of work.
- The objectives it aims to cover.
- The addressees of the work.
- Information about the terminological and bibliographical situation of the area.
- Information about the linguistic situation .
- The structuring of the area of work.
- The compilation of the corpus for term extraction.
- The proposal of work organization:
  - The working agents: authors, collaborators, informants: names and distribution of responsibilities.
  - The methodology: general stages, specific operations for each stage.
  - The schedule.
  - The resources: budget, material, infrastructure].

5) The selection of the information and the fixation of the corpus for term extraction. In this stage, in which the corpus has already been compiled, a series of actions have to be undertaken with

the aim of successfully selecting the necessary information for accomplishing two basic objectives: term extraction (documentation for term extraction) and reference (reference documentation).

The documentation for term extraction constitutes the material basis for the detection, extraction and analysis of the terms of the discipline, whereas the reference documentation provides information about different aspects of the subject matter.

The corpus for term extraction (*corpus de vaciado*) is the group of documents that allows the list of terms of the work to be established and has to be carefully compiled since it constitutes the basis for the detection of the terminological units; the final results are therefore highly conditioned by this corpus.

Accordingly, a series of criteria were followed for the elaboration of the corpus, that is to say, a number of parameters were taken into account in order to guarantee the quality of the textual samples and their adequacy to the objectives established.

In general, the information contained in the documentation and included in the corpus must be relevant or representative of the field of knowledge, and complete, which means it includes all the aspects directly related to the subject matter. In the same way, updating is another basic requisite because the lists of terms obtained must reflect the current linguistic reality existing in the area under study (in the case of technological/scientific branches it is quite liable to change). These criteria thus determined that the texts were suitable for constituting and being called a "corpus" and, more particularly, for being compiled and forming part of the bilingual corpus of this study, given the linguistic objectives established. However, the more theoretical criteria taken into account for the selection of the documents (that is, those to be used for term extraction or reference) and their inclusion in the corpus are specified below as a key issue in this work preparation stage.

Hence, Rondeau (1984) puts forward a series of criteria in order to evaluate the documentation that might be used as a source for terminological work but making a further distinction between the criteria regarding lexicographical works and the criteria to be taken into account for the rest of the sources. In each of his lists, Rondeau establishes the elements that positively determine the documental evaluation, which are the ones that have been taken into account, among others, for the selection of the documentation in this work (mainly used to verify term extraction):

Positive criteria for lexicographical works:

- Specification of the method for data compilation.
- Presence of cross references.
- Presence of an alphabetic index.
- Ease of consultation.
- Presence of illustrations.
- Presence of definitions or contexts.
- Indication of the sources of terms.
- Authority of the author.
- Indication of the thematic domain for each term.

Criteria that must be taken into account for the evaluation of non-lexicographical works:

- Language in which the work is written (original/translation).
- Authority of the author.
- Date of publication.
- Public to whom the work is addressed (general/specialised).
- Level of the language in relation to the addressees of the work (specialised/popularising).
- Geographic area to which it is addressed.
- Importance of the editor (if there is one).

8.2.1. Criteria for corpus compilation: general considerations for text selection in corpus design

Corpus-based specialised lexicography can be easily justified if we consider that the language used by the different members of a scientific community is materialised both in oral and written communication. These written forms are the ones that are electronically kept and stored as text card indexes (Gómez and Vargas, 2002) and are thus the ones forming part of the corpora compiled for different studies and with different objectives.

Therefore, the group of texts created by the specialists in a given domain are the "raw material" from which to extract the different kinds of linguistic data (terms, definitions, contexts, and so forth), since these texts contain most of the terminology of the field being dealt with and report the knowledge shared by the professionals from this field (Gómez and Vargas, 2002). However, these texts must be in agreement with the aims posed for the terminological extraction process and not every text will be valid for such purposes or show the quality level required for specific terminographical purposes. This is the reason why there are many different factors to be taken into account when compiling a specialised corpus (Gómez and Vargas, 2002), namely:

- Its final size before starting with the extraction of terminological units.
- The languages of the texts.
- The original reproduction mode (oral or written).
- the original reproduction format (printed or electronic).
- The sample size.
- Copyright considerations, and so on.

To better understand the specific criteria followed for the compilation of the texts forming part of the corpus used in this study, in the following subsections a complete account of the corpus-related issues considered here regarding its design and compilation are provided.

According to Ahmad and Davies (1992: 22) "A corpus-based approach enables the terminologist to identify, study and record terms in their natural habitat, and translators, as users of the termbank, to have customised access to a full set of information about all the terms and related terminological data of a domain". However, before starting to use any corpus, it is fundamental that linguists are aware of the importance of a good corpus design.

As has already been mentioned, if one intends to work with a corpus, two possibilities are presented: to work with one that has already been compiled or to compile it so that it can be designed in the way that best fits the objectives and necessities posed (a tailored corpus).

In both cases, the quality of the corpus will determine the results of the linguistic research so that it is worth taking into account a series of parameters that may, to a certain extent, guarantee this quality (and that may also guarantee that a corpus is actually that and not just a collection of texts gathered at random). The accomplishment of these parameters is easier if, as in the case of this study, corpus composition and design depends on the same linguist undertaking the linguistic investigation afterwards. No-one can better determine the accomplishment of the criteria to be adopted than the person in charge of compiling the corpus and, thus, the one who chooses what to include and what to dismiss. According to this, there are certain issues that must be and in fact have already been considered for the design of the corpus and, as such, they are regarded here as forming part of the theoretical considerations behind the methodology used for corpus compilation.

When designing a corpus the first step is to clearly determine the intended purposes of the research in order to try to construct a corpus that fits these purposes. Departing from the fact that a corpus is not just the aforementioned collection of randomly selected texts but a collection of texts that has been compiled according to a series of given criteria with the aim of being used for specific purposes, then the appropriateness of this corpus will be mainly determined by its representativeness in terms of the area under study. "The appropriate design for a corpus therefore depends upon what it is meant to represent" (Biber, Conrad and Reppen, 1998: 246).

What seems obvious, whatever the topic area or the research objectives of a given corpus may be, is that the representativeness criterion is crucial when designing it since it will determine the kind of research questions to be posed as well as the level of generalisability and reliability that can be given to the results obtained in the research.

However, representing a language or a part of it is not at all an easy issue because it is impossible to know "the full extent of variation in language or all the contextual variables that need to be covered in order to capture all variation in texts" (Biber, Conrad and Reppen, 1998: 246).

In spite of this, taking into account a series of methodological issues can and has helped me to attain what I think is a satisfactory corpus design. In this specific case, I have taken into account and combined the criteria of corpus composition and design proposed by various authors. What follows is an account of the main methodological proposals in this respect and, in fact, the ones that have been considered in this specific project.

Firstly, I have made use of the guidelines proposed by Biber, Conrad and Reppen (1998) for selecting the textual samples of the corpus. Broadly speaking, these authors suggest that for a good corpus design, apart from representativeness, two additional parameters (diversity and size) must also be considered when undertaking text selection and compilation:

a) Diversity is important and several aspects are of crucial importance as regards diversity, mainly:

- Register variation and dialect: a well-designed corpus must represent the different registers of the language. However, in the analysis of PAL or a specific specialised language these factors tend not to be very significant.
- Subject matter: it is especially important in lexicographical studies like this one since, as the results of this study show, the frequency of many words varies depending on the subject matter. For all studies, a variety of subject matters, understood as sub-areas of the main area under analysis, need to be included within the corpus (the field diagram has been the most useful tool in this respect).

b) Size: the issues of size in corpus design do not only refer to the number of total words in the corpus but also to the number of texts from different categories, the number of samples from each text, and the number of words in each sample.

Obviously, if the total number of texts included is very low (although a single text is very long and includes a large number of words), this can have an undue influence on the results of an analysis. The personal linguistic features of a given author or expert on the topic may then be taken for granted as a characteristic of the language or register analysed when, in reality, it is just the reflection of the way of speaking or writing of an individual. According to Biber (1990), enough texts must be included in each category to encompass variation across speakers or authors. More specifically, Biber (1990) investigated how many texts were needed for a category and concluded that ten texts represented the categories of the LOB corpus well for many grammatical features.

In the same way, the number of samples from each text can make the characteristics of a text vary dramatically internally. The example that Biber (1990) proposes to clarify this issue is the following: experimental research articles follow a structured scheme in which the Introduction, Method, Results and Discussion sections have quite different patterns of language use. Thus, if all these sections are not included in the sampling, then the results obtained from the corpus would misrepresent the real language patterns of the research article as a genre.

Finally, the number of words in each sample is also important in order to provide a reliable count of features in a text. Biber (1990) states that counts are relatively stable across 1000-word samples from a text, although some other features which are rarer in nature would require larger samples for quantitative studies.

One important conclusion to mention here is that, usually, lexicographical studies are thought to require particularly large corpora.[35] It can be deduced from the results section in this study that many words and collocations occur with low frequencies (some of them because they are highly specialised) and a corpus must be really large and shaped by many different texts coming from different sources and authors to enable reliable investigations and results regarding use. In spite of this, size cannot act as a substitute for diversity because both features are necessary for good and reliable corpus design.

Following Sinclair (1996, in Vargas, 2005: 339), a corpus must accomplish four basic criteria to be considered as such. If any of these criteria are not accomplished the corpus would be called a *special corpus*. These characteristics, closely related to those mentioned earlier, are the following:

a) Quantity: "el valor por defecto de esta característica es grande" [The value by default of this feature is big]. (Vargas, 2005: 339). It may not be stated explicitly but it is commonly assumed that a corpus must contain a great number of words.

35 There is no general agreement in this respect either. For more information regarding size and to be able to analyse discordant opinions, see section 8.2.1B.

b) Quality: "el valor por defecto es auténtico" " [The value by default is authentic]. (Vargas, 2005: 339). All the material compiled in a corpus must come from genuine communication developed in normal situations (the term "normal" would vary if the corpus is a rather specialised one like the one used here because what is a normal situation in the context of the ceramic tile industry may not be so, for instance, in the context of a hospital).

c) Simplicity: "el valor por defecto es texto plano" [The value by default is plain text]. (Vargas, 2005: 339).

d) Documentation: "el valor por defecto es documentado" [The value by default is documented]. (Vargas, 2005: 339). The complete details and documentation of the texts must be kept separately from these.

Taking these features into consideration, the parameters I have focused on for the elaboration of the English and the Spanish corpora could be summarised in two big groups (Vargas, 2005), namely, representativeness and equilibrium, on the one hand, and size, on the other. Moreover, Vargas (2005) also proposes to take into account the channel of production of the texts, the period of time, and so on. In this study these other parameters have not been analysed in depth (although they have been taken into account for the composition of the corpus) but sections 8.2.1 A, 8.2.1 B and 8.2.1 C provide a more detailed account of the factors that have been most widely considered for the specific compilation of the corpus of industrial ceramics: representativeness and equilibrium, size and reliability of Internet documents respectively.

a) Representativeness and equilibrium in the corpus compiled for this study

Tognini-Bonelli (2001) explains that the determination of the function of a corpus is inherent to the methodology chosen for the compilation of textual samples.

Therefore, for a study like the one presented here, which aims to cover the terminology of a very specific industrial district like the ceramic one, it has been necessary to elaborate a specialised corpus by compiling textual samples that coherently represent and characterise the specialised language under study. However, "es un hecho asumido entre los lingüistas de corpus la imposibilidad de definir y crear un corpus totalmente representativo"[36] (Clear, 1992, 1997; Kennedy, 1998; Torruella and Llisterri, 1999).

From the quotation above it can be deduced that the notion of representativeness is not an easy issue to define or delimit. As Gómez and Vargas state (2004), the notions of equilibrium and representativeness have been widely debated and dealt with by corpus linguistics (Atkins *et al.*, 1992; Biber, 1993, among others).

The controversy it generates is an "old friend" of linguists, who have just approximate ideas of what a representative corpus could be. In addition to this, there is no way of guaranteeing this feature of representativeness and neither can it be subject to objective evaluation (Tognini-Bonelli, 2001; Berber Sardinha, 2000).

What seems clear is that, although a corpus may vary depending on its design, its size, its nature (Kennedy, 1998) and its intended purposes (they may be used for general or specific description), it must always be representative. This notion of representativeness is close to that of diversity introduced by Biber, Conrad and Reppen (1998) in many senses because, in Summers' (1993: 186) words, the term "representative" refers to:

> Representative of the standard language in a very general sense, not restricted to a regional variety (e.g. British English or a local dialect) or a narrow range of text types (e.g. scientific texts, newspaper writing, language of a particular social class).

Tognini-Bonelli (2001: 57) summarises this issue of the representativeness of the corpus as follows:

> Thus there seems to be general agreement among scholars who choose to work on a corpus that this should be representative of a certain population and that the statements derived from the analysis of the corpus will be largely applicable to a larger sample or to the language as a whole.

36 "The impossibility of defining and creating a wholly representative corpus is a fact assumed among corpus linguists."

The main problem presented by the notion of representativeness is that, given that a corpus is a finite sample from an infinite population, the linguistic samples that can be compiled never reach an end because "there are always new ones coming along that we haven't seen yet" (Leech, 2002: 4). For this reason, complete, perfect representativeness will never be reached because, according to Leech's (2002) views, this will never be possible. However, in spite of all the difficulties, there are a series of guidelines that facilitate the creation of representative (and also balanced) corpora. For a corpus to be balanced and representative, the field diagram plays a fundamental role, since it allows the balanced inclusion of the necessary number and kind of texts dealing with each specific area or sub-area that go to make up the domain as determined by this diagrammatic representation. This is crucial since the notion of representativeness refers, mainly, to the texts normally given in the specialised area in question. Thus, in the stage of corpus design or compilation it is necessary to include the different situations (whether they are academic or professional) in which specialists in the field normally produce their discourse, so that the different kinds of texts representing the professional field in question can be covered. Following Bowker's views (1996: 45), a representative corpus must include, broadly speaking, the same number of samples of four different kinds of texts that represent or account for the level of specialisation (Gómez and Vargas, 2004):

- Very specialised
- Specialised
- Didactic
- Popularising

At the same time, this classification is closely related with, on the one hand, the author's level of specialisation (expert, semi-expert and professor) and, on the other hand, the addressees (specialist, semi-specialist, student and general public) (Gómez and Vargas, 2004). In order to illustrate this, the textual types that can be compiled according to the category of "level of specialisation" (*nivel de especialización)* have been classified by Gómez and Vargas (2004: 17), on the basis of Bowker's (1996) views, as shown in figure 23, most of which have been included in the corpus used in this study.

Level of specialisation	*Textual types*
Highly specialised	Specialised journal article
	Academic journal article
	Norms
Specialised	Specialised journal article
	Academic journal article
	Technical manual
Popularising	Specialised journal article
	Newspaper article
	Reference work
	Advertising brochures
Didactic	Specialised journal article
	Academic journal article
	Technical manual
	Reference work
	Encyclopaedic article
	Text books

Figure 23. Adaptation of Gómez and Vargas' (2004) views on the levels of specialisation and kinds of texts (textual types) included in each level.

Each textual type will contain different conceptual and linguistic information, and terms and concepts will vary depending on whether a text has been written by a specialist or a layman. However, if the quality of the text is adequate, every textual type can accomplish a function in the different phases of the terminographical process depending on the level of specialisation it shows and, therefore, on the communicative purpose it aims at. For instance, manuals turn out to be very effective in the early stages of terminographical work in order to become familiar with the speciality field, whereas norms provide highly specialised and technical normative information so that their use is (and has been) more advisable in subsequent and more advanced stages of the work.

As has already been mentioned, equilibrium is another key issue for those corpora designed to represent the specific language of a specialised field, but also for the representation of the language in general terms (Kennedy, 1998; Tognini-Bonelli, 2001). However, it is not difficult to deduce that this feature is not taken into account, for instance, in those corpora referring to the complete works of an author (Kennedy, 1998) even though this has not been the case in this study, in which the equilibrium of the textual samples gathered and compiled for the corpus has necessarily been considered.

Regarding equilibrium, or what some authors prefer to call balance, Atkins *et al.* (1992) define a balanced corpus as a corpus that is so finely tuned that it offers a manageably small-scale model of the linguistic material which the corpus builder wishes to study. In this sense, in the context of specialised corpora and with the aim of achieving the aforementioned equilibrium, Gómez and Vargas (2004) consider it more appropriate to talk about conceptual balance. This notion, introduced by Bowker (1996: 45-46) develops on the already mentioned convenience of gathering within the corpus every subfield into which a field of knowledge is divided, as well as every professional or academic area related to it. In this sense, the already-mentioned field diagram becomes the perfect tool for achieving this conceptual balance, since it comprises the different aspects involved in a knowledge field and may help to represent it thoroughly.

b) Size in the corpus compiled for this study

In general terms, and as will be explained in the section devoted to results, Sinclair (1991) recommends, from a lexicographical point of view, that the corpus should be as large as possible and always allow the inclusion of new samples (the corpus is a linguistic tool that is constantly growing). He grounds this view in the so-called Zipf's law about lexical distribution (Zipf, 1935; Sinclair, 1991), according to which the majority of words are used with a very low frequency and a small number of the most common words (*the*, *of*, *to*, and so on) constitute the biggest part of any text because they appear with a high frequency.

Therefore, the terminographer needs to have quite a large number of occurrences available in order to study the behaviour of words inside texts. Vargas (2005: 345) explains, however, that size may be dependent on the objectives for which the corpus is compiled:

Recientemente se ha considerado necesario construir córpora más pequeños, centrados en áreas específicas de la lengua, especialmente destinados a ámbitos como la docencia de la traducción (Bowker, 1998, Zanettin, 1998), de idiomas (Ghadessy, Henry and Rosberry, 2001) y la terminología (Ahmad and Rogers, 2001). Podemos realizar, por tanto, una división de los córpora según el tamaño. A un lado se sitúan los grandes corpora, que se utilizan para analizar la lengua general y que, además, tienen en su mayoría un fin lexicográfico. Al otro lado se sitúan los córpora utilizados para examinar áreas más específicas del uso lingüístico, de menor tamaño y con fines más variados y concretos.

[Recently, the compilation of smaller corpora focused on specific areas of language has been considered necessary, especially corpora addressed to fields such as translation teaching (Bowker, 1998, Zanettin, 1998), language teaching (Ghadessy, Henry and Rosberry, 2001) and terminology (Ahmad and Rogers, 2001). Hence, a classification of corpora according to their size may be established. On the one hand we find the big corpora, those used in order to analyse general language and that, in addition, have in their biggest part a lexicographical target. On the other hand we find corpora used for examining more specific areas of linguistic use, smaller and with more varied and specific aims.]

Berber Sardinha (2000: 346) suggests a classification of the size of corpora in terms of the number of words based on the observation of certain corpora used in different studies and investigations over a four-year period. According to Berber Sardinha's (2000) classification (figure 24), the corpus presented in this study can be considered to be a medium-sized / big corpus, since nearly 1,500,000 words have been compiled:

Size	*Number of words*
Big corpus	10 millions or more
Medium-sized / big corpus	1 million to 10 million
Medium-sized corpus	250,000 to 1 million
Small / medium-sized corpus	80,000 to 250,000
Small corpus	Less than 80,000

Figure 24. Classification of corpora size according to the number of words.

A special mention must be made of the Internet, as a "megasource", which is a universal supplier of documents of any kind. However, this "universality" also makes it a dangerous source to resort to if adequate selection criteria are not followed. Anyone can contribute to the Net's megacorpus and that is the reason why, in the next section, a series of specific guidelines in the methodology used for corpus compilation have been included in order to avoid possible issues derived from a bad selection of documents.

As Gómez and Vargas (2004) point out for some of their own terminographical works and their corresponding corpus-based studies, the volume in terms of size of the corpus used for this study may seem modest or even insufficient if compared with the number of words (normally millions) traditionally used in corpus linguistics. However, in general, this is due to a basic difference between specialised and non-specialised corpora: specialised texts are much denser from the point of view of lexical terms than texts from general language (Ahmad and Rogers, 2001). This implies that texts with a high degree of technicality like the ones normally included in specialised corpora present what is known as "terminological density", that is to say, a large number of words that transmit specialised knowledge. In addition to this, in spite of presenting a number of words that is generally inferior to the figure for general language corpora, truly revealing and satisfactory results can be obtained from specialised corpora if equilibrium and representativeness are achieved and if the texts compiled present a high degree of technicality.

c) Reliability of Internet documents in corpus design

One of the main sources for corpus compilation and composition in this study has been the Internet. The Internet constitutes a worldwide forum in which everyone's opinions can be expressed and included. The Net is nowadays the most important and easiest distributing medium for authors who want their work and studies to be known worldwide. However, there is a fundamental difference between having an article published, for instance, in a specialised journal and having it published on a personal homepage on the Internet: anyone can contribute to the Internet's megacorpus whereas the criteria for publishing in more traditional media (books, manuals, specialised journals) are normally much more difficult to comply with. Consequently, this may be a dangerous fact for those who use the Internet as a source for their daily work or research, and a factor to be widely considered.

In the specific case of this study, the Net has been a main source for corpus compilation because it has been regarded as an essential part of real language use and transmission both in specialised or general fields of knowledge. However, many documents that can be found during a search on the Net are neither edited nor checked by organisations, institutions or any other mechanism that could at least to a certain extent guarantee the quality of the information contained therein. This is why the Internet, in spite of being a very useful tool, is still not a completely reliable source if the appropriate criteria are not used to distinguish between reliable and non-reliable materials. In general terms, as this study reflects, the Internet may be considered a reliable means or resource for many kinds of research if we are aware of the factors to be taken into account for accepting a document as valid or disregarding it.

Codina (2000) enumerates a series of factors to be considered when attempting to establish the adequacy and quality of digital resources. He proposes a series of parameters and tries to justify and reason them out, although there is no general agreement regarding the criteria or the indicators to be followed in order to evaluate the adequacy of these digital resources. In general terms, however, there is some agreement on the following: content, authorship, ergonomics and representation of the information. In the author's opinion, this list can even be reduced to the first two parameters, content and authorship, which are analysed in depth below:

The *content* criterion must include, in Codina's (2000) views, indicators both on the quality and quantity of the information. The indicators on quality are mainly:

- The rigour or care with which the information has been treated. Some indicators of this rigour, which is usually not easily perceived by non-specialists, are: mention of other sources, mention of specific data (dates, authors, statistics), the non-inclusion of factual mistakes, the absence of orthographic mistakes, the separation between opinion and information, and so forth.

- The exhaustivity or degree to which the information is presented in a more or less complete manner. For example: a bibliographical datum may be just a title and a name of an author or incorporate, as a positive indicator, the date of edition, the place, the publisher's name, the number of pages or the ISBN number.

- Updating: the inclusion of the date of the last update is also a positive indicator, since the more up-to-date information is, the more valuable it is. Updating has been important in this study because, for its purposes and given that the speciality domain is a highly technical one and thus constantly evolving, the information needed to be up-to-date. Especially in fields like industrial ceramics (involving new technologies, engineering and sciences in general), knowledge is in constant evolution and consequently its terminology is as well. The indicators observed for including only up-to-date information are: looking for the date of the last update (if it is included, it is usually worded as "last updated") and for the date of the author's rights, if he/she has them (usually worded as "copyright").

- Edition, or the degree to which the information has been treated, revised and completed before being published.

- Systematisation: a directory is systematised if each web is defined in the same way.

- Intrinsic interest: the intrinsic interest of the information provided by websites must always be taken into account more than other more superficial considerations. Consequently, websites on trivial topics and lacking research or documentary interest must be avoided.

- Originality or the degree to which a resource offers information which is unique or exclusive in any sense. For instance, many websites offer digital resources but perhaps only a couple of them offer an evaluation of these resources.

Among the indicators of quantity, it is important to pay attention to the degree to which the information is covered, or the exhaustiveness with which it is done, with respect to the field under study. However, this refers to the amount of useful, valuable information, not to indiscriminate quantities of information.

The *authorship* criterion can be measured or evaluated by three aspects or indicators:

- The reliability or competence of the author and/or the institution that has created, produced or edited the resource.

- The existence of explicit declarations of authorship. A well-conceived website must have a section which states without any kind of ambiguity and in detail to whom the authorship of the resource must be attributed and who is or are its distributor(s) and editor(s). Apart from this, it should be complemented with information about the author(s) and the editor(s), the institution they work for, their address, and so forth.

- The life span of the resource. It seems much more reasonable to resort to resources supported by some sort of institution or company than to personal websites, which usually present many more irregularities, in general, both in their life span and in their quality and reliability. This is why in this study these pages have been avoided. However, an author of recognised prestige can also be considered a guarantee of the quality of a given material.

Figure 25 would constitute an example of a reliable Internet document because it accomplishes the criteria proposed throughout this section and, as such, it has been included in the corpus together with many others of the same sort.

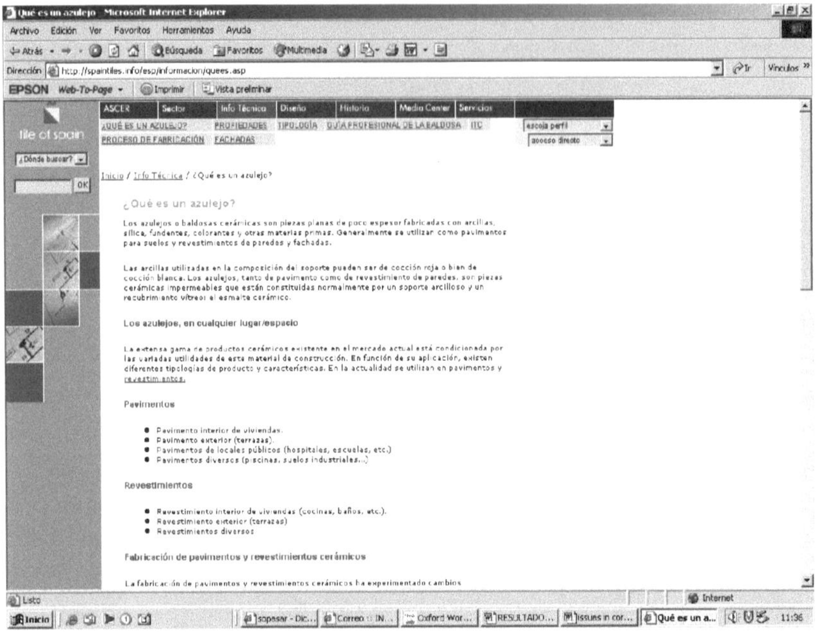

Figure 25. Example of a reliable website included in the Spanish corpus which meets the quality and quantity criteria proposed by Codina (2000) (ASCER's website in http://spaintiles.info/esp/informacion/quees.asp).

The example in figure 25 meets the content reliability requirements of rigour, exhaustivity and edition among others, as well as the authorship reliability requirement by identifying, for instance, the institution which created it, in this case the *Asociación Española de Fabricantes de Azulejos y Pavimentos Cerámicos (ASCER – Association of Ceramic Tile Manufacturers of Spain)*, among many other data.

8.2.2. Stage of work preparation and corpus compilation

The second stage strictly speaking of the dictionary-making process is that of work preparation and corpus compilation. As has been mentioned in the theoretical considerations, it has consisted of gathering documentation about the speciality field with the aim of compiling an adequate corpus for the purposes targeted.

However, a series of criteria have been observed in order to guarantee up to a certain extent the adequacy of the corpus. According to the theoretical considerations mentioned, in this stage, for the corpus design to be adequate, it must show representativeness and equilibrium, an adequate size and finally, it is important that the internet documents included are reliable, this reliability depending on rigour, systematicity, authorship, updating and originality among other criteria. Thus, as its own name indicates, the preparation of the kind of work to be developed, the compilation of the aforementioned corpus documents and their storage in an ordered and systematised way before the stage of documentary corpus management constitute the stage of work preparation and corpus compilation.

8.3. Considerations for the elaboration of the field diagram

A *field diagram* constitutes, an organising/organised structure of the concepts that integrate a speciality domain and the ones that are, to different extents, directly related to it. This kind of diagram is a graphic representation in diagrammatic form of the fields and subfields that are comprised in a given subject/activity. It is a useful tool due to its associative and classificatory nature. The relationships it shows make of the field diagram a coherent whole determined by the notion of *semantic field*. According to Auger and Rousseau (1987), a semantic field is a group of notions that can be grouped under the heading of a key notion. Each terminological unit of a semantic field is conditioned by the others and its value is determined by the position it occupies in the structure. In the same way, every terminological unit has as a function to establish the relationship between a linguistic form (word or term) and a reality (abstract or specific) through a notion. The elaboration of this field diagram has also been useful in order to select the terms to be included in the dictionary and to establish the first element of definition of the different terminological units by means of abbreviations that indicate the semantic field the term belongs to (Vargas, 2005). The *field diagram* is thus a tool to establish an ontological system, that is, a structured list inside which the different activities belonging to the sector under analysis can be included and classified and the mental structure of the terminographer can be organised in a meaningful way.

8.3.1. Stage of elaboration of the field diagram

In the case of the elaboration of the ceramics dictionary, the third stage has dealt with the elaboration of a definitive graphic representation of the field under study illustrating the conceptual system of the area, that is, a field diagram, which allows the terminographer to:

- Delimit the field of work by means of specifying its parts and their relationship within the whole showing thus hierarchical relationships among TUs.
- Elaborate and determine a list of notion categories which are used as a guide for selecting the terms during term extraction.
- Place the terms inside a structured group, which has helped in the correct classification and treatment of the terminological units.

The result of this elaboration process are the field diagrams as such (see figures 26 and 27), elaborated in the two languages with which we are working. In these field diagrams it may be noticed how the domain has been firstly subdivided into characterisation (*caracterización*), productive processes (*procesos productivos*), applications (*aplicaciones*) and related subjects (*temas relacionados*), and the abbreviations of the different fields and subfields have been included and subsequently used as the first element of semantic reference for the entries, as may be observed in the illustrative entries presented in section 9.

1.CHARACTERISATION	1.1 Raw materials [RAWMAT] 1.2 Properties of the raw materials [PROPRAWMAT] 1.3 Geology/ Mineralogy/ Crystallography [GEOL-MIN-CRYST] 1.4 Chemistry [CHEM]	
2. PRODUCTIVE PROCESSES	2.1 Extraction of raw materials	2.1.1 Exploitation and quarrying [EXPL-QUARR] 2.1.2 Extraction and exploitation machinery [EXTRACTMCHN]
	2.2 Transformation of raw materials	2.2.1 Transformation processes of raw materials [TRANSPROC] 2.2.2 Transformation materials [TRANSMTRLS] 2.2.3 Transformation machinery [TRANSMCHN]
	2.3 Transformations for obtaining the product	2.3.1 Productive processes for the elaboration of the product [ELABPROC] 2.3.2 Glazes and related products [GLAZEREL] 2.3.3 Materials [MTRLS] 2.3.4 Elaboration machinery [ELABMCHN] 2.3.5 Elaboration instruments [INSTR] 2.3.6 Final product [FINALPRODUCT] 2.3.7 By-products[BYPROD] 2.3.8 Testing [TESTING] 2.3.9 Chemical and physical properties [CHEM-PHYSPROP] 2.3.10 Quality [QUALITY] 2.3.11 Design [DESIGN]
	2.4 Commercialisation	2.4.1 Management [MNGMNT] 2.4.2 Trade [TRADE] 2.4.3 Distribution [DISTRIB]
	2.5 Security measures/occupational health [SFTY]	
	2.6 Environmental management [ENVRMENT]	
3. APPLICATIONS	3.1 Maintenance [MNTNCE] 3.2 Installation [INSTAL] 3.3 Construction [CONST]	
4. RELATED SUBJECTS	4.1 Allied industries [ALLIEDIND] 4.2 Measures [MEASURE] 4.3 Organisations and institutions [ORG-INST] 4.4 General [GEN]	

Figure 26. English field diagram.

1.CARACTERIZACIÓN	1.1 Materias primas [MATPRI] 1.2 Propiedades de las materias primas [PROPMATPRI] 1.3 Geologia/ Mineralogia/ Cristalografia [GEO-MIN-CRIST] 1.4 Química[QUIM]	
2. PROCESOS PRODUCTIVOS	2.1 Extracción de las materias primas	2.1.1 Explotación y cantería [EXPL-CANT] 2.1.2 Maquinaria de extracción y explotación [MAQEXTRAC]
	2.2 Transformación de las materias primas	2.2.1 Procesos de transformación de las materias primas [TRANSPROC] 2.2.2 Materiales para la transformación [TRANSMTRLS] 2.2.3 Maquinaria de transformación [MAQTRANS]
	2.3 Transformación para la obtención del producto	2.3.1 Procesos productivos para la elaboración del producto [ELABPROC] 2.3.2 Esmaltes y productos relacionados [ESMREL] 2.3.3 Materiales [MTRLS] 2.3.4 Maquinaria de elaboración [MAQELAB] 2.3.5 Instrumentos de elaboración [INSTR] 2.3.6 Productos resultantes/finales [PRODFIN] 2.3.7 Subproductos [SUBPROD] 2.3.8 Ensayos [ENSAYO] 2.3.9 Propiedades químicas y físicas [PROPQUIM-FIS] 2.3.10 Calidad [CALIDAD] 2.3.11 Diseño [DISEÑO]
	2.4 Comercializacion	2.4.1 Gestión [GESTION] 2.4.2 Comercio [COM] 2.4.3 Distribución [DISTRIB]
	2.5 Medidas de seguridad y salud laboral [SEG]	
	2.6 Gestion medioambiental [MEDAMB]	
3. APLICACIONES	3.1 Mantenimiento [MANTNMO] 3.2 Instalación [INSTAL] 3.3 Construcción [CONST]	
4. TEMAS RELACIONADOS	4.1 Industrias afines [INDAFIN] 4.2 Medidas [MEDIDA] 4.3 Organismos e instituciones [ORG-INST] 4.4 General [GRAL]	

Figure 27: Spanish field diagram.

The inclusion of the semantic field in the entries and thus the previous elaboration of this ontological representation is fundamental in the SLA because of its user-friendly, active character aimed at meaningfully placing the terms in the domain, providing thus the first element of definition of such terms.

8.4. Considerations for documentary corpus management

The general-theoretical considerations dealt with in this study regarding documentary corpus management have been covered in an integrated way in subsection 8.4.1, that is, jointly with their practical application in the method, because of the clearly applied nature of this stage of the work.

8.4.1. Stage of documentary corpus management

In the fourth stage of the method, in order to process the textual samples that have been previously compiled and that form part of the corpus, these samples have to be "stored" as a collection of files in the computer. For this, texts have had to be rendered machine-processable and compatible with the programs to be used in subsequent stages. With this aim, the texts with an electronic format, are quickly incorporated to the computer by means of "optical reading" or the keyboard. On the contrary, those texts in paper format have to be incorporated through digitalisation by means of a scanning process using *Omnipage Pro.12.0* Afterwards, using the same Omnipage program, the sections of text to which the OCR (Optical Character Recognition) process wants to be applied are manually selected. Through OCR, the program optically recognises the characters of these textual samples so that what the program has recognised (the useful text as such) may be exported to other programs in a compatible format.

Texts are saved at this point in txt. extension. The next step is to correct orthographic mistakes and reconstruct in Word the text format that is lost at certain points in the OCR process. The resulting corrected text is saved again in *.txt* so that textual samples are ready for working with them in subsequent stages of the method.

In a more graphic way, figure 28 summarises this process which is crucial in order to be able to work with the corpus previously compiled.

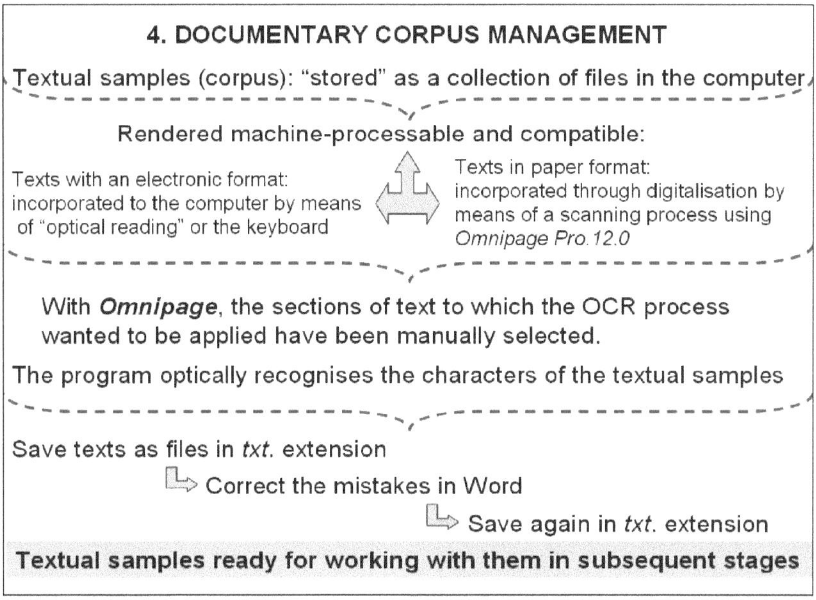

Figure 28. Diagram summarising the stage of documentary corpus management.

8.5. Considerations for term extraction

Term extraction is a fundamental stage in any termiographical work because it implies retrieving and selecting the terms to be presented and analysed in it as belonging or characterising a specific domain.

From a theoretical point of view, there are a series of aspects that must be widely considered when undertaking the term extraction process if accurate and adequate results are to be obtained.

The stage of term extraction deals with extracting from the corpus all the segments that can be considered to be terms belonging to the speciality field being dealt with.

Broadly speaking, in order to undertake this technical operation one must, according to Cabré (1993):

- locate the terms in the texts and delimit the segment representing them, and
- determine their relevance to the work.

Term extraction consists in selecting those segments of text belonging to the specialised area that, according to the topic and objectives posed, must be extracted from the corpus and subsequently included to form part of the work as the prototypical terminology of the subject area. However, as Cabré points (1993: 303) out:

> No todos los términos que aparecen en los textos especializados de una disciplina deben figurar en la terminología que se quiere abordar. A veces, porque aunque aparezcan en un texto especializado, no pertenecen propiamente a la disciplina en cuestión, en otros casos, porque son propios del léxico general.
> La pertinencia de los términos no es una cuestión tan objetiva ni matemática como podría parecer de entrada. Los objetivos y los destinatarios de un trabajo son factores que pueden modificar la selección de las unidades terminológicas del trabajo en curso.
>
> [Not all the terms appearing in the specialised texts of a discipline must figure in the terminology to be studied. Sometimes, because in spite of appearing in a specialised text they do not properly belong to the discipline as such; in other cases because they belong to general language. The pertinence of terms is not such an objective or even mathematical question as could seem at first sight. The objectives and addressees of a work are aspects that may modify the selection of the terminological units of the work in progress.]

In this case, the extraction (understood as recognition/detection, delimitation and retrieval of these terms or candidates for terms) has been undertaken on the basis of a series of lists elaborated with the software concordance program *WordSmith Tools 4.0.* (*WST*).

Following Estopà (1999), the mechanisms for term extraction used by automatic term detectors or concordance programs are of three kinds:

- Mainly statistical: those using statistical (independent from language) information, that is, they use frequency criteria and measure the degree of association between the words of a potential term.
- Mainly linguistic: those using linguistic (depending on language) information in order to determine the probability of a word to be a potential term.
- Hybrid: those combining different kinds of data such as statistical, morphological, syntactic and semantic.

A key aspect in terminological extraction is the detection of not only single terms but also phraseological units or collocations. This issue, closely related to segmentation (see section 8.5.1) requires the theoretical consideration of certain factors like the Mutual Information score (MI). In layman's terms, the polylexical listings have been designed to detect the "strength" or the degree of mutual dependence of the words forming collocations, the ruling principle being that the word that appears more frequently with another word than in any other way or position within the corpus is viewed as being a significant combination and therefore deserves special consideration. These "mutually dependent" LUs can be said to "collocate". Thus, from all the parameters offered by Wordlist in these polylexical lists, I have focused on the MI score in order to detect the "strength of the bond" among collocates and thus the "strength" of collocations. Following the definition and explanation provided by the Wikipedia (http://en.wikipedia.org/wiki/Mutual-information) on probability and information theory, the mutual information of two random variables is a quantity that measures, in bits, the independence of the two variables. However, more informally speaking, mutual information measures the information of X that is shared by Y. If X and Y are independent, then X contains no information about Y and vice versa, so their mutual information is zero. If X and Y are identical then all the information conveyed by X is shared with Y: knowing X reveals nothing new about Y and vice versa, and therefore the mutual information is the same as the information conveyed by X (or Y) alone. In a specific sense, mutual information quantifies the distance between the joint distribution of X and Y and the product of their marginal distributions.

8.5.1. Segmentation

Regarding the factors considered in term segmentation, Halliday's (2004) reflections on what a word is point out as being potentially difficult in some cases the decision as to where a word begins and ends, and even more deciding whether two forms are instances of the same word or not or whether variants like *take, takes, took, taking* or *taken* are different words or just a single word, in this case *take*, with many forms. In this respect, this same author explains that different decisions can be adopted depending on the dictionary, despite the fact that, most probably, there is no single right answer to these questions.

If the detection or extraction of a term as such is not at all easy due to the fact that a deep knowledge of the subject matter is necessary, the delimitation of the segment, statement or utterance representing a TU – especially in those cases in which it has a syntagmatic structure – is an especially complicated and delicate task.

In Cabré's (1993) views, in order to form new terms, both linguists and specialists tend to resort to lexical procedures that allow them to transcribe the formal units of language in the most transparent way possible. Syntagmation is one of the most widely used resources for the creation of new transparent units. However, this kind of structure presents two big problems for the terminologist: the difficulty of formally recognising the term and the difficulty of exactly delimiting the segment representing it. Regarding the aforementioned transparency of terms, terms may present different degrees of semantic opacity according to the formal and structural resources with which they have been created. The highest degree of opacity is normally attributed to those terms whose meaning cannot be deduced from form (acid, atom…). On a second degree we find those terms formed by morphemes, whose meaning contributes to the understanding of the meaning of the whole (machining). The third degree of opacity comprehends transparent units as in the case of descriptive syntagmas: telephone directory or lifeboat.

As this author goes on explaining, when we face a terminological syntagma that corresponds to the description of the content of a term, it is certainly difficult to decide without any additional proof whether we are before a term or a combination of terms since, apparently, there is no observable difference between a free combination and a fixed structure.

That is why starting out from the analysis of a representative number of syntagmatic terms, practice has established a series of proofs whose application altogether helps (and has helped here) to determine whether an expression corresponds to a term, and even indicates where the denominative segment representing it starts and finishes. Although not all these proofs are equally productive, and although they are not relevant to the same degree either, certain proofs applied to a lexical combination indicate to the specialised lexicographer whether he/she is before a combination of terms or dealing with a single terminological unit. These proofs which were applied for the segmentation of dubious-to-delimit units in this study are, in Cabré's (1993, 304-305) words:

- El hecho de que un conjunto se organice léxicamente en torno a una base única: unidad central de proceso, etc.
- La imposibilidad de insertar otros elementos lingüísticos en el interior del sintagma terminológico: *enfermedad muy mortal, etc.
- El hecho de no poder complementar separadamente ninguna de las partes del conjunto: *ataque de corazón enfermo.
- El hecho de poder sustituir el conjunto por un sinónimo: coste de enlace /coste de conexión.
- El hecho de poseer un antónimo en la misma especialidad: lenguas vivas vs lenguas muertas.
- La frecuencia de aparición del mismo sintagma terminológico en los textos de una determinada especialidad.
- El hecho de que en otras lenguas el sintagma en cuestión sea una sola unidad lexemática: soporte lógico (ESP)-software (EN).
- El hecho de que el significado del conjunto no se deduzca del significado de los elementos que lo forman (cuando el significado de un sintagma no es igual a la suma de significados de sus partes, suele tratarse de un conjunto lexicalizado): pelota de partido (no se trata de una pelota como tal).
- Complementariamente, la presencia de determinadas unidades lingüísticas en el interior del sintagma revela que muy probablemente se trata de una combinación libre.

- [The fact that a whole is lexically organised around a unique basis: central processing unit, etc.
- The impossibility of inserting other linguistic elements within the terminological syntagma: *highly deadly illness, etc.
- The impossibility of separately complementing any of the parts of the whole: *ill heart attack.

- The fact of being able to substitute the whole by a synonym: furnace atmosphere/ kiln atmosphere.[37]
- The fact of having an antonym in the same speciality: alive languages vs dead languages.
- The frequency with which a terminological syntagma appears in the text of a given speciality.
- The fact that in other languages the syntagma is a unique lexematic unit: soporte lógico (ESP)-software (EN).
- The fact that the meaning of the whole may not be deduced from the meaning of the elements forming part of it (when the meaning of a syntagma does not result from the sum of the meanings of its parts, it is normally a lexicalised whole): match ball (it is not a ball strictly speaking).
- Complementarily, the presence of certain linguistic units within the syntagma reveals that it is highly likely that we are in front of a free combination.]

Consequently, what can be deduced from all the ideas mentioned in this respect is that recognising whether a segment corresponds or not to a terminological unit and the delimitation of its "boundaries" are not easy-to-solve questions, especially due to the problems generated, above all, by phraseology or descriptive syntagmas.

8.5.2. Quantitative techniques for term extraction in a corpus

Although not all the statistical tests and quantitative techniques enumerated and explained here have been used for term extraction in this specific study, I have considered it positive to provide a brief analysis of the quantitative tools that linguists and terminologists may resort to nowadays in order to make the most of term extraction in a corpus. At the same time this also makes it possible to evaluate what would constitute a good term extraction system.

For this, before extracting a term it is necessary to know what a term is. According to ISO standard 1087 (1990), a term is *la designación de un concepto definido en un lenguaje especializado mediante una expresión lingüística,*[38] the term being composed by a single word, two words or more.

37 The example provided is different to the one provided by Cabré in Spanish.

38 "The designation of a concept defined in a specialised language by means of a linguistic expression."

Despite the benefits that automatic term extraction has brought with it, it is also true that there are two main "problems" that this kind of extraction has to face:

- Automatic extraction does not provide operational criteria
- World and domain knowledge are needed

In this section it can be observed how the best possible solution nowadays to solve this kind of problem posed by automatic extraction is to combine techniques and measures with the terminologist's observation and intuition. Such a combined approach leads to the semi-automatic term extraction process implemented in this study (and explained from the point of view of its application here throughout section 8.5). That is why, as a final step for term extraction – and after segmentation issues have been considered from a theoretical point of view (see section 8.5.1) – a series of additional quantitative techniques have also been observed in this study to determine the adequacy and accuracy of the term extraction process. The theoretical explanation of these quantitative techniques has been set out in the paragraphs that follow.

The already mentioned Zipf's law, for example, refers to word distribution in a corpus and according to this law, if we order the words in a text from the commonest to the rarest, frequency decreases or diminishes exponentially. Zipf's law is represented by the formula f=k/r, in which f stands for the frequency of a word and r stands for its position in the rank (Ferrer, 2003). On consulting the Wikipedia (2007), we find that:

> Originally, Zipf's law stated that, in a corpus of natural language utterances, the frequency of any word is roughly inversely proportional to its rank in the frequency table. So, the most frequent word will occur approximately twice as often as the second most frequent word, which occurs twice as often as the fourth most frequent word, etc. The term has come to be used to refer to any of a family of related power law probability distributions.
> For example, in the Brown Corpus "the" is the most frequently-occurring word, and all by itself accounts for nearly 7% of all word occurrences (69971 out of slightly over 1 million). True to Zipf's Law, the second-place word "of" accounts for slightly over 3.5% of words (36411 occurrences), followed by "and" (28852). Only 135 vocabulary items are needed to account for half the Brown Corpus.

Confusion matrixes are also used to measure the predictions of a system. Hence, the comparison of the predictions of a system with the real classes results in four different groups:

- True positives (TP): terms which have been successfully recognised by the system.
- False negatives (FN): terms which the system does not recognise and consequently does not consider to be terms.
- False positives (FP): non-terms that are considered as terms by the system.
- True negatives (TN): non-terms which have been recognised as such, that is, as non-terms.

These four classes are highly useful when it comes to evaluating the results obtained after term extraction and can be easily and meaningfully grouped in what has been called a confusion matrix:

		Predicted class	
		Term	Non-term
Real class	Term	TRUE POSITIVES (TP)	FALSE NEGATIVES (FN)
	Non-term	FALSE POSITIVES (FP)	TRUE NEGATIVES (TN)

Figure 29. Example of how to create a confusion matrix.

These nomenclatures are thus useful in order to group terms in a coherent manner and measure the quality of the term extraction process and the "good choice"/"error" rates through mathematic formulae. This is, of course, especially useful if we want to empirically prove the efficacy of a term extractor and, obviously, if we have the "correct answer" beforehand, so that we can check that the system presents more or less the same results.

The "good choice" rate is the percentage of examples that are well or successfully classified and is calculated with the formula:

$$\text{Good choice rate} = (TP + TN) / N$$

The error rate is the percentage of ill-classified examples and is calculated with the formula:

$$\text{Error rate} = (FP + FN) / N$$

In both formulae:

$$N = TP + FN + FP + TN$$

The way to interpret the numeric result of such formulae is simple: if the resulting value is close to 1 the "good choice" rate is high. Obviously we can multiply the result by 100 in order to obtain a percentage – for instance, a term extractor may have a "good choice" rate of 89%.

There are two other very useful parameters that can be measured arithmetically by again resorting to formulae. These are *coverage* – which is commonly known as *recall* – and *precision*. Both parameters share an inverse relationship as is explained in figures 30 and 31:

Recall: are all the terms that are indeed terms present?
Recall is the number of correctly recognised terms of the total number of terms.

Recall = correctly recognised terms /total number of real terms = TP/ (TP + FN)

Figure 30: Representation of recall (coverage).

Precision: are terms all the units that are present?

Precision = correctly recognised terms / total of predicted terms = TP / (TP + FP)

Figure 31: Representation of precision.

There is also another measure that combines both recall (understood as coverage) and precision in a single formula, the F-measure:

$$F = (2 \times \text{recall} \times \text{precision}) / \text{recall} + \text{precision}$$

As has been already mentioned, recall and precision share, in general, an inverse relationship which can be summarised as follows:

If recall increases ➔ precision diminishes
- More terms are recognised
- But "things" which are not terms are also recognised

If precision increases ➔ recall diminishes
- False terms diminish
- Some proper terms are not recognised

Total recall (coverage) ➔ no precision
- Every single "term" is recognised
- But also those which are not

There are two other measures: sensitivity and specificity.

Sensitivity is responsible for determining how many terms are recognised as such and, accordingly, it is another name for or another way to refer to recall (coverage):

Sensitivity = terms correctly recognised /total of real terms = TP/ (TP + FN)

Specificity, however, introduces a new aspect to be calculated, i.e. the coverage or recall of non-terms. It aims at calculating how many non-terms have been classified as if they were terms:

Specificity = correctly recognised "non-terms" / total of real "non-terms" = TN / (TN + FP) = 1 – FP / (FP + TN)

Finally, two of the most common and widely used measures for evaluating the adequacy of a term extractor and, in general, for the extraction of terminology, are the parameters of "noise" and "silence".

Noise refers to the number of false terms included among predicted terms. As happened with recall and precision, noise and silence also share an inverse relationship, since diminishing silence implies provoking more noise and diminishing noise implies increasing silence. Noise and silence are calculated with the following formulae:

Noise (= 1 – precision) ➔ noise = false terms / predicted terms = FP / (TP + FP)
Silence (= 1 – recall) ➔ silence = no recognised terms / real terms = FN / (TP + FN)

Of all the measures and rates explained here, "noise" and "silence" are the ones that have received the greatest attention in this study.

8.5.3. Theoretical considerations on collocations and concordance lines: Concord application in the method

A correct and natural-sounding use of language has many implications and involves many factors that must be accurately and proficiently combined. As Pedersen (1995) states, paraphrases and non-conventional wording tend to make a text unnecessarily long and wordy. In addition, if we focus on specialised texts, their lack of appropriateness becomes even more acute given the precise and concise nature of this kind of texts and the economical wording they use as one of the most distinctive features of technical writing.

Among the different issues analysed throughout this book, the study of collocates giving way to collocations or polylexical terms and the concordance lines in which they are contained has been one of the mainstays of this work. As the CTT states, technical terms do not occur in isolation but in combination with other LUs and they must also be studied and presented in accordance with this fact in a technical or specialised dictionary. Conceiving and presenting LUs in another way would lead to an artificial view of language, whether specialised or not.

The term *collocation* was first introduced by Firth (1957: 14), and was defined as "actual words in habitual company". As Pedersen (1995: 63) explains "by analysing the language used in poems, Firth (1957) demonstrated the expediency of operating with several modes of meaning, one of them being meaning by collocation". However, as

Pedersen (1995) goes on to explain, over the years, Firth's collocation theory underwent further development. Already in 1991, Sinclair (1991: 170) defined collocation as "the occurrence of two or more words within a short space of each other in a text [...] Collocations can be dramatic and interesting because unexpected, or they can be important in the lexical structure of the language because of being frequently repeated". Following Alcaraz and Martínez Linares' (1997: 117-118) definition of collocation:

> En la tradición SEMÁNTICA inglesa (Halliday, 1973: 32) se emplea el término 'colocación' para aludir a la CONCURRENCIA, o tendencia que tienen nombres y verbos, y determinados nombres y adjetivos a "co-aparecer" en construcciones sintácticas, como ladrar y perro, relinchar y caballo, talar y árbol, etc.
>
> [In the English SEMANTIC tradition (Halliday, 1973: 32), the term 'collocation' is used to make reference to the CO-OCCURRENCE, or tendency shown by some nouns and verbs, and certain nouns and adjectives to "co-appear" in syntactic constructions, such as bark and dog, neigh and horse, fell and tree, etc.]

Other definitions of collocations, although coming from less academic sources, also concede that:

> Within the area of corpus linguistics, collocation is defined as a pair of words (the node and the collocate) which co-occur more often than would be expected by chance, that is to say, a collocation can be defined as a sequence of two or more consecutive words that has characteristics of a syntactic and a semantic unit, and whose meaning cannot be derived compositionally, i.e. it cannot be derived directly from the meaning of its components. (Wikipedia, 2007)
>
> In Manning and Schütze's words (1999: 151) "a collocation is an expression consisting of two or more words that correspond to some conventional way of saying things". Accordingly, the study of collocations and their correct usage in discourse, whatever the degree of specialisation of such discourse may be, constitutes the difference between comprehensible and natural-sounding language and language that is artificial and does not sound natural. Accordingly, technical dictionaries should help their users to form grammatically and lexically correct word combinations since an infelicitous combination may cause discordance and even irritate the receiver (Cop, 1988).

The object of our analysis of collocations in this terminographical study is clear if we consider the theory on which it has been based (CTT). But it is also important to know that collocations present many and varied applications apart from terminology or lexicography, among which we find:

- Machine translation (multi-word translation pairs)
- Text simplification
- Word sense disambiguation ("one sense per collocation" principle)
- Parsing (symbolic, statistical)
- Information retrieval

Thanks to the concept of collocation, it is possible to determine empirically which pairs or groups of words can be said to have a substantial amount of "glue"[39] between them. Before going any further, however, it is interesting to notice Khellmer's (1991) views in this respect, according to which our mental lexicon is made up not only of single words but also of larger phraseological units, both fixed and more variable – what has also been called "collocation" and even more consistently "polylexematic term" in this study. However, as McEnery and Wilson (1996) point out, it is not as easy as it may seem at first sight to distinguish which word groups are collocations and which are not: "it is not easy to determine which co-occurrences are significant collocations, especially if one is not a native speaker of a language or language variety". Yet, a number of methods and formulae have been developed with this aim in mind. Subsequent sections offer an analysis of such approaches by explaining a series of formulae and processes that have helped to detect the "glue" of collocations in this study.

Nevertheless, apart from mathematical formulae, the study of collocations must necessarily be conducted in context, and thus the role played by concordances in terminological data retrieval is fundamental. According to Martínez de Sousa (1995: 65) a concordance is an "índice de palabras en su contexto, en el cual la palabra analizada figura en el centro de una línea rodeada a derecha e izquierda de otras con las que aparece en un contexto determinado".[40] Following this same author,

39 This "glue" can be measured, for instance, by means of the aforementioned Mutual Information Score (MI) (see section 8.5.4)

40 "Index of words shown in their context in which the word under analysis appears in the middle of a line surrounded on its right and on its left by other words with which it appears in a given context."

in computerised lexicography concordances are fundamental for the analysis of language and this is why, although quantitative techniques definitively have been used in this study, the observation and the intuition of the terminographer when observing these concordance lines have played a fundamental role.

With this aim in mind, I decided to use Concord, the pure concordance application of WordSmith Tools. This tool generates concordance lines, also known as Key Word in Context (KWIC), both for a sequence or group of words (clusters) or for a word, a part of it, a phrase, and so on. A concordance is, according to another definition by Sinclair (1995), a collection of all the occurrences of a word-form, each in its own textual environment, that is to say, it is the list of all the occurrences of a given word in a corpus together with its contexts, and Concord highlights the search word in the centre, thus allowing rapid detection and analysis of its collocates or words that appear around it.

> The point of a concordance is to be able to see lots of examples of a word or phrase, in their contexts. You get a much better idea of the use of a word by seeing lots of examples of it, and it's by seeing or hearing new words in context lots of times that you come to grasp the meaning of most of the words in your native language. It's by seeing the contexts that you get a better idea about how to use the new word yourself. A dictionary can tell you the meanings but it's not much good at showing you how to use the word (…). (Scott, 1998: 55)

One of the main (and final) goals of this research has been to avoid what Scott (1998) states in the last sentence from the quotation above. Since the role of context in the definition, characterisation and understanding of any word or term is playing an increasingly important role in current lexicographical/terminographical studies, Concord and all its complementary applications have facilitated a realistic approach to the pragmatic aspects involved in this research. This tool has made it possible to identify the linguistic patterns that most frequently appear in the corpus and which, as such, determine and characterise the phraseology of the speciality field of industrial ceramics. Basically, what Concord does through its application Concordance is to produce the concordances of terms, that is to say, lists of a given term called a search word (or key word or node) together with its surrounding text or co-text. The most common concordance is the aforementioned *Key*

Word in Context (KWIC), presented in the form of KWIC lists that gather every appearance of a search word or node (highlighted in the middle) and allow the terminographer to detect and analyse its collocates or words that appear in their textual environments with a significant frequency. The analysis of these recurrent linguistic patterns reflects the behaviour of the speciality language under analysis in a given context.

8.5.4. Stage of term extraction

From a practical point of view, in the elaboration of our (or any) dictionary the stage of term extraction is one of the most demanding steps to be carried out. In this stage of term extraction, WordSmith Tools 4.0 has been used for the processing of the texts in the corpus in order to identify characters or chains of characters that could be potential terms and for the subsequent analysis of such terms in context in order to verify or revoke their "term status" (specialised character) in real use.

Thus, with WST, the first part of the terminological extraction process is carried out on the basis of frequency and statistics data with the application Wordlist, whereas in a second part of this process, a more textual-oriented approach has been provided by Concord (see figure 32). What follows is a more detailed account of this term extraction process.

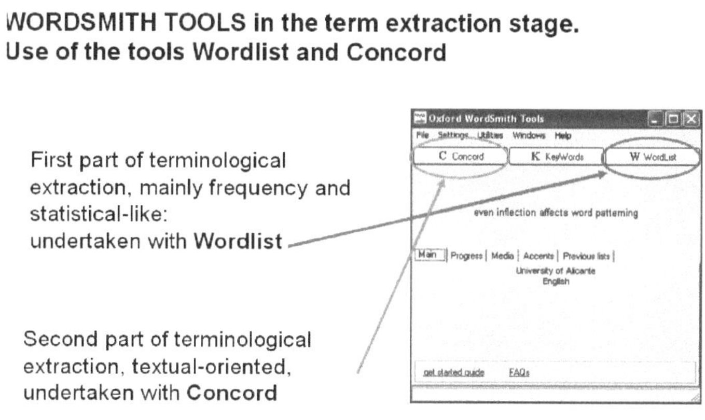

Figure 32. Use of WordSmith Tools in the term extraction stage, more specifically of the tools Wordlist and Concord.

With Wordlist, the first approximation to semi-automatic (both human and technical means are involved) term extraction has consisted in generating a monolexical frequency list of the words in the corpus. Since our dictionary is bilingual, the whole term extraction process will have to be carried out both in English and Spanish. Then, a preselection process has been undertaken in order to get rid of useless data, such as grammatical words and clearly non-terminological units. In order to get rid of grammatical or functional words, *stopwordlists* or lists of these kinds of "empty" words have been loaded in the program (in this case WordSmith Tools) acting as a filter when retrieving frequency. The frequency lists generated after applying these lexical filters will not show the grammatical words contained in the list, offering then "cleaner" data. For instance, for the English corpus, figures 33 and 34 show the difference between the kind of results to be found before and after preselection respectively and it is noticeable how the results obtained after preselection have ignored the useless data provided by grammatical words and are clearer, easier, more relevant and more pertinent to work with.

Wordlist results for semi-automatic term extraction before preselection:

N	Word	Freq.	%	Texts	%	N	Word	Freq.	%	Texts	%
1	THE	42206	5,9657	38	81	21	WHICH	2912	0,4116	35	74
2	#	32260	4,5598	38	81	22	IT	2901	0,41	32	68
3	OF	25813	3,6486	42	89	23	CAN	2770	0,3915	31	66
4	A	17824	2,5194	36	76	24	CERAMIC	2698	0,3814	39	83
5	AND	16500	2,3322	40	85	25	AN	2564	0,3624	33	70
6	IN	13904	1,9653	38	81	26	USED	2416	0,3415	28	59
7	TO	13019	1,8402	37	79	27	GLASS	2202	0,3112	17	36
8	IS	11849	1,6748	34	72	28	C	2119	0,2995	27	57
9	FOR	7401	1,0461	45	96	29	TEMPERATURE	1951	0,2758	30	64
10	ARE	6091	0,8609	34	72	30	HIGH	1903	0,269	24	51
11	BY	5445	0,7696	35	74	31	SEE	1847	0,2611	28	59
12	OR	5101	0,721	34	72	32	MATERIALS	1799	0,2543	25	53
13	AS	4892	0,6915	34	72	33	HAS	1737	0,2455	21	45
14	BE	4702	0,6646	34	72	34	SURFACE	1719	0,243	34	72
15	WITH	4679	0,6614	37	79	35	MATERIAL	1690	0,2389	22	47
16	THAT	3681	0,5203	34	72	36	HAVE	1613	0,228	33	70
17	ON	3260	0,4608	37	79	37	CERAMICS	1568	0,2216	16	34
18	AT	3093	0,4372	25	53	38	ALSO	1556	0,2199	24	51
19	THIS	3029	0,4281	33	70	39	TILES	1478	0,2089	34	72
20	FROM	2912	0,4116	35	74	40	TILE	1465	0,2071	30	64

Figure 33. Wordlist results for semi-automatic term extraction before preselection (functional words included) in the form of frequency lists.

Wordlist results after preselection

N	Word	Freq.	%	Texts	%
1	CERAMIC	2698	0,3816497	39	83
2	GLASS	2202	0,31148726	17	36
3	TEMPERATURE	1951	0,27598166	30	64
4	HIGH	1903	0,26919177	24	51
5	MATERIALS	1799	0,25448027	25	53
6	SURFACE	1719	0,24316376	34	72
7	MATERIAL	1690	0,23906152	22	47
8	CERAMICS	1568	0,22180383	16	34
9	TILES	1478	0,20907274	34	72
10	TILE	1465	0,2072338	30	64
11	GLAZE	1435	0,20299011	20	42
12	PROCESS	1408	0,19917078	19	40
13	CLAY	1357	0,19195651	22	47
14	PROPERTIES	1244	0,17597191	26	55
15	SIZE	1157	0,16366519	32	68
16	THERMAL	1119	0,15828985	23	49
17	METAL	1087	0,15376323	19	40
18	PHASE	1058	0,149661	13	28
19	MADE	986	0,13947614	29	62
20	FIRING	966	0,136647	29	62

Figure 34. Wordlist results for semi-automatic term extraction after preselection (functional words removed) in the form of frequency lists.

Then, a second step of the term extraction process has dealt with the close observation of the monolexical frequency lists free from grammatical words just generated in order to start selecting potential terms. Normally and advisably (as figure 34 shows) the top-frequent terms in the corpus after preselection will be closely related to the domain delat with, in this case industrial ceramics and could, most likely, be considered potential terms. This is also an indicator that the corpus is, broadly speaking, representative and adequate.

On a third step, Wordlist also offers the possibility of resorting to polylexical lists containing mutual information (MI) scores that "measure" the strength or degree of mutual dependence of the LUs forming collocations in order to start determining if the co-occurrence of a node and a collocate(s) is purely by chance or statistically significant. The combinatorial aspect of terms is a key feature in the SLA and accordingly polylexical or polylexematic terms must also be correctly identified. MI scores help to detect these plylexical terms and allow their inclusion as subentries in the dictionary.

Therefore, the three steps described above generate huge lists of potential TUs, both monolexical and polylexical, which Concord contextual analysis will subsequently corroborate or revoke as real terms. Hence, in the second part of the term extraction process, Concord allows the terminographer to observe the concordance lines in which these prospective terms retrieved with Wordlist appear, and analyse from different perspectives the way potential TUs are used in real contexts. For a contextualised analysis in Concord, the applications Concordance (see figure 35), Collocates (see figure 36), Patterns (see figure 37) and Source Text (see figure 38) have been the ones mainly used.

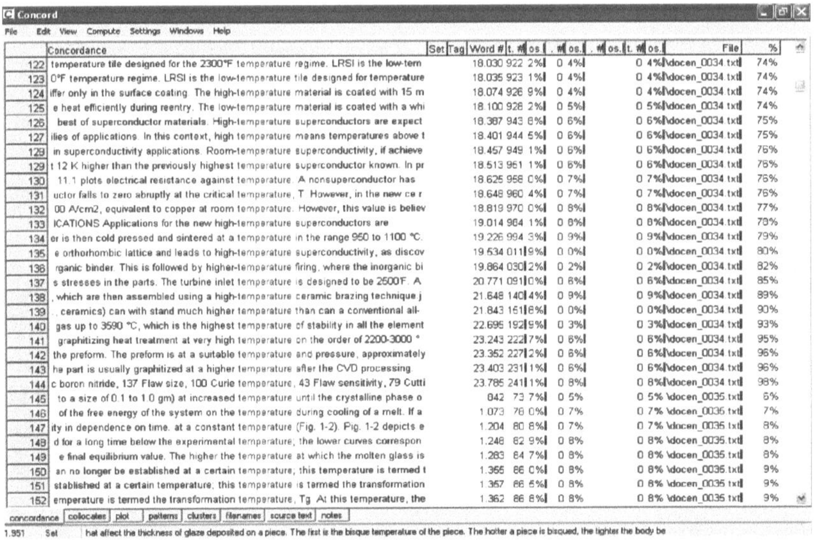

Figure 35. Concord application Concordance

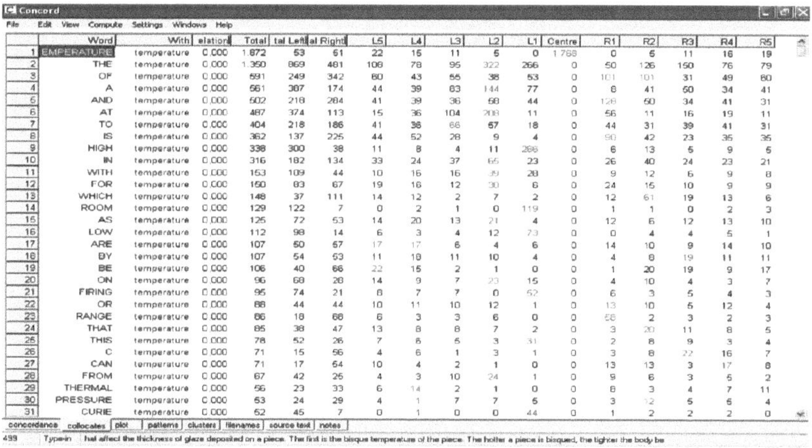

	Word	With	elation	Total	tal Left	al Right	L5	L4	L3	L2	L1	Centre	R1	R2	R3	R4	R5
1	EMPERATURE	temperature	0.000	1.872	53	61	22	15	11	5	0	1.768	0	5	11	16	19
2	THE	temperature	0.000	1.350	869	481	108	78	95	322	266	0	50	126	150	76	79
3	OF	temperature	0.000	591	249	342	60	43	55	38	53	0	101	101	31	49	60
4	A	temperature	0.000	561	387	174	44	39	83	144	77	0	8	41	60	34	41
5	AND	temperature	0.000	502	218	284	41	39	36	58	44	0	128	50	34	41	31
6	AT	temperature	0.000	487	374	113	15	36	104	208	11	0	56	11	16	19	11
7	TO	temperature	0.000	404	218	186	41	36	66	57	18	0	44	31	39	41	31
8	IS	temperature	0.000	362	137	225	44	52	28	9	4	0	90	42	23	35	35
9	HIGH	temperature	0.000	338	300	38	11	8	4	11	266	0	6	13	5	9	5
10	IN	temperature	0.000	316	182	134	33	24	37	65	23	0	26	40	24	23	21
11	WITH	temperature	0.000	153	109	44	10	16	16	39	28	0	9	12	6	9	8
12	FOR	temperature	0.000	150	83	67	19	16	12	30	6	0	24	15	10	9	9
13	WHICH	temperature	0.000	148	37	111	14	12	2	7	2	0	12	61	19	13	6
14	ROOM	temperature	0.000	129	122	7	0	2	1	0	119	0	1	1	0	2	3
15	AS	temperature	0.000	125	72	53	14	20	13	21	4	0	12	6	12	13	10
16	LOW	temperature	0.000	112	98	14	6	3	4	12	73	0	0	4	4	5	1
17	ARE	temperature	0.000	107	50	57	17	17	6	4	6	0	14	10	9	14	10
18	BY	temperature	0.000	107	54	53	11	18	11	10	4	0	4	8	19	11	11
19	BE	temperature	0.000	106	40	66	22	15	2	1	0	0	1	20	19	9	17
20	ON	temperature	0.000	96	68	28	14	9	7	23	15	0	4	10	4	3	7
21	FIRING	temperature	0.000	95	74	21	8	7	7	0	52	0	6	3	5	4	3
22	OR	temperature	0.000	88	44	44	10	11	10	12	1	0	13	10	5	12	4
23	RANGE	temperature	0.000	86	18	68	6	3	3	6	0	0	58	2	3	2	3
24	THAT	temperature	0.000	85	38	47	13	8	8	7	2	0	3	20	11	8	5
25	THIS	temperature	0.000	78	52	26	7	6	5	3	31	0	2	8	9	3	4
26	C	temperature	0.000	71	15	56	4	6	1	3	1	0	3	8	22	16	7
27	CAN	temperature	0.000	71	17	54	10	4	2	1	0	0	13	13	3	17	8
28	FROM	temperature	0.000	67	42	25	4	3	10	24	1	0	9	6	3	5	2
29	THERMAL	temperature	0.000	56	23	33	6	14	2	1	0	0	8	3	4	7	11
30	PRESSURE	temperature	0.000	53	24	29	4	1	7	7	6	0	3	12	5	6	4
31	CURIE	temperature	0.000	52	45	7	0	1	0	0	44	0	1	2	2	2	0

Figure 36. Concord application Collocates

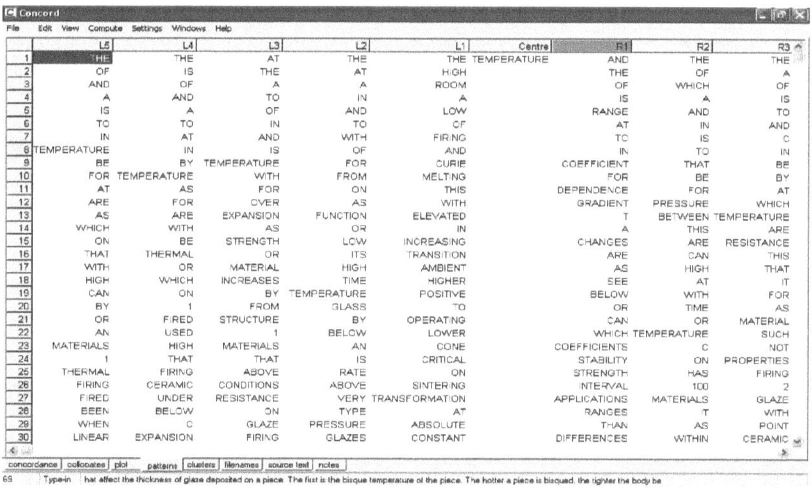

	L5	L4	L3	L2	L1	Centre	R1	R2	R3
1	THE	THE	AT	THE	THE	TEMPERATURE	AND	THE	THE
2	OF	IS	THE	AT	HIGH		THE	OF	A
3	AND	OF	A	A	ROOM		OF	WHICH	OF
4	A	AND	TO	IN	A		IS	A	IS
5	IS	A	OF	AND	LOW		RANGE	AND	TO
6	TO	TO	IN	TO	OF		AT	IN	AND
7	IN	AT	AND	WITH	FIRING		TO	IS	C
8	TEMPERATURE	IN	IS	OF	AND		IN	TO	IN
9	BE	BY	TEMPERATURE	FOR	CURIE		COEFFICIENT	THAT	BE
10	FOR	TEMPERATURE	WITH	FROM	MELTING		FOR	BE	BY
11	AT	AS	FOR	ON	THIS		DEPENDENCE	FOR	AT
12	ARE	FOR	OVER	AS	WITH		GRADIENT	PRESSURE	WHICH
13	AS	ARE	EXPANSION	FUNCTION	ELEVATED		T	BETWEEN	TEMPERATURE
14	WHICH	WITH	AS	OR	IN		A	THIS	ARE
15	ON	BE	STRENGTH	LOW	INCREASING		CHANGES	ARE	RESISTANCE
16	THAT	THERMAL	OR	ITS	TRANSITION		ARE	CAN	THIS
17	WITH	OR	MATERIAL	HIGH	AMBIENT		AS	HIGH	THAT
18	HIGH	WHICH	INCREASES	TIME	HIGHER		SEE	AT	IT
19	CAN	ON	BY	TEMPERATURE	POSITIVE		BELOW	WITH	FOR
20	BY	1	FROM	GLASS	TO		OR	TIME	AS
21	OR	FIRED	STRUCTURE	BY	OPERATING		CAN	OR	MATERIAL
22	AN	USED	1	BELOW	LOWER		WHICH	TEMPERATURE	SUCH
23	MATERIALS	HIGH	MATERIALS	AN	CONE		COEFFICIENTS	C	NOT
24	1	THAT	THAT	IS	CRITICAL		STABILITY	ON	PROPERTIES
25	THERMAL	FIRING	ABOVE	RATE	ON		STRENGTH	HAS	FIRING
26	FIRING	CERAMIC	CONDITIONS	ABOVE	SINTERING		INTERVAL	100	2
27	FIRED	UNDER	RESISTANCE	VERY	TRANSFORMATION		APPLICATIONS	MATERIALS	GLAZE
28	BEEN	BELOW	ON	TYPE	AT		RANGES	IT	WITH
29	WHEN	C	GLAZE	PRESSURE	ABSOLUTE		THAN	AS	POINT
30	LINEAR	EXPANSION	FIRING	GLAZES	CONSTANT		DIFFERENCES	WITHIN	CERAMIC

Figure 37. Concord application Patterns

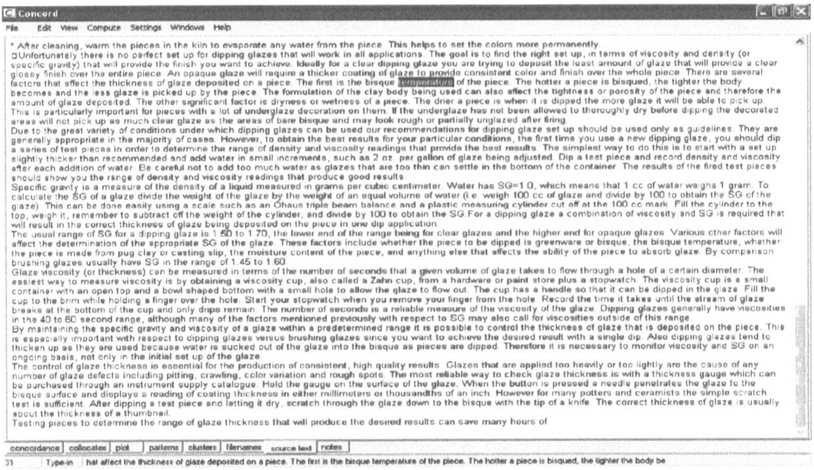

Figure 38. Concord application Source Text

So with Concord work, on the basis of monolexical frequency lists and the data obtained in polylexical ones, further information is provided by a close observation of, first of all, “Collocates” results. With Collocates, the most significant collocates in terms of frequency (mainly in the positions indicated on the slide) of the LUs regarded as potential terms with Wordlist have been retrieved.

For instance, after having introduced the prospective, high-frequency term *horno* (kiln) for “Collocates” analysis, we find that one of the most frequent collocates of this term in the corpus is *atmósfera* (atmosphere) (see figure 39). As such, they appear together or in a close position a total of 45 times. The word a*tmósfera* (atmosphere) appears with a frequency of 6 in position R2 (second on the right), as happens in concordance lines such as: “*en un horno de atmósfera templada…*” (“in a warm atmosphere kiln…”). However, the preferred position of the collocate *atmósfera* (atmosphere) with respect to the node *horno* (kiln) in the corpus is L2 (second on the left), with a total of 18 instances, which gives way to concordance lines such as: “*dependiendo de la atmósfera del horno, la pieza…*” (“depending on the kiln atmosphere, the piece…”)

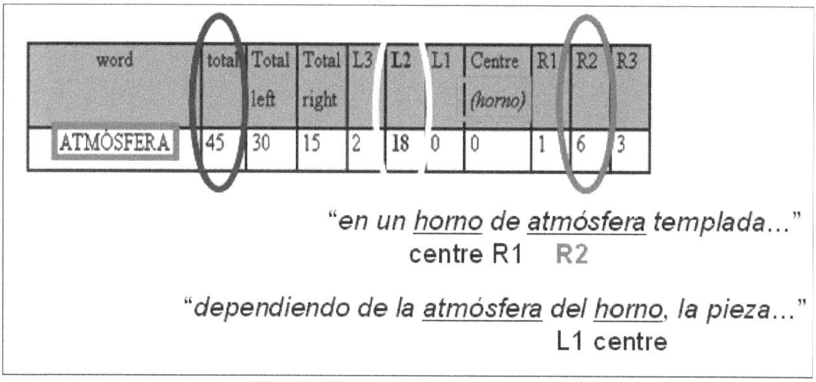

Figure 39. Graphic representation of the results obtained with Collocates for the search word *horno* (kiln) with respect to the collocate *atmósfera* (atmosphere) in the corpus.

Then, in a subsequent stage of Concord work for semi-automatic term extraction, those prospective polylexical and monolexical terms which, considering the analysis undertaken so far with Collocates, have been empirically regarded as significant, are introduced, one by one, in Concord's search window for further analysis. For instance, for *atmósfera de horno* (kiln atmosphere), a complementary analysis in the form of a KWIC list may be provided and the same can be done with the options "source text" and even "patterns" (see again figures 38 and 37 to see the kind of analysis to be provided by these applications). As has already been mentioned in the theoretical considerations for term extraction, a special attention must be paid to the segmentation of the lexical units.

After all this process, which must be given with every single instance of potential term, the terminographer, normally has data enough for corroborating or dismissing the "term status" of a lexical unit. It is at this point that, provided the bilingual nature of the work, the matching of the equivalents takes place. In order to match the equivalents in one language and the other, a series of procedures and tools may be used, namely: the comparison of parallel documents in English and Spanish, the comparison of frequency lists in English and Spanish, resorting to previously elaborated bilingual/plurilingual lexicographical works, the search in the net, the search in terminological databases, etc.

After these processes, a complete list of terms (prospective entries) is obtained and ready for being included in a data base together with all the pieces of information necessary for their correct understanding and use on the part of the user of the specialised lexicographical work.

8.6. Considerations for data processing

In databases the traditional concept of a terminological card on which to store all the data about the terms extracted is usually called a register, and this is a fundamental concept in the data processing stage of any kind of terminological work:

> Una ficha terminologica es una pauta estructurada que permite consignar de forma ordenada las informaciones sobre cada término que serán necesarias para llevar a cabo el trabajo. La ficha terminológica se elabora a partir de las informaciones que contienen las distintas fases de vaciado sobre un mismo término. (Cabré, 1993: 308)
>
> [A terminological card is a structured guideline that allows the terminologist to keep in an ordered way the pieces of information which will be necessary to carry out the work. The terminological card is elaborated departing from the information obtained in the different "emptying out"/extraction stages about a given term.] (Cabré, 1993: 308)

A terminological card can be designed or produced on paper – thus constituting a manual index card – or with a computerised medium using terminotic tools and thus creating an automatic index card or database, which is the most advisable. The latter offers a series of search and information retrieval facilities which are clearly superior to manual ones and which facilitate enormously the treatment and organisation of information along the different stages of the work.

Terminological cards may follow different designs depending on the particular features of each kind of work, but, generally speaking, there are a series of basic data or information which are usually present in every case (Cabré, 1993):

i. The entry
ii. The reference of the term
iii. The grammatical category of the term
iv. The thematic area to which the term belongs
v. The definition or context
vi. The equivalents in other languages (if it is a plurilingual work)
vii. The remissions or cross references
viii. The management data of the terminological index card: author of the card, elaboration date, etc.
ix. Different notes
x. The weighting mark or the reliability code of the term or the card

It is important, however, to bear in mind that each piece of information must be represented on the terminological card following a series of normalised, systematic and coherent conventions without which it would be very difficult to retrieve and interchange information afterwards. Normally, the document containing the instructions on how to fill in a card is called the protocol of use or writing guide (*guía de redacción*), which is crucial because only by respecting the instructions can a certain degree of systematicity and internal coherence be guaranteed in the elaboration of the terminological cards in the data base. These instructions will cover, for instance, the inclusion or not of full stops at the end of the definition or the context of use, the defining rules to be followed, the kind of context which is preferred (explanatory, associative, etc.), etc.

8.6.1. Stage of data processing

The stage of data processing deals then with the characterisation of the TUs and their storage in an ordered and systematised repertoire or database. For this, the resulting bilingual lists of terms obtained during term extraction are stored in the database TermStar XV together with their relevant terminological data. With this objective, two terminological repertoires, one in English and the other one in Spanish have been created. Figure 40 shows an empty register from this study in TermStar and illustrates how a personalised format according to the necessities detected has been created, this favouring a specific, user-oriented structuring of the data as the specialised lexicographical approach states. The fields so contained are, both in the English and Spanish part of the registers, the subject (semantic field), part of speech, abbreviation, context, xontext reference, data source, cross reference, definition, definition source, synonym, headword and category. The observation of these fields gives an idea of the kind of final entries to be obtained at the end of the process and the information contained in them.

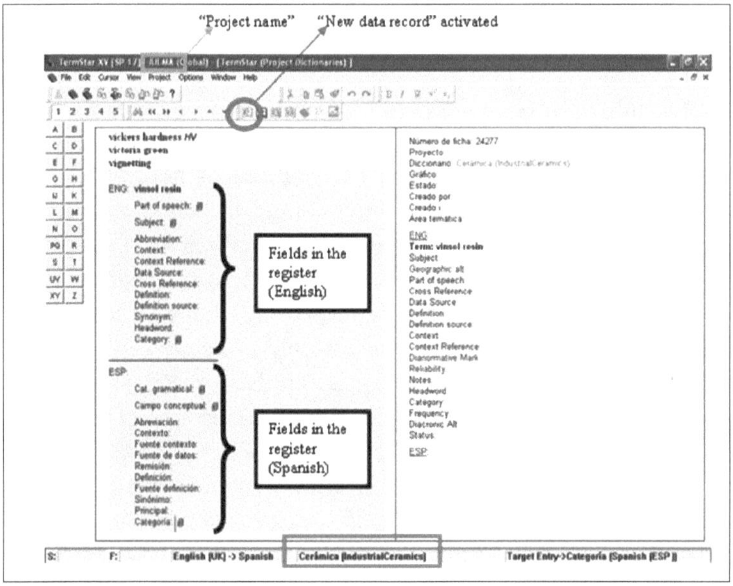

Figure 40. Empty register from the database used in the elaboration of the dictionary on industrial ceramics.

Finally, in order to fill in TermStar registers, it has been necessary to adopt the aforementioned protocol of elaboration of the terminological cards which has added systematicity and internal coherence to the elaboration of the different registers in TermStar by establishing a series of general criteria to be respected when filling in the different fields of the registers. Figure 41 shows a register from the database used in the elaboration of the dictionary on industrial ceramics illustrating the way fields have been filled in for the term “accessory mineral(s)” or *mineral(es) accesorio(s)*.

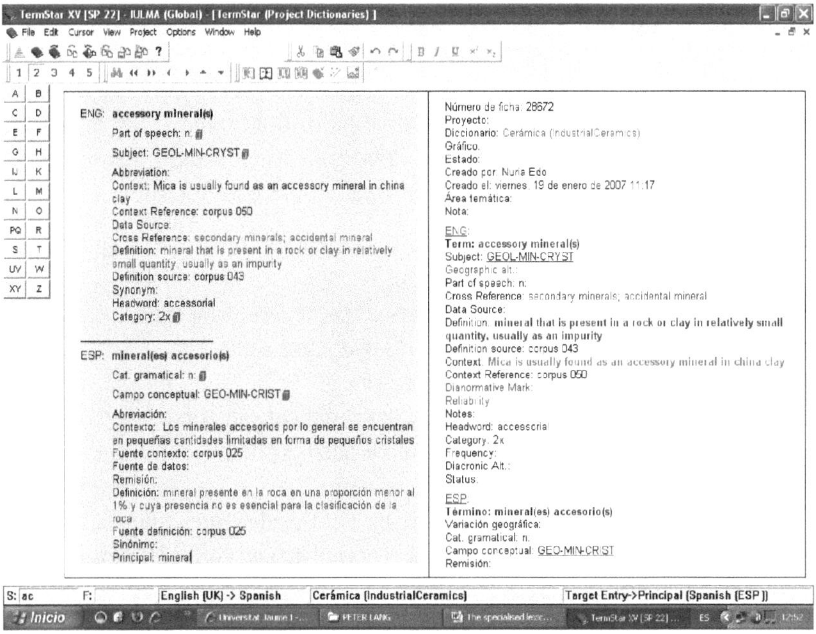

Figure 41. Register from the database used in the elaboration of the dictionary on industrial ceramics illustrating the way fields have been filled in for the term “accessory mineral(s)” or “mineral(es) accesorio(s)”.

8.7. Considerations for revision, normalisation and edition

Finally, as happened with the considerations for documentary corpus management, the general-theoretical considerations concerning revision, normalisation and, edition, have been covered in section 8.7.1, that is, jointly or in an integrated way with their practical application in the method in order to avoid repetition and because of the clearly applied nature of this stage of the work.

8.7.1. Stage of revision, normalisation and edition

Stage seven has been that of revision and normalisation of the information gathered and any possible neologism in Access, where TermStar data have been exported with the aim of checking, correcting and appropriately arranging the information for then exporting the data again to an rtf. document in the final stage of the method. For instance, in the Access board (see figure 42) one must check that, according to the protocol of elaboration of the entries we have adopted:

- Every term has the mandatory categories "principal" and "tipo" completed and correctly assigned.
- That no context starts with lower-case setter and ends with a full stop;
- That every definition starts with lower-case setter.
- That no definition ends with a full stop.
- That every term has the correct grammatical category.
- That contexts and definitions have been correctly stated and contain no spelling mistakes.
- That synonyms and cross-references are well-written and spaced out.
- That the category semantic field is complete and correct for every term.

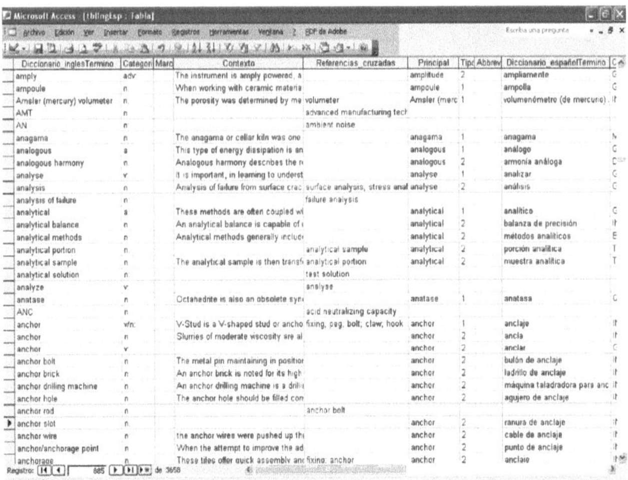

Figure 42. Access board generated before edition for correcting possible mistakes. In this case, for instance, the red circle signals that unlike the rest of contexts, this one starts with lower-case setter. This kind of mistakes should be corrected in Access.

Finally, in the edition stage, an *rtf.* (rich text format) document with the final version of the entries is created with the dictionary generator GENDIC, developed by Vargas, which generates from the Access board and thanks to a complex Visual Basic programming, the final *rtf.* version of the dictionary entries. This final version of the entries obtained with Gendic is presented with an illustrative sample in the next section, results.

Words – so innocent and powerless as they are,
as standing in a dictionary,
how potent for good and evil they become
in the hands of one who knows howto combine them.
Nathaniel Hawthorne

9. Results: Illustrative final entries

Final results illustrating the kind of results to be obtained with the SLA and more specifically the kind of results obtained for the specialised bilingual dictionary on industrial ceramics can be easily summarised with the view and explanation of, first of all, a single final dictionary entry. Figure 43 shows the main entry OVEN together with its three subentries: OVEN DRYING, OVEN ROOF and OVENWARE. We see how, according to the principles of the SLA and therefore as an active dictionary requires, this entry includes real contexts illustrating the way terms are used, the semantic field for each entry and subentry, the equivalents, so necessary for a translational bilingual tool, definitions including notes on the use, the part of the speech and contexts illustrating the use of terms and the habitual company with which they appear.

oven *n:* MAQELAB horno; término un tanto obsoleto para referirse a horno; compartimento cerrado utilizado para calentar, cocer o secar cuya energía calorífica puede ser proporcionada por la combustión de algún combustible o por otros medios (electricidad, etc.) ◊ *ASTM C484 is a test for ceramic tiles, which are removed from an oven at 145°C and placed on a sheet of aluminium at room temperature.* [Exp: **oven drying** (ELABPROC secado en el horno (proceso de)), **oven roof** (MAQELAB techo de la cámara (del horno) ◊ *The uppermost layer of the oven roof is formed by common red brick*), **ovenware** (PRODFIN utensilios para horno, utensilios termorresistentes ◊ *Ceramic whiteware or glassware (casseroles etc.) of good thermal shock resistance for use in cooking is called ovenware*)].

Figure 43. Final dictionary entry generated in the last stage of the method.

Finally, the next pages include a small but representative sampe of the first entries forming part of the final specialised dictionary on industrial ceramics in its English-Spanish version. The entries themselves, the data included in them, the way of presenting the information and implicitely the theoretical positioning and method of work adopted for their elaboration constitute the best summary of what the SLA is and why it may constitute a step-further in specialised dictionary making.

A

A *abbr:* MEDIDA V. *amp, ampere.*

a/c *abbr:* GESTIÓN V. *account.*

A/F *abbr:* DISTRIB V. *advance freight.*

AAC *abbr:* INDAFIN V. *autoclaved aerated concrete.*

AAS *abbr:* ELABPPROC/ENSAYO V. *atomic absorption spectroscopy (liquid solution).*

AAS *abbr:* ELABPROC/ENSAYO V. *atomic absorption spectrometry.*

abac *n:* GRAL V. *nomogram.*

abaciscus *n:* PRODFIN abacisco; piedra/baldosa pequeña, generalmente cuadrada, que se emplea para formar pavimentos de mosaico *-tessellated pavement-* V. *abaculus; tessera, tessella.*

abaculus *n:* PRODFIN abáculo, loseta; abaculus; pequeña baldosa de mármol *-marble-*, cristal, o cualquier otro material utilizada para hacer pavimentos de mosaico V. *tessera; tessella.*

abacus *n:* PRODFIN loseta rectangular.

abasement *n:* CONST asiento; referido a muros, terreno, cimentación, etc.

abatement *n:* MEDAMB reducción, disminución, recorte ◊ *Examples of applications of ceramics in the automobile include their use in safety and tempered glass for windows and catalysts and catalyst supports for emission abatement.*

Abbe number, V number *n:* PROPQUIM-FIS número de Abbe, constringencia; valor utilizado para caracterizar el poder de dispersión de una materia ◊ *The Abbe number of a glass mixture is carefully monitored and controlled by manufacturers to achieve target dispersion values, which usually range between 20 and 60*; V. *Abbe value.*

Abbe value *n:* PROPQUIM-FIS V. *Abbe number.*

ABC *abbr:* GESTIÓN V. *activity-based costing.*

Aberson machine *n:* MAQELAB máquina (de) Aberson V. *soft-mud process.*

ablate *v:* PROPQUIM-FIS erosionar-se, destruir-se ◊ *Whereas the carbon composites ablate during reentry, the ceramic tiles merely get hot, with no material loss at all.* [Exp: **ablating** (PROPMATPRI/PROPQUIM-FIS ablativo, erosionable; erosivo), **ablating agents** (ELABPROC agentes erosivos/ ablativos o de erosión/ablación), **ablating body** (PROPQUIM-FIS materia/ cuerpo erosionable), **ablating material** (ELABPROC material ablativo; material, especialmente de recubrimiento *-coating material-* utilizado para proporcinar protección térmica *-thermal protection-* a un cuerpo mediante la pérdida de masa *-loss of mass-* ◊ *Ablating materials absorb heat by increasing in temperature and changing in chemical or physical state*), **ablation** (ELABPROC ablación; eliminación de material de alguna superficie o capa protectora mediante algún proceso erosivo ◊ *The picture shows a tile with two clean areas where laser ablation has been used*; V. *zircon ablation; laser ablation*)].

ablution *n:* GRAL lavabo ◊ *Private ablution facilities with hot & cold water, showers, toilets and even your private ablution and storage lodge.* [Exp: **ablution facilities** (GRAL instalaciones sanitarias, lavabos; instalaciones para el aseo personal ◊ *The Clubhouse is a modern building with full ablution facilities*; V. *ablution*)].

ABM *abbr:* GESTIÓN V. *activity-based management.*

above *adv:* GRAL encima de, arriba; sobre; por encima de; "la planta de arriba" se traduciría como "*the floor above*" ◊ *Above a certain temperature, called the Curie temperature, the ferroelectric nature of the crystal disappears.*

abrade *v:* ELABPROC desgastar, bruñir, corroer (metal), erosionar (roca), esmerilar, frotar, lijar, pulir, raspar ◊ *The sandpaper abraded the wood until it was smooth*; V. *abrase.* [Exp: **abradability** (PROPQUIM-FIS abrasividad; capacidad para desgastar por fricción elementos en contacto con un cuerpo y que guarda relación con la cantidad y dureza de la materia mineral que contiene dicho cuerpo ◊ *The low abradability of a pavement tile (0.06 g\sm) and staying power to sliding in winter are important features*), **abradability index** (PROPQUIM-FIS índice de abrasividad ◊ *AS 1774.23.1-2001 Refractories and refractory materials - Physical test methods - Abradability index - Oblique method*; V. *abrasion resistance*), **abradant** (MTRLS abrasivo; material usado para abrasar -*abrade*-, molturar/triturar -*grind*-, desgastar -*wear down*- suavizar -*smooth*- o pulir -*polish*-tal que el esmeril -*emery*-, la arena -*sand*- o el vidrio en polvo -*powdered glass*-), **abrader** (INSTR V. *abraser*), **abrader** (INSTR abrasímetro; máquina de/para ensayos de abrasión), **abrading tool** (MAQTRANS/MAQELAB V. *abrasive tool*)].

Abrams' law *n:* PROPQUIM-FIS ley de Abrams; ley que establece la relación entre la resistencia del concreto -*concrete*- y la relación agua/cemento ◊ *According to Abram's law, low water-to-cement ratios produce high strengths.*

abrase *v:* ELABPROC desgastar V. *abrade.* [Exp: **abraser** (INSTR abrasímetro; máquina de/para ensayos de abrasión)].

abrasion *n:* PROPQUIM-FIS abrasión, desgaste por fricción/rozamiento; desgaste -*wear*- o erosión -*erosion*- causado/a en una superficie por una acción continua y producido por fricción -*friction*-, por impacto -*impact*- o por agentes erosivos -*erosive agents*- como el viento, la lluvia etc. durante largos periodos de tiempo ◊ *Among the advantages* *of ceramics tile are an ability to withstand damage from heat, and resistance to abrasion*; V. *corrosion; wear; erosion.* [Exp: **abrasion by sandblast/sand-blast** (PROPQUIM-FIS abrasión mediante chorro de arena ◊ *Physical properties were determined on specimens prepared under laboratory conditions using applicable ASTM procedures and showed, for instance, an excellent resistance to abrasion by sandblast*; V. *sand-blast*), **abrasion finish** (ELABPROC acabado con abrasivos; proceso de eliminación de las rebabas de los objetos moldeados y/o deslustrado de sus superficies, sometiéndolas al impacto de materias como huesos de albaricoque machacados, cáscaras de nuez o gránulos de plástico, con suficiente fuerza como para fracturar la rebaba V. *surface finish; sand blasted finish*), **abrasion hardness** (PROPQUIM-FIS V. *abrasion resistance*), **abrasion resistance** (PROPQUIM-FIS resistencia a la abrasión, dureza a la abrasión; resistencia al desgaste [por rozamiento]; propiedad que presenta una superficie a la hora de resistir el desgaste -*wearing*- producido por frotamiento -*rubbing*- con un material extraño que puede producir la erosión de dicha superficie ◊ *Abrasion resistance is determined by abrasion tests, and tiles are grouped accordingly*), **abrasion resistance classification** (ENSAYO/CALIDAD clasificación de resistencia a la abrasión; clasificación en la que se determina la resistencia a la abrasión -*abrasion resistance*- de un producto/material; la clasificación de baldosas esmaltadas para piso según su resistencia a la abrasión es: CLASE 1 (PEI I): uso individual ligero como cuartos de baño doméstico y dormitorios sin acceso directo desde el exterior; CLASE 2 (PEI II): uso individual normal como cualquier zona de vivienda particular a excepción de cocinas y entradas; CLASE 3 (PEI III): uso individual elevado o uso colectivo moderado como todas las zonas de una vivienda privada; CLASE 4 (PEI IV): uso colectivo normal como cocinas, restaurantes, exposiciones, boutiques, peluquerías; CLASE 5 (PEI V): uso colectivo elevado como centros comerciales, bares, tiendas con mucho tránsito, zonas peatonales y aplicaciones industriales V. *PEI rating; resistance to surface abrasion; abrasion resistance test*), **abrasion resistance test** (ENSAYO ensayo de resistencia a la abrasión, ensayo de abrasión; test de resistencia al desgaste; ensayo consistente en someter a la loseta cerámica sobre la parte vidriada a una acción abrasiva compuesta de una mezcla de esferas de acero, arena de Corindón y agua destilada; a este tipo de prueba se le conoce también como prueba de P.E.I. y da lugar a una clasificación de los azulejos en 5 grupos V. *abrasion resistance classification; PEI rating; resistance to surface abrasion*), **abrasion test** (ENSAYO ensayo de abrasión V. *abrasion resistance test*), **abrasion/abrasive hardness, HA** (PROPQUIM-FIS dureza a la abrasión, resistencia al desgaste [por rozamiento]; propiedad o grado de resistencia que presenta un material al desgaste por abrasión ◊ *Granite is a well known building stone and has high abrasion hardness, with very high resistance to weathering and extreme resistance to chemical attack*)].

abrasive[1] *n/a:* MTRLS/TRANSMTRLS abrasivo; material usado para lijar -*sand*-, alisar -*smooth*-, cortar -*cut*- o pulir -*polish*- otra sustancia; entre los abrasivos más utilizados se encuentran la arena -*sand*-, la piedra pómez -*pumice*-, el corindón -*corundum*- , el cuarzo -*quartz*- , la alúmina -*alumina*-, el carborundo -*carborundum*- y el diamante -*diamond*- ◊ *The one major area in which conventional abrasives still play the primary role is polishing.* [Exp: **abrasive**[2] (PROPQUIM-FIS abrasivo; capaz de provocar abrasión ◊ *Abrasive materials used in blasting can generally be classified as sand, slag, metallic shot or grit,synthetic, or other*), **abrasive action** (PROPQUIM-FIS acción abrasiva; acción producida por la abrasión ◊ *Mechanical wear can be caused by the abrasive action of hard inclusions in the workpiece on the tool*), **abrasive agent** (TRANSMTRLS agente abrasivo ◊ *Baking soda is a gentle abrasive agent*; V. *abrasive*), **abrasive bead** (TRANSMTRLS perla abrasiva ◊ *If the abrasive bead started to penetrate the substrate, coating delamination started, and the coating was going to be removed*), **abrasive belt/band** (MTRLS cinta abrasiva, banda abrasiva; cinta cubierta con abrasivo utilizada para esmerilar ◊ *The sharp corners are removed by an abrasive belt to form a semirounded edge*), **abrasive blade** (INSTAL cuchilla abrasiva ◊ *You can use an abrasive blade to cut tile, but it throws an immense amount of dust and chips the edge of the tile*; V. *grinding disk*), **abrasive blasting** (ELABPROC limpieza por chorro abrasivo; proceso caracterizado por el uso de materiales abrasivos (arena, abrasivos minerales, metálicos y sintéticos) para limpiar u otorgar una determinada textura a un material o a una superficie ◊ *Industries that use abrasive blasting include the shipbuilding industry, automotive industry, and other industries that involve surface preparation and painting*), **abrasive**

charge (TRANSMTRLS carga abrasiva ◊ *An abrasive charge consisting of steel balls, alumina grit and deionized or distilled water is rotated on the surface whose abrasion resitance is to be assessed*), **abrasive cleaning** (TRANSPROC limpieza abrasiva, limpieza con abrasivos ◊ *The use of water in combination with grit may also be classified as abrasive cleaning*), **abrasive cloth** (ELABPROC/MTRLS tela abrasiva, lija, tela para pulir; tela dura a cuya superficie se ha ligado un abrasivo tal que arena -*sand*- o esmeril -*emery*- para su uso), **abrasive collector** (MAQELAB depósito colector de abrasivo ◊ *Place the abrasive collector beneath the wide abrasion wheel*), **abrasive disk** (MAQELAB V. *grinding disk*), **abrasive finish** (PRODFIN acabado abrasivo/mate; acabado con una cierta textura, no reflectante -*non-reflective*- y plano -*flat*- de una superficie; normalmente se recomienda para exteriores debido, entre otras, a sus características antideslizantes -*non-slip features*- ◊ *Unglazed tile or tiles that have an abrasive finish or textured surface are less slippery than bright glazed tile or tiles with a very smooth surface*), **abrasive flow** (ELABPROC/TRANSPROC flujo abrasivo/de abrasión ◊ *The material removal through abrasive flow takes place by flowing the media, mixed with abrasives, across the surface to be machined*), **abrasive grain** (MTRLS/TRANSMTRLS grano abrasivo; partícula pequeña y dura usada con fines abrasivos, por ejemplo para eliminar el material sobrante de una pieza, y que incluye, por ejemplo, gravilla -*grit*-, granalla metálica -*metal shot*- o perlas de vidrio -*glass beads*- ◊ *Sandpaper is made by bonding an abrasive grain like aluminum oxide, garnet or silicon carbide to a backing material*; V. *abrasive powder*), **abrasive grinder** (TRANSPROC/MAQTRANS muela abrasiva ◊ *The machines employed in the honing process normally comprise a series of arms carrying heads equipped with abrasive grinders*; V. *grinding disk*), **abrasive machining** (TRANSPROC/ELABPPROD mecanizado con abrasivos; procesos de molienda/molturación -*grinding*-, perforación -*drilling*-, conformado -*shaping*- o pulido -*polishing*- mediante abrasión utilizando maquinaria especial ◊ *Abrasive machining can achieve the highest qualities of surface finish*), **abrasive material** (TRANSMTRLS/MTRLS material abrasivo ◊ *The general cleaning of metal castings is normally done by placing them in a revolving drum, or barrel, together with coarsely crushed abrasive material such as broken biscuit-fired ceramic ware*; V. *abrasive*), **abrasive method** (GRAL método abrasivo ◊ *Shot blasting is an abrasive method of removing floor tile* *mastic*), **abrasive paper** (MTRLS papel de lija, papel abrasivo), **abrasive paste** (MTRLS pasta abrasiva), **abrasive powder** (TRANSMTRLS/MTRLS polvo abrasivo ◊ *In this machine, used to define the quality of tile, tile is subjected under revolution with abrasive powder at the rate of 30 cycless/min. and it is revolved 100 times from both sides*; V. *abrasive grain*), **abrasive product** (MTRLS/TRANSMTRLS producto abrasivo ◊ *A method of abrading a work surface includes applying an abrasive product to it in an abrading motion to remove a portion of the work surface*; V. *abrasive*), **abrasive rock** (EXPL-CANT roca abrasiva ◊ *To cut particularly abrasive rocks, the wire is completely immersed in plastic*), **abrasive sand** (TRANSMTRLS/MTRLS arena abrasiva; gravilla/arenilla -*grit*- usada como abrasivo ◊ *Abrasive sand is particularly applicable for the removal of heavy rust, epoxy paints, concrete, and paint from steel surfaces*), **abrasive slurry** (MTRLS/TRANSMTRLS mezcla abrasiva, lodo abrasivo; compuesto acuoso de materiales abrasivos empleado en el proceso de corte ◊ *This tool combines with abrasive slurry to microscopically grind the workpiece*), **abrasive strength** (PROPQUIM-FIS V. *abrasion/abrasive hardness*), **abrasive substance** (MTRLS/TRANSMTRLS sustancia abrasiva, abrasivo V. *abrasive*), **abrasive tool** (MAQTRANS/MAQELAB herramientas abrasivas, herramientas para abrasión; instrumento utilizado para erosionar, lijar, esmerilar, etc.), **abrasive wear** (PROPQUIM-FIS desgaste por abrasión; desgaste producido por partículas abrasivas que se deslizan sobre una superficie causando el desprendimiento de material -*material detachment*- y rayaduras profundas -*deep scratch*- ◊ *When material is removed by contact with hard particles, abrasive wear occurs*; V. *Taber abrasive test*), **abrasive wheel** (MAQTRANS rueda abrasiva, muela abrasiva; rueda consistente en partículas abrasivas adheridas mediante el uso de sustancias orgánicas e inorgánicas como la resina ◊ *The risk of breakage is inherent in every abrasive wheel*), **abrasiveness** (PROPQUIM-FIS abrasividad; propiedad de un material para producir desgaste -*wear*- sobre una superficie por fricción ◊ *Abrasiveness is the property of a material to remove matter when scratching or grinding another material*; V. *abrasion*)].

abridge *v:* GRAL reducir, abreviar; acto de acortar o condensar, especialmente referido a reducir documentos escritos. [Exp: **abridged** (GRAL abreviado ◊ *The present document is an abridged version of the comprehensive document submitted to the Board*), **abridged**

specification (GRAL especificación abreviada), **abridgement** (GRAL resumen, extracto; abreviación; sinopsis)].

abroad *adv:* GRAL extranjero (en el); to go abroad: ir-se al extranjero ◊ *We specialize in manufacturing, processing and trading abroad ceramic tiles.*

abrupt *a:* GRAL/EXPL-CANT abrupto, accidentado; escarpado ◊ *The sides of the specimen shall be smooth and free from abrupt irregularities.*

abscissa *n:* GRAL abcisa; coordenada horizontal en un plano cartesiano rectangular designada mediante la letra X ◊ *The weight fraction of water is represented by the abscissa and specific volume quantities are given by the ordinate*; V. *ordinate.*

absence *n:* GRAL ausencia, falta ◊ *The first term is obtained from a measure of the sample density in the absence of appreciable porosity.* [Exp: **absent** (GRAL ausente ◊ *Residual stress is reduced with this process and may sometimes even be totally absent*)].

absolute *a:* GRAL absoluto; total ◊ *We need to ensure an absolute fit between one step and the next.* [Exp: **absolute humidity** (PROPQUIM-FIS humedad absoluta; masa total de agua existente en el aire por unidad de volumen expresada en gramos por metro cúbico -*grams per cubic meter*- de aire V. *atmospheric humidity; relative humidity; specific humidity*), **absolute porosity** (PROPQUIM-FIS porosidad absoluta; diferencia entre volumen aparente y volumen real (término aplicado generalmente a rocas)), **absolute temperature, T** (PROPQUIM-FIS temperatura absoluta; uno de los parámetros principales empleados en termodinámica y mecánica estadística y que indica el valor de la temperatura medida con respecto a una escala iniciada en el cero absoluto (-273,15 °C); se representa generalmente en kelvin), **absolute temperature scale** (MEDIDA escala de temperatura absoluta ◊ *The absolute temperature scale is a scale with which temperatures are measured relative to absolute zero*), **absolute value** (GRAL valor absoluto; en un número real, su valor después de quitarle su signo negativo: si el número es positivo, su valor absoluto es él mismo mientras que si es negativo, el valor absoluto es el número opuesto ◊ *El valor absoluto de un número "n" siempre es positivo o* *cero, y se escribe como* $|n|$), **absolute volume** (PROPQUIM-FIS volumen absoluto; volumen total de las partículas en un material granular -*granular material*- incluyendo los huecos permeables e impermeables -*permeable and impermeable voids*- pero no tomando en consideración los espacios entre las partículas; en un fluido, volumen total ocupado por éste; volumen de desplazamiento -*displacement volume*- de un ingrediente del concreto o mortero)].

absorb *v:* GRAL absorber ◊ *The factors include whether the piece to be dipped is greenware or bisque, the bisque temperature, and anything else that affects the ability of the piece to absorb glaze.* [Exp: **absorbed moisture** (PROPQUIM-FIS humedad absorbida; humedad que ha penetrado en un sólido por absorción y que cuenta con propiedades físicas que no difieren de las del agua común a la misma temperatura y presión ◊ *If you are in a freeze area some tiles could crack or crumble due to freezing absorbed moisture*; V. *absorption*), **absorbent** (PROPQUIM-FIS/MTRLS absorbente; sustancia/material con la capacidad de extraer otras sustancias de otro medio con el cual está en contacto; que posee la capacidad de absorber/extraer sustancias ◊ *The absorbent plaster pulls water from the slurry*), **absorbing** (PROPQUIM-FIS absorbente; que posee la capacidad de absorber o empapar -soak up- algo ◊ *Clay green is the most absorbing clay, generally used for face masks in cases of acne, oily and neglected skin*), **absorbing filter** (INSTR filtro de absorción), **absorption** (PROPQUIM-FIS absorción; proceso de absorber o ser absorbido, esto es, retención de un gas o vapor por un líquido, o de un líquido por un sólido; aumento de masa de un sólido poroso -*porous solid*- producida como resultado de la penetración de un líquido en sus poros permeables -*permeable pores*- ◊ *Absorption is the relationship of the weight of the water absorbed by a ceramic specimen subjected to prescribed immersion procedure, to the weight of the dry specimen, expressed in percent (ASTM C 242)*; V. *absorbed moisture; adsorption*), **absorption by capillary action/by capillarity** (PROPQUIM-FIS absorción por capilaridad, absorción capilar; propiedad de sorción entre un material poroso y un fluido y consecuencia de estar el material en contacto con el líquido por una de sus caras, y resultante de la penetración y ascensión de éste por la red capilar del cuerpo debido a la tensión superficial del líquido, dependiendo la velocidad de penetración de la intensidad de dicha tensión y del valor del radio medio de la red capilar; la propiedad de absorción por capilaridad, tiene una extraordinaria importancia en las arcillas, piedras, ladrillos, etc ◊ *The addition of this product to Portland cement prevents water absorption by capillary action*), **absorption by immersion** (PROPQUIM-FIS absorción por inmersión; propiedad de sorción entre un material poroso y un fluido y resultante de la absorción de un líquido por un cuerpo poroso inmerso en él), **absorption coefficient** (PROPQUIM-FIS coeficiente de absorción, coeficiente de atenuación; cociente (normalmente expresado en Sabines dentro de una escala de 0 a 1) entre la energía incidente y la energía absorbida por una superficie o sustancia ◊ *White Glass has a uniform low absorption coefficient over the whole visible spectral range*), **absorption rate** (PROPQUIM-FIS tasa de absorción, velocidad de absorción ◊ *The absorption rate of a tile measures the relationship of the weight of the water absorbed by that tile to the weight of the dry tile, expressed in percentages*), **absorption resistance** (PROPQUIM-FIS resistencia a la absorción ◊ *Reinforced tiles are tiles of two layers, the face layer containing chemical or mineral materials to improve its water absorption resistance and abrasion resistance*), **absorption spectrum** (PROPQUIM-FIS espectro de absorción; espectro de los fotones absorbidos por una sustancia, clasificados según su longitud de onda ◊ *An absorption spectrum is, in a sense, the opposite of an emission spectrum*), **absorption test** (ENSAYO ensayo de absorción, prueba de absorción; método para determinar la absorción-retención -*uptake*- de un líquido por parte de un material en el que el tiempo y la temperatura son considerados ◊ *Absorption test is valuable as a fairly reliable indication of the ability of tile to resist frost action*), **absorptive** (PROPQUIM-FIS/MTRLS V. *absorbent*), **absorptive power** (PROPQUIM-FIS V. *absorptivity*), **absorptivity** (PROPQUIM-FIS poder absorbente; factor que determina la capacidad de una sustancia de absorber otra sustancia o forma de energía ◊ *Grout compositions may be used in any width joint with tile of any absorptivity, including nonabsorptive tile*)].

abstract[1] *n/a:* GRAL/DISEÑO abstracto; estilo artístico en el que se enfatizan los aspectos cromáticos, formales y estructurales sin tratar de representar -*depict*- modelos o formas naturales ◊ *This funky abstract tile is full of colors and designs that cause the eye to bounce around in a visual feast*. [Exp: **abstract**[2] (GRAL extracto, resumen; síntesis, compendio, sinopsis)].

abuilding *a:* CONST en construcción; en proceso de ser construido o en construcción ◊ *He supervises motels and restaurants abuilding.*
abundance *n:* GRAL abundancia ◊ *The price of the oxides is markedly dependent on natural abundance and on product purity.* [Exp: **abundant** (GRAL abundante ◊ *Crystalline silica in the form of quartz sand is an abundant raw material*)].

abut[1] *v:* GRAL lindar, colindar ◊ *In property law, when two parcels abut it means they are adjacent to each other and up against each others' borders.* [Exp: **abut**[2] (INSTAL/CONST unir a tope, empalmar; colocar a tope dos piezas de construcción ◊ *Abut the tile to the integrated joint spacer to ensure a uniform joint of 1.5 mm*), **abutment** (CONST contrafuerte, estribo, machón; parte de una estructura o pilar que soporta el peso o la presión de un arco V. *buttress*), **abutting** (CONST contiguo, colindante; en contacto V. *adjoining, adjacent*), **abutting joint** (INSTAL junta a tope ◊ *It is very difficult to lay the tiles without the abutting joint of adjacent tiles being seen to the naked eye by a casual observer*), **abutting surface** (INSTAL superficie de contacto ◊ *On residential floor installations, movement joints should be located anywhere the tiles meet an abutting surface like a wall, a post or column*)].

acc *abbr:* GRAL/CALIDAD V. *accepted.*

Research is the process of going up alleys
to see if they are blind.
Marston Bates

10. Conclusion

It is commonplace and necessary in any kind of research to "end up" by offering a series of concluding remarks which summarise ideas and account for the accomplishment of the objectives established at the outset. As I understand it, this book, like any other, is only the point of departure for further research on an interesting and profitable field like specialised lexicography but may be useful for the reader in order to understand a bit better what specialised lexicography is and implies both from a theoretical and practical perspective.

Throughout this book, I have focused on the development of a corpus-based, bilingual (English-Spanish, Spanish-English), specialised dictionary, within the framework specialised lexicographical approach. Hence, a representative number of terms have just been presented in the previous section to illustrate the final results that have been obtained, and which reflect the kind of lexicographical work that has been undertaken. In this regard, many aspects have been considered, both from a theoretical and practical point of view, in order to provide a coherent, systematic and logical approach to specialised lexicography and, more particularly, to the specific dictionary of the ceramic tile industry. Among other aspects, the SLA described in this book has tried to highlight the fact that terminology is of key importance for specialised languages (even though its terminology is not the only feature identifying specialised languages or PAL) and that specialisations in language and linguistic disciplines are not "watertight compartments" within language but, instead, aspects forming a *continuum*. In the same way, right from the very beginning the work has highlighted the need to approach terminology from a communicative, not artificial, dimension which conceives it as an interdisciplinary field of work stemming from the pure necessity of professionals working in specialised domains.

Likewise, it has also underlined the multifaceted nature of terms. Accordingly, the corpus has enabled the observation and analysis of the discourse in which ceramics terminology is naturally given and the use of, consequently, real texts has allowed the retrieval of not only single terms but also of phraseological units that characterise the terminology used in the field and, thus, deserve a dictionary entry. Hence, the specialised lexicographical approach (SLA) adopted (which goes beyond terminography) and the observance of the principles of the CTT it implies have made it possible to develop a user-friendly, active, bilingual specialised dictionary on ceramics industry. This theory of terminology fits the SLA because of the sound, realistic conception of terminology it presents, which has made it widely accepted nowadays. This realistic conception takes the text as the natural starting point for the analysis of terminological units in real use. In the same way, the SLA makes it necessary to use a corpus-based approach and to describe not only monolexical terminological units but also other polylexical specialised units and/or collocations which explain the phraseological character of specialised terminology.

In the following paragraphs, I have summarised the main concluding remarks that can be extracted from this study. First of all, the conclusions regarding the theoretical framework of the SLA have been presented in the form of items dealing with and summarising the different aspects analysed in the different chapters. Finally, some concluding remarks regarding the method of work have also been provided.

Chapter 2 examined the constant interchange between common and specialised language, their characterisation as differentiated phenomena or a continuum (depending on the author), and the stated need for conscious mediation between them. In this regard, then, the main conclusions reached in this chapter were:

1. The only way to facilitate effective communication between experts and the laymen and between experts from different areas is to make efforts from a linguistic point of view in order to achieve it by means of identifying, analysing and solving the linguistic questions and needs posed, especially from a terminological perspective.

2. There is no universal agreement regarding the way of conceiving the general and the specialised in language but, after having analysed the way different authors approach the topic, the viewpoint adopted has been to consider that between the specialised and the non-specialised there is a continuum and so the difference between general and specialised is only a matter of degree. Thus, there is a set of rules and units (which may be phonological, morphological, lexical, semantic and discursive) that are common and necessary for every speaker of a language no matter what communicative situation they are in. This group of rules, units and restrictions that form part of the knowledge of the majority of the speakers of a language constitutes the so-called common or general language. The units of this common language are used in situations that can be described as "unmarked", as opposed to "marked" situations (which may be marked to a greater or lesser extent) in which specialised languages are necessary. This is so because specialised languages are used to refer to a group of subcodes, which partially coincide with the subcode of general or common language and are characterised by a series of peculiarities that make them "special". These peculiarities are specific to each specialised language and refer to the topic, the communicative situation, the kind of interlocutor, the speaker's intention and the medium in which the communicative interchange takes place, for example. Consequently, specialised languages make use of part of this assumed general language but also draw on special technical terms and, in some cases, register-specific structures. Therefore, no clear-cut division can be made between the general and the specialised, which leads us to the continuum view as being the most realistic one.

3. It has been analysed how, within the continuum, specialised languages are functional varieties of general language that are differentiated from it by a group of characteristics that are activated when a series of specific communicative circumstances converge. Such conditions include: the topic is specialised, the speakers are specialists (a subgroup of a community of speakers defined by their profession or by the knowledge acquired after

a learning process), the situation is formal and professional, attempts are being made to transmit some information from a discursive point of view, and so forth. Thus, it is more accurate and convenient to talk about specialised discourse. However, the term *language* has traditionally been used even when it would be more accurate to use *discourse*, that is, even when dealing with a linguistic situation developed in a context with a given communicative goal.

4. The notion of "specialised" in a text involves not only a lexical consideration and, in spite of being its paradigmatic aspect, other pragmatic, functional, thematic, textual-linguistic and cognitive criteria must also be present. The reason for this is that, even though specialised languages are born within natural common language, they differ from it in that their ultimate goal is to solve specific communicative needs, both from the formal and functional point of view, that arise in the professional world of the different scientific and technical fields. Accordingly, the term "specialised language" refers to the kind of language used by specialists and professionals in order to transmit information and negotiate the terms, concepts and knowledge of a given field of knowledge.

5. The denomination PAL (understood as an umbrella term covering the different specialised languages that arise in the academic world and during the practice of the corresponding professions) has been preferred to that of LSP since any use of language is always specific because it is targeted towards accomplishing a given goal. As a result, throughout this work the term "specialised language" has been the denomination adopted in order to refer to a single specific specialised language – in this case, that of industrial ceramics – whereas PAL has been the preferred denomination for referring to specialised languages as a whole.

6. Terminological units can be considered as the communication units of specialised discourse and PAL, since they are the units that best concentrate specialised knowledge and the only ones capable of correctly representing and transferring the concepts (the

content) of a speciality. They are created to satisfy the need to refer to and hence name things properly and accurately. From a semantic and conceptual point of view, terms guarantee the precision necessary in every specialised communication and also the interchange of knowledge among the members of a professional community.

7. In order to gain a correct understanding of the cognitive structure of a specialised language or the functioning of its terminology, the isolated artificial study of terms is not enough. As the SLA concedes, the conceptual relations existing between the terminological units are therefore fundamental to be able to realistically account for a phenomenon like PAL and the terminology of specialised languages in general. The combinatorial syntactic aspect of terminological units is a reality that cannot be ignored, no matter what field we are dealing with.

All the factors underlined in previous paragraphs regarding the true nature of specialised languages and their conception, inevitably lead to the implementation of an approach (the SLA) that allows PAL to be studied and presented from a realistic, coherent point of view. In this light, corpus linguistics emerges as the best option for obtaining real terminological data, and the most relevant conclusions that can be drawn from Chapter 3 in this respect can be summarised as follows:

1. The rejection/corroboration of hypotheses for explaining certain aspects of reality, including any linguistic phenomenon, must be strongly based on the data that this very same reality offers. Accordingly, linguistics in general needs elements of true reference as much as natural sciences do in order to analyse real language use and therefore real behaviour in context. Specialised languages are no exception in this respect and also need a "tool" that makes it possible to identify and characterise the terms that form part of and shape a given speciality field. It is in this light that the use of corpora becomes fundamental for observing the communicative dimension of use (pragmatic aspects and real contexts) of terminology and thus the real nature of PAL.

2. One of the greatest potentials of corpora is that they offer naturalistic data for analysis, that is, unmonitored data that are the product of real social interactions which are always given in context. A corpus (with the help of concordance software programs) allows terminological units to be identified but it can also be used to detect their frequencies of use, their collocates and thus the collocations they form, as well as the strength of the bond between these collocates and, in sum, the way in which these (specialised) linguistic units group together in order to form phraseological units which deserve the terminographer's attention. For "specialised dictionary makers", this approach also allows the researcher to examine the linguistic and non-linguistic associations a given word may have.

3. Although the discipline of corpus linguistics as such is rather recent, it has had its opponents since it began. The most important of these detractors was Chomsky, for whom a corpus could never be a useful tool for the linguist since language must seek to model language competence rather than performance. For this author, because a corpus is performance it is therefore a poor guide on which to model linguistic competence. He also claimed that the number of sentences in a language is potentially infinite because of the number of combinatorial choices that can be made when producing a sentence. Accordingly, for Chomsky, if the number of statements of a language is non-finite, then the existence of a finite data repertoire that is adequate for explaining all the mechanisms of linguistic production was not possible. He elaborated on the fact that the object of study of linguistic research is the "underlying mental reality" and thus observation must not be considered, thereby invalidating the usefulness of corpora as sources of true data in linguistic investigation.

4. In spite of Chomsky's attempts to invalidate the action and value of corpus linguistics as a reliable source for extracting linguistic evidence and making linguistic enquiries, from the point of view of scientific method, a corpus has proved to be a powerful methodology since it is open to objective verification of results and

allows language to be studied in actual, proven, authentic instances of use produced by specialists, in opposition to intuitive, invented, isolated sentences.

5. Using (good quality) samples of the actual language employed by specialists in naturally occurring texts is also important, in general, for identifying the kind of linguistic-terminological needs the prospective users of the specialised dictionary may have. Once these needs are known, they can be used as the basis on which to select the terms to be analysed and included in terminographical works and to make decisions on how they are to be presented. In the specific case of this book, this has also been associated with the aim of creating an active dictionary intended at providing the user with all the information necessary to successfully cope in real-world specialised communication, with a special emphasis on those aspects that are more directly related with real users' demands (which are reflected in the corpus).

6. Corpora allow the complete meaning of a word to be analysed by examining large numbers of language instances collected from varied sources, which also emphasises the view that every study of meaning needs to set out from a complete context.

7. Most of the flaws that corpus linguistics had in its beginnings were dismissed when computer technology spurred its revival and offered new, reliable possibilities. The wider availability of institutional and private computing facilities resulted in computerised/electronic corpora that allowed corpora to increase their size exponentially. Hence, the possibility of storing and analysing huge amounts of data and complex patterns of language use, as well as the possibility of retrieving all the examples of a given word in just a second or examining thousands or millions of words easily, quickly and accurately are capabilities that must be taken advantage of. Apart from all the aforementioned factors, the use of modern corpora has also enhanced the conception and management of terminological work by using computer science to make the most repetitive tasks much easier, quicker

and even more accurate and reliable, since human "weaknesses" like changing one's mind or getting tired are ruled out. The advancement and rapid evolution of computer science have given rise to powerful computer aids and software applications that are capable of carrying out work with no errors and processing large corpora almost instantly.

8. The "marriage of machine and corpus" means that, today, the term *corpus* is nearly a synonym for the terms "electronic corpus" or "computer-readable corpus". Electronic corpora have proved to be essential nowadays in order to shed light on the corroboration/dismissal of linguistic hypotheses, to know the different meanings that words acquire depending on the context in which they appear, and to develop technologies for processing natural language. These technological advances in the field of corpora analysis allow data to be exploited effectively; at the same time, meaningful results can also be obtained by performing difficult calculations and the data be displayed in different forms that can be adapted to the user's needs, according to different parameters or filters. Data may therefore be arranged, for instance, alphabetically or on a frequency basis.

9. The benefits a corpus presents are always determined by the quality of the documents it is made up of, which is determined by a series of criteria to be observed while the corpus is being designed and compiled. The importance of designing a good corpus is fundamental if we consider the fact that it is to constitute a smaller but representative sample of the linguistic phenomenon or language under study. A corpus must be varied in its composition so that no conclusions are wrongly based on just a few speakers' idiosyncrasies. Hence, taking into account and measuring the representativeness of the linguistic samples compiled for the corpus is the only way to obtain a linguistic tool that realistically describes a linguistic variety or a language.

10. Apart from the advantages mentioned above, this book has tried to show the benefits resulting from ease of access to corpora, that is to

say, current technological advancements in the field of terminotics for the exploitation of corpora make it easy and fast to access, manage and analyse the data contained in a corpus, thanks to the development and use of concordance programs. This ability to call up and retrieve word combinations (and not just single individual words) and to carry out frequency and statistical analyses of different kinds makes it possible to treat and analyse phrases and collocations more systematically and from different aspects of the terminological reality. Sampling is another positive aspect of working with corpora since a corpus is compiled bearing representativeness in mind as a major goal for ensuring that any findings extracted from it can be generalised to the larger population. The technological means available for corpora exploitation are essential fot the SLA, as the working method for dictionary-making has shown.

In the light of the conclusions presented so far, the following paragraphs gather the most relevant concluding remarks reached with regard to the importance *of terminology as a key element in the study of specialised languages (chapter 4)*. These conclusions attempt to summarise the fundamental relationship that exists between PAL and terminology, as well as the relevance of the role played by corpus linguistics as an instrument for its analysis and characterisation. Terminology is the most prototypical (although not the only) "feature" of specialised language/discourse, which originates in the real world due to the real communication needs of experts in different technical fields. As such, the SLA considers it necessary, advisable and realistic to approach it from a corpus-based perspective.

Furthermore, this work has underlined the need to approach terminology from a coherent, well-sustained theoretical conception. It is important to define the way terminology is conceived since this determines the way it can be analysed as well as the way terminologies can be presented in specialised lexicographical works. Throughout this book the Communicative Theory of Terminology has played a "satellite role" over the rest of the theoretical aspects addressed, shaping thus the SLA in a big extent. Therefore, the conclusions that can be drawn regarding the conception of terminology and the theory of terminology adopted by the SLA may be summarised as follows:

1. The SLA considers that terminology arises from practice and from the explicit necessity of specialists to order the denominations of their conceptual systems. Professional communication and effective knowledge transmission are fundamental for scientists and technicians and can only be guaranteed by normalising their disciplines both from a conceptual and denominative perspective. Accordingly, from a strictly terminological point of view, terms should be approached as elements from natural language to be found in specialised texts produced by experts/specialists in the field.

2. This chapter has described how no universal agreement has been reached about the way of conceiving terminology or a theory of terms, and has illustrated this by tracing back its evolution. The first meaningful look at the topic was provided by Wüster with his General Theory of Terminology, the principles of which, however, do not take into account the communicative and pragmatic aspects inherent to the lexicon of different specialised languages. The GTT is grounded on the view that concepts exist independently of the term that designates them, that the nature of terms is bi-univocal (there is a single form for each concept and a concept for each form), and that terms are independent of context. Therefore, because of its lack of interest in any pragmatic and communicative aspect of terms, the GTT has been considered a reductionist theory which reduces the terminological unit to its denominative condition. The GTT assumes a uniformity in communication which reality shows is not so and it ignores the communicative dimension every interaction has, whether it is specialised or not. The goals attributed to the GTT are limited to ensuring the univocity of professional communication, something which contradicts the complexity and the intrinsic interdisciplinary character of speciality areas and the wide range of socio-professional necessities that require suitable terminological activity, as was proved through the needs analysis carried out for this research. Most of the criticism that the GTT has received over the years basically refers to its unrealistic idealisation of reality, knowledge and communication, as well as its limited

scope, which is reduced to standardisation. The Classical Theory is grounded on the principles of univocity and monosemy and advocates a method of work with a prescriptive basis as being valid for every kind of investigation – no matter what the topic or subject of the work may be. This book has tried to show that this way of approaching reality does not fit the reality of specialised communication.

3. The belief that the GTT could not accurately and completely account for the complex nature of terminology and the terminological object gave rise to the appearance of a new theory that displayed a more "sensitive" approach to terminology and its implications, namely, the Communicative Theory of Terminology (Cabré, 1999 b). This theory rests firmly on the corroboration of its principles by contrasting them with empirical data that allow them to be maintained, qualified or revoked. It is also in this light that the use of corpora takes on its meaning.

4. There are a series of basic principles which account for the way the CTT conceives terminology, namely, the principle of the multifaceted nature of terms; the principle of the communicative character of terminology (every terminological unit pursues, in either an immediate or a remote way, a communicative goal); the principle of variation; the condition of natural language (terminologies are given within a specific area of knowledge where its object is defined); and the specialisation condition. The intention of this book has been to show how all these principles are necessary in order to understand the true nature of terminology.

5. The essentially *representational* terminology defended by the GTT can (although not necessarily *must*) be artificial and arbitrary and can control variation, thus preserving the principles of univocity and monosemy it defends. However, the essentially *communicational* natural terminology, like that defended by the CTT and targeted in this research, must be real, show actual usage and, accordingly, present variation. This fact determines the dichotomy between representational and communicational

terminology, that is, between "*in vitro*" knowledge and "*in vivo*" knowledge, the latter being the one adopted here. If terms are analysed *in vitro*, they are studied from outside their natural context and in an isolated way, whereas if they are analysed *in vivo*, they are characterised from the natural habitat in which they are given in specialised communication/discourse (the text being the point of departure). Accordingly, the fundamental pillar upholding the CTT is the specialised text and its observation, leading to the *in vivo* analysis of terms that this book defends as the most consistent and advisable way of addressing the matter.

6. In accordance with the CTT, this book has emphasised the understanding of terminological production from a descriptive point of view, since specialised lexical units are real linguistic items and not ideal homogeneous entities that are free of any kind of conceptual ambiguity. However, this more modern conception of terminology does not imply the complete rejection of terminological standardisation, but rather its understanding as a way of intervention whose adoption will be regarded as positive or not dependent on each situation and on each communicative context.

7. The CTT explains the interdisciplinarity of terminology. Thus, it conceives terminological units as multifaceted units made up of the three disciplinary aspects that describe them, namely, linguistic, cognitive and pragmatic, and as such these units have been presented in the entries. The essentially communicational terminology defended by this theory highlights the multifaceted linguistic-cognitive-social character of all the units of language, including terminological ones. Accordingly, in this research, terminology (understood as the group of terms from a speciality) has been approached as a group of denominative-conceptual units from natural language which represent specialised knowledge within a precise subject area and which, therefore, act as a vehicle conveying natural professional communication. Terminology has been understood as an interdisciplinary and multi-entry field of knowledge in which terms cannot be explained in an autonomous way that ignores other denominative signs with which they share

the "space" of specialised communication. Neither can it be accounted for independently from them or isolated from the rest of the signs of natural language made up of a form and a meaning.

8. In accordance with the previous item, every object of study is interdisciplinary *per se* and as such it can be tackled or approached from different subject matters. This has given rise to the "Theory of Doors" (*La Teoría de las Puertas*), a theory which allows terms to be treated in a multidimensional manner and, according to which, a term is a unit made up of three different aspects: a semiotic-linguistic aspect, a cognitive aspect and a communicative aspect.

9. The CTT has originated new and more appropriate ways of carrying out the terminographical task since it assumes linguistic diversification, which depends on various factors such as the kind of situation, the level of specialisation of texts, the addresser, the degree of formality, the final goal of the discourse and the topic, among others.

10. The CTT designates the specialised text as the base unit for the analysis of specialised lexical units so that terminological research takes on a textual dimension that allows the specialised lexicographer to observe terms in context. At the same time this leads to the adoption of a phraseological dimension. Due to this, the results presented in this research do not only show single terms but also polylexical specialised units that work as complete wholes within the specialised text.

11. Terminology has been approached as having two main objectives: to formally, semantically and functionally describe the lexical units that may acquire a terminological value and thus become terminological units, and to account for the way in which this terminological value is activated.

12. Regarding the "distinction" between term and word, the CTT supports the hypothesis that the lexical unit is not a term or a word

per se but a lexical form that, according to the communicative situation in which it is given, activates a specialised value or not. Thus, the selective activation of information, either through formally specialised units (units used exclusively in specialised contexts although with a potential general value) or through units that are specialised in meaning (lexical units used with a specific sense in specialised contexts and with an open sense in non-specialised ones), is determined by the features and the discursive-communicative situations in which lexical units occur within specialised discourse. Likewise, the lexical competence of a speaker is not made up of words or terms but of lexical units and semantic traits that may activate (or not) specialised values according to the contexts in which they are found. The lexical unit is therefore an abstract unit which is not *per se* a word or a term and which goes beyond them because it is a form associated to a great amount of (more abstract) semantic information and because it gathers, under a single notion, both the values that constitute a non-specialised use (potential words) and those which constitute a specialised use (term).

13. According to the aforementioned conception of the terminological unit, terms do not differ much from words from a formal and semantic point of view, but the differences between the two become more apparent whenever pragmatic and/or communicative criteria are adopted. Consequently, terminology, in contrast to common lexicon, is used to designate the concepts belonging to specialised disciplines and activities; terms are seen as units of a lexical system forming part of the wider general grammatical system, which includes the common/general lexicon and the diverse specialised lexicons.

14. Terms, like any other significant unit of a linguistic system, belong to natural language and form part of a structured system in which they occupy a particular level (the level of lexical units). Thus, on the one hand, they relate to the rest of the units on the same level and, on the other hand, to the units on the rest of the levels, together shaping and participating in the construction

of discourse. Hence, the way terms relate with both the lexicon in general and the rest of the grammatical components does not make it possible to observe any specificity that makes them systematically different from the relationships that, at the same time, words maintain with their grammatical environment. However, within the lexical component of language, it has also been observed and acknowledged that terms relate more and more closely to the other terms from the same discipline (with which they constitute specific structured subsystems) than with terms from other thematic areas. Consequently, from a functional perspective, terms are units that occur in a very specific or determined linguistic environment and which, most frequently, appear in combination with other specific lexical units or terms within discourse, thus giving rise to phraseology.

15. It has been repeatedly noted that the terminological character of a unit is a pragmatic value that is conferred or activated by the discursive conditions in which it is given. In other words, this specific value activation depends on its use in a given, specific expressive and situational context. Consequently, a lexical unit is made up of a group of semantic parameters, some of which will be activated while others are not, depending on the use made of them in a specific domain. However, the word-term distinction is sustained on a more traditional conception which also deserves some consideration. Given the fact that any discipline is distinguished from others by the specificity of its object of study, in order to be considered a discipline, terminology needed to distinguish its object from that of linguistics and drew a distinction between "term" and "word". This traditional (and rather abrupt) distinction, not adopted in this research, has also been the reason why the denomination "field of work" has been used throughout this study rather than "discipline".

16. Even though any unit with a reference has the potential of being either a term or a word, it is also possible that some highly specialised units in very specific subjects are only given as terms, since they are always used to denominate special

concepts. This would be technical vocabulary in the strictest sense, in opposition to the more sub-technical one, which may be found in less specialised contexts or even in contexts showing no specialisation at all (let us think about the words *water, oven* or *adhere*, for instance, and even polylexical formations like *orange peel*). Despite this, purely technical vocabulary may eventually become part of the general language due to the spread of specialised knowledge.

17. In the light of the previous item, this book has tried to show that terminology is an interdisciplinary field of work which is best described by a linguistic theory, like the CTT, which includes linguistic aspects as well as cognitive and pragmatic ones. The CTT also provides an explanation for the fact that a term may be used in the field of a speciality area and transferred from one speciality to another or from the general language to a specialised language. This theory therefore accounts for the possibility of specialised units' losing that specialised character in a given moment, as well as the possibility of the continuous "terminologising" of units from the general language or the constant and observed entry of terms from one speciality field to another ("pluri-terminologising").

18. On analysing terms *in vivo* (that is, as they appear in different communicative situations and, therefore, subject to change), close observation of specialised knowledge in specialised texts shows that these specialised lexical units or terminological units may occur at different levels of specialisation and can be described at different levels of representation. This is the only way to account for the whole reality of these units, both from a communicative and representational point of view.

19. In accordance with the CTT and with the reality shown by the results obtained, the existence of synonymy as a real phenomenon within natural specialised communication seems to have been confirmed.

To sum up, terminology has experienced a necessary evolution with the CTT, in which the former privileged position of the conceptual schemata in the scientific-technological fields defended by the GTT has given way to the pre-eminent role of observing specialised lexical units in real specialised texts. Therefore, terminology has been conceived throughout this research as a "theory of terms" (understood as units of the lexicon) and not as a "theory of concepts".

Regarding *specialised lexicography* (see Chapter 5) as such, a series of reflections on terminology-related disciplines and the adequacy of their theoretical and applied approaches have been presented so that the overall conclusions that can be drawn are the following:

1. In general, it has been assumed that the word *terminology* designates at least three different concepts: when referring to the discipline, it is the conceptual basis and the group of principles governing the study of the terms; regarding methodology, it refers to the guidelines used during terminographical work; and, finally, it is used to designate the group of terms in a given speciality area.

2. When the question of whether terminology is linguistics has been posed, this work has assumed that whereas linguistics is in charge of the study of a grammatical and/or social system consisting of components on different levels (phonology, morphology, lexicon, syntax and discourse) and known as language, terminology only deals with one of these component aspects of language – the lexical one. Hence, terms/terminology, as an integrating part of this lexical component, form part of language and can thus be studied by linguistics, and more specifically by lexicology and terminology.

3. Terminology is language (it deals with one of the aspects/ perspectives of linguistics: the lexicon, and more specifically specialised lexicon) but, as an intersection discipline, it can be considered from different perspectives. From the linguistic perspective, terminology is a part of the lexicon which becomes specialised due to thematic and pragmatic criteria; from the users' perspective, terminology is a group of communication

units to be used and evaluated in terms of economy, precision and accuracy criteria; and from the perspective of the scientific-technical disciplines, terminology is the formal reflection of their conceptual organisation and an unavoidable means of expression and communication within discourse communities.

4. According to the CTT, terms are not isolated units forming an individual, perfectly delimited system but units that are incorporated into the speakers' lexicon as soon as they acquire the role of specialists (after a process of learning specialised knowledge). This is also the main reason behind the need to use real texts produced by specialists (as the only true knowers of terms) to analyse terminology.

5. Terminology has been approached as an interdisciplinary field of work, since it is determined by the characteristics of the terminological units that are at the same time language units (linguistics), cognition elements (cognitive science) and communication "vehicles" (communication theory). In addition to this, these specialised lexical units appear in specialised communication (documentation) and are usually treated by a computer in the terminographical activity (computer science).

6. Throughout this research it has been stressed that terminological theory must develop in close relation to practice with the ultimate goal of solving actual communicative linguistic problems, as the CTT postulates. However, terminology is not just a practical activity that can be justified in itself, but must be considered within a wider scope in which it acquires its full significance. In this wider view, terminology is understood as a subject concerned with the compilation, description, management and presentation of the terms that belong to speciality fields and as such it has to establish as a priority the solving of social needs by optimising and guaranteeing effective communication between specialists and professionals. As an activity closely linked to real, socio-communicative needs and which reflects the state of the art in the different speciality fields, terminology is and must be constantly

developing parallel to the evolution of science and technology, since knowledge cannot develop independently from language and hence from the lexical units used to refer to new concepts.

7. In order to refer to the practical aspect of terminology dealing with the elaboration of dictionaries, vocabularies, glossaries, databases and any other kind of terminological application in a given specialised field, the term "terminography" has traditionally been used. It has also been noted how "terminology" and "terminography" have often been utilised without distinction, and how even more frequently the word "terminology" has been assumed to entail or include both a theoretical (terminology) and practical/applied (terminography) dimension (apart from being the actual group of terms forming part of a speciality field). Therefore, at times *terminology* is used when referring exclusively to terminography simply because it may be understood as an integral part of it (in its widest sense). However, throughout this study (and even when the term "terminographical work" could be, in general terms, valid in order to describe the kind of work here presented) a different nomenclature has been adopted for considering it to be more pertinent, preferable and more coherent with the theoretical positioning adopted and hence more accurate to define the kind of work developed, i.e. specialised lexicography. From a linguistic perspective, and to be coherent with the way terminology has been approached as a whole in this book, the terminographical work presented here is more appropriately defined by the label "specialised lexicology" or a lexicology of specialised units. Moreover, specialised lexicography constitutes a step further with respect to plain terminology because of its objectives, method and overall approach to specialised lexicon.

8. There are many different kinds of prospective or potential users of specialised lexicographical products and the same occurs with the professional profile of the specialised lexicographer. Nevertheless, the question of whether the method used in terminography is always the same presents multiple shades of meaning and has also been addressed in this study. It has been stated that two different

answers or options can be provided, each with its corresponding methodological implications: if specialists in the field (who are familiar with the conceptual scheme of the domain in which they work on a daily basis) are the ones in charge of the terminographical work, it has to be assumed that they know the concepts of their speciality beforehand. This allows them to take concepts as their starting point in order to later look for the linguistic forms representing them, using what has been called an onomasiological method of work (i.e. going from the concept to the form). However, the specialised lexicographer may not be a specialist in a scientific-technical area but a linguist who must progressively acquire the knowledge related to the speciality field being dealt with. In this case the terminographer will have to document himself/herself in order to acquire the necessary cognitive competence, and this documentation (in the form of texts) will become the source for the subsequent extraction of the terms that are to be included in the actual terminographical work. Accordingly, the method of work used here has started out from the linguistic forms and the target has been to discover their corresponding concepts; this has been called a semasiological method of work, going from the form to the concept. In this light, traditionally, if the clear-cut distinction between lexicology and terminology and thus between lexicography and terminography were accepted, then the onomasiological method of work would be the one assigned to terminography and the semasiological method would be the one attributed to lexicography. However, in this study and following the current conceptions of terminology, this distinction between the lexicographical and terminographical methods of work has not been of much use for two fundamental reasons. The first reason is that here I have adopted a view of language as being a continuum. The other reason is that terminology is a part of linguistics that deals with the lexicon, in the same way as lexicology does, but it does so more specifically, with the lexical units that become specialised in context. This is so because in the descriptive works aimed at the compilation of lexical units, whether they are specialised or not, the method of work normally used nowadays is also semasiological: the departure point is the identification of the terms in the texts in which they are used (this is usually done by means of a corpus). The onomasiological method is only used in those specialised terminographical works carried out by real specialists in the field. Therefore, due to all the reasons mentioned above, this research has adopted a semasiological method. I was not an expert in the field when the elaboration process commenced and so a corpus was compiled for the extraction of terms. Terms were thus identified from the texts in which real experts use them (the corpus) and this natural use was employed to characterise and define them in the entries by means of contexts of use, collocates, definitions, etc. As a result, in general, semasiology is the most common and probably the most reliable process for decoding information (because of its empirical basis provided by the corpus): the user selects a term (denomination) and afterwards pays attention to the information associated to it (definition, contexts of use, notes, etc.).

9. In this book, the view according to which terminology is prescriptive whereas lexicography is descriptive has not been adopted because it was considered to be an excessively sharp division between disciplines or fields of work. It was also deemed to place terminography too close to the classical prescriptive model adopted by the GTT. It is here again that the term "specialised lexicography" rather than "terminography" also seemed to be more appropriate for a work like this.

10. Specialised lexicography as such can thus be understood as the branch of lexicography which is practised by PAL lexicographers responsible for preparing and developing specialised dictionaries. Terminology can then be more associated with the mere study of terms, which may be complemented by the wider projection of specialised lexicography for the compilation and elaboration of specialised, user-oriented and user-friendly quality products in the form of dictionaries. Consequently, terminography has been understood as that part of terminology concerned with the production of terminological dictionaries in their most basic, purely linguistic sense (and thus this way of naming the word presented here is not incorrect either). But again, specialised lexicography has

been considered as a more accurate label because of the theoretical approaches adopted and the active, user-friendly feature that I have sought to emphasise in the ceramics industry dictionary. Thus, specialised lexicography goes beyond pure terminography even when most linguists would identify it with terminography.

11. Throughout this research, according to the SLA, attention has been drawn several times to the importance of phraseology and collocations, understood as the natural tendency of words to group together in a meaningful way. Thus, the study of collocations has been taken very much into account for the elaboration of the different entries. The identification of collocational patterns indicates semantic relationships among terms, which is always important for achieving natural, accurate and effective communication among experts. "Sounding natural" may not sound very scientific, but it is a real need which can only be achieved by taking these factors into account.

Specialised lexicographical tools (like the dictionary here presented) are created to meet specific needs and to provide effective solutions from a communicative point of view. Hence, the study of the socio-economic study of the domain to be dealt with is a fundamental aspect to consider. From a *socio-economic point of view* (see Chapter 6), both regarding the benefits that a study like this may imply and the state of the art in the ceramic industrial district, the conclusions that can be drawn from this research are the following:

1. Globalisation is imposing a real need for communication and for interaction with other discourse communities in society and all around the world. As a result it has become necessary to have an adequate knowledge of the language that, in general terms, most frequently allows this global understanding to take place, i.e. English (Johnson and Bartlett, 1999; Alcaraz Varó, 2000). It could, however, be any other language which effectively acts as a vehicle to convey (specialised) communication among communities. Hence, due to the great number of advancements in the ceramic field that take place in Spain (as a leader country in the sector) and

owing to the importance of the sector in the country, an ordered repertoire of ceramic terms should also be created in Spanish as has been done in English, because of its being a *lingua franca*.

2. Works like this are centred upon an immediate application and are anchored in real-world needs. Thus, one of the main grounding beliefs for undertaking a work like this was the real conviction that this study can be a good linguistic tool that is both necessary and beneficial for the economy of this area. Why? Because it can help to establish a neat, ordered and contextualised repertoire of English and Spanish terms showing actual, appropriate use which could provide firms with the capability to become more competitive worldwide. Hence, this study has been conceived as a step forward in the field of dictionaries by constituting a linguistic tool designed to enhance the production of adequate specialised discourse and to "fight" against communicative pressures that professionals may find difficult to solve in their everyday life.

3. The ceramic tile industry is a district with a huge potential and importance worldwide and more especially within the Spanish area of the Valencian Region. Therefore, rather than dealing with an abstract phenomenon that cannot easily be accounted for, shaped or represented, this study has considered a phenomenon that shows a linguistic dimension and a real-world application and which must be dealt with and analysed as such. The need for a good knowledge of ceramics industry terminology, understood as the group of terms used for communication in this very specific domain, is a real fact that takes place in a real socio-economic context and for real people who have to use it on a daily basis while performing their professional activities.

4. The final active dictionary developed according to the SLA has been designed and elaborated with the intention of its becoming a useful and complete linguistic tool. Including the definition and the real contexts in which the terms are used fosters the reliability of the information. At the same time, other information of a linguistic, conceptual and pragmatic character, such as synonyms,

significant variations imposed by the context of use, grammatical category, conceptual relationships, etc., is also included to help the user to employ these terms properly.

Finally, it may be conceded that the SLA constitutes a step further in specialised dictionary-making because of the sound and realistic theoretical positioning it describes, because of the kind of lexicographical works it aims at and because of the working methodology it establishes. As this book aims to show, PAL cannot be reduced to the technical terms that have traditionally formed part of specialised dictionaries. It is also necessary to incorporate phraseology that illustrates the use of terms in context because the terminological unit activates specific knowledge depending on the context in which it is found. Hence, an active dictionary like the one presented here sets out from the premise that every term is always accompanied by certain words or terms more frequently than with others and this will determine the activation of certain traits and thus the activation of a particular knowledge rather than another.

An active dictionary – key notion in the SLA – goes beyond other dictionaries of the sort in many senses, for instance, by giving the context the importance due to it in order to determine meanings and by paying greater attention to the word inside the sentence, and not as an isolated element. Active dictionaries show far more complementary contextual information in accordance with the pragmatic principles by offering grammatical and technical information, possible collocations and examples both in the source term and in the target language. In this respect, this study has been considered necessary in order to go a step forward in lexicographical and terminological work and to better meet and solve the current needs in the sector. Basically, from the linguistic point of view, it is necessary to renew the conception of speciality language dictionaries applied to the ceramic industry by introducing the benefits of an active dictionary that may become a source of information for professionals. This renewal is achieved here through the use of a corpus-based approach which fits within the pragmatic emphasis on context that the lexicographical concept of active dictionary implies (Salerno, 1990). Specialised lexicography is thus based on the development of bilingual user-friendly technical dictionaries like the one presented here.

Consequently, current specialised dictionaries like the one presented in this study reflect a considerable degree of progress regarding the information provided on patterns of use and collocational behaviour or phraseology. The aim of including this data is, as the SLA has tried to convey, to foster the active use of language, to help to construct specialised discourse in an appropriate manner, and to sound natural. In this way, acknowledging the need to study the phraseological component in ceramics terminology has made it necessary to set out from professional and academic discourse in order to extract the required phraseological data from the analysis of contexts.

With respect to the *method of work for the elaboration of a specialised dictionary* (see Chapters 7 and 8), the items below constitute a brief summary regarding the effectiveness of the method of work adopted according to the SLA and its contributions to the study as a whole:

1. It has been observed that, if one intends to work with a corpus, there are two possibilities open to us: either we can work with one that has already been compiled or a new one can be created. The second possibility allows us to design a corpus that better fits the objectives and necessities posed but, in both cases, the quality of the corpus will determine the results of the linguistic research. This has made it advisable, in the specific case of this study, to take into account a series of parameters that guarantee (at least up to a certain extent) the quality of the corpus and thus the quality of the results that can be extracted from it. Hence, it was crucial to determine the intended purpose of the research from the very beginning in order to try to construct a corpus that fitted these purposes. Thus, the appropriateness of the corpus was mainly determined by how well it represented the domain it characterises, which means that most of the statements obtained from the analysis of the corpus can be applicable to a larger sample or to the language as a whole. In addition to this, diversity and size were also considered when text selection and compilation were undertaken to ensure that enough text has been included in each category to cover the range of variation across speakers or authors. Thus, in the stage of corpus compilation, different text genres (specialised journals, articles, magazines, books, etc.) representing the professional field in question

were included. However, it was also assumed throughout the study that it is impossible to create a completely representative corpus and that it is unfeasible to give an absolute guarantee of this representativeness, which cannot be subject to objective evaluation. In the same way, it had to be assumed that a corpus is a finite sample from an infinite population, and therefore new linguistic samples are always appearing and could be included.

2. It seems to have been proved that specialised texts are much denser from the point of view of lexical terms than texts from general language (Ahmad and Rogers, 2001). This implies that the texts compiled in the corpus used for the study presented (and, because of the goals aimed at, had to present) what is called "terminological density", that is, a high degree of technicality or words that transmit specialised knowledge.

3. The value of the field diagram in corpus compilation can be seen by the fundamental role it played in achieving a balanced inclusion of the necessary number and kinds of documents comprising the different areas or subareas the domain is made up of, as determined by this diagrammatic representation. Furthermore, this field diagram was, on the one hand, a key element in carrying out the terminological extraction, that is, in selecting the terminological units to be included as dictionary entries and in establishing the first element of their definition, as is explained in more detail below. The *field diagram* was used as an ontological system that represents the different areas and subareas of the field graphically. That is to say, it consisted of a structured list in the form of a diagram inside which the different activities belonging to the sector under analysis were included and classified in such a way as to allow me to internalise a clear and meaningful system of the area to work with. On the other hand, regarding other more tangible benefits of this diagram, this system provided the first element of definition of the terminological units in the dictionary by means of abbreviations that indicate the semantic field the term belongs to so that the dictionary user can coherently place the term within the professional area/subarea to which it belongs right from the very beginning. The "bare skeleton"

of the field offered by this diagrammatic representation of reality is in direct contact with this reality and can be filled with the terms extracted from the linguistic data of the corpus. The key aspect in a field diagram is that it is determined by the notion of *semantic field* (Auger and Rousseau, 1987), which represents a group of notions that can be grouped under the heading of a key notion. This was a useful tool for delimiting the field of the work, for coherently organising and presenting the information, and for placing the terms inside a structured group which will be a valuable aid when it comes to classifying and treating them.

4. With the aim of identifying the most frequent terms both in English and Spanish, a process of semi-automatic term extraction and data analysis was employed, in which both human and technological means were necessarily involved. Therefore, one of the main aims throughout this study has been to offer a methodological proposal based on a solid theoretical basis and grounded on a very particular conception of terminology sustained on the corpus as the means for obtaining a comprehensive terminological representation of the field under study.

5. In the semi-automatic term extraction process, collocational behaviour and the general relationships between words inside texts, that is, in context, were widely considered. The analysis of phraseology in this study was considered a fundamental part aimed at facilitating the acquisition of a good level of competence on the part of prospective users of the dictionary. The terminology of specialised languages is not correctly analysed by simply extracting the terms that form part of the specialised field (Scott, 1998) and this would not have been logical either within a study like this.

6. Apart from the (purely human) work done "by hand" that I have mentioned earlier, the use of a concordance software program like WordSmith Tools 4.0 benefited the whole work presented here by allowing close observation and analysis of corpus data as well as their retrieval. Nowadays, terminographical or specialised lexicographical works owe most of their development not only to

advances from the point of view of the evolution of terminological theories, but also to the technological advances in the field which allow much quicker and more reliable analyses to be conducted. In addition to this, displaying the data in different formats, taking into account different parameters depending on the necessities of each terminographer or each stage of the work, contributed positively by allowing terminological units to be analysed according to different parameters (frequency, MI, etc.). This possibility is always enriching in order to gain a more complete view of the terminological unit as a whole, as well as within the wider dimension of the text in which it is found. In the same line and also within terminotics, the use of TermStar XV also benefited the working method and the results obtained enormously by allowing the logical management of the ordered repertoire of terms, which would have been almost impossible to achieve otherwise. Likewise, without GENDIC, final entries could never have been generated in the desired format

To sum up, this book has tried to show a proposal aimed at disclosing the SLA and the development of a specialised lexicographical tool in accordance with this approach. In this specific case, the ceramics industry called for a renewal in the conception of specialised dictionaries on the topic, mainly because of the need to respond to the linguistic pressures stemming from the socio-economic demands of a globalised society and an increasingly international market. Establishing a systematised, structured, coherent and contextualised inventory of terms is a necessity in most industrial sectors, especially if the rapid development these fields undergo is taken into account. The relationship between socio-economic context and specialised lexicography is therefore reciprocal and mutually beneficial and originates real tools (specialised dictionaries) with a practical, immediate application deeply grounded on real needs and a coherent treatment of terminology like the one proposed by the SLA. Nonetheless the truest conclusion of all regarding lexicography was wisely summarised by Samuel Johnson more than four centuries ago:

Every other author may aspire to praise;
the lexicographer can only hope to escape reproach,
and even this negative recompense has been yet granted to very few.

The greatest part of a writer's time
is spent in reading, in order to write;
a man will turn over half a library to make one book.
Samuel Johnson

References

Abercrombie, D. 1963. *Studies in phonetics and linguistics,* London: Oxford University Press.

Adelstein, A. 2004. *Unidad léxica y valor especializado. Estado de la cuestión y observaciones sobre su representación,* Barcelona: Institut Universitari de Lingüística Aplicada, Universidad Pompeu Fabra (ISBN: 84-89782-15-6, Serie Tesis 5, <http://www.iula.upf.edu/publi036.htm> [Last search date: June, 2007].

Aguado de Cea, G. 2001. "Panorama de la investigación en lenguas aplicadas en España", in Aguado de Cea, G. and Durán, P. (eds): *La investigación en lenguas aplicadas: enfoque multidisciplinar*, Madrid: Universidad Politécnica de Madrid.

Ahmad, K. and Davies, A. 1992. *Knowledge Processing 7: Methods of Corpus Linguistics and Terminology Extraction*, Department of Mathematical and Computing Sciences, University of Surrey CS-92-10.

Ahmad, K. 1995. "Document Management: The Role of Terminology", Conference by invitation in the Document Conference, 22-24 March, Ede, The Netherlands. Online document: <http://www.mcs.surrey.ac.uk> [Last search date: September, 2007].

Ahmad, K. and Rogers, M. 2001. "Corpus Linguistics and Terminology Extraction" in Wright S. and Budin G. (eds): *Handbook of Terminology Management,* vol. (2). John Benjamins Publishing Company, 725-760.

Alcaraz Varó, E. 1990. *Tres paradigmas de la investigación lingüística*, Alcoy: Marfil.

Alcaraz Varó, E. and Martínez Linares, M. A. 1997. *Diccionario de lingüística moderna*, Barcelona: Ariel Referencia.

Alcaraz Varó, E. 2000. *El inglés profesional y académico*, Madrid: Alianza Editorial.

Alcaraz, E. and Hugues, B. 2004. *Diccionario de términos económicos, financieros y comerciales*, Ariel.

Arntz R, Picht H. 1995. *Introducción a la terminología*. Madrid: Fundación Germán Sánchez Ruipérez.

Atkins, S. and Clear, J. 1992. "Corpus Design Criteria", *Literary and Linguistic Computing,* vol. 7, n.1, 1-16.

Auger, P. and Rousseau, L. J. 1987. *Metodologia de la recerca terminològica*, Sant Adrià de Besòs, Departament de Cultura de la Generalitat de Catalunya.

Balboni, P. 1986. "LGP versus LSP: Which Way to the Razor's Edge?", ALSED-LSP NEWSLETTER, 22, 2-8.

Beaugrande, R. 1987. "Special purpose language and linguistic theory". ALSED-LSP NEWSLETTER 10/2(25), 2-11.

Becattini, G. 1990. "The Marshallian industrial district as a socio-economic notion", in Pyke, F., Becattini, G. and Sengenberger, W. (eds): *Industrial Districts and Local Economic Regeneration*, Geneva: International Institute for Labour Studies, 37-51.

Berber Sardinha, A. P. 2000. "Lingüística de Corpus: histórico e problemática", *D.E.L.T.A 16* (2), 323-367. Online document: <http://www.scielo.br/pdf/delta/v16n2/a05v16n2.pdf> [Last search date: March, 2006].

Bergenholtz, H. and Tarp, S. 1995. *Manual of Specialised Lexicograpy: The Preparation of Specialised Dictionaries,* Amsterdam/ Philadelphia: John Benjamins.

Berkenkotter, C. and Huckin, T. N. 1995. *Genre knowledge in disciplinary communication: Cognition / Culture / Power,* Hillsdale, N.J.: Erlbaum.

Biber, D. 1990. Methodological issues regarding corpus-based analyses of linguistic variation. *Literary and Linguistic Computing* 5, 257-269.

Biber, D. 1993. "Representativeness in Corpus Design", *Literary and Linguistic Computing,* Vol. 8, No. 4, Oxford University Press.

Biber, D., Conrad, S. and Reppen, R. 1998. *Corpus Linguistics. Investigating Language Structure and Use*, Cambridge University Press.

Boas, F. 1940. *Race, Language, and Culture,* New York, MacMillan.

Bongers H. 1947. *The history and principles of vocabulary control*, Worden: Wocopi.

Bowker, L. 1996. "Towards a Corpus-Based Approach to Terminography", *Terminology*, 3(1), 1996, 27-52.

Cabré Castellví, M. T. 1993. *La Terminología : Teoría, metodología, aplicaciones,* Editorial Antártida/Empúries.

Cabré Castellví, M. T. 1994. "Terminologies et dictionnaires". *Meta* XXXIX (4), 584-597.

Cabré Castellví, M. T. 1999 a. *La terminología, representación y comunicación: elementos para una teoría de base comunicativa y otros artículos*, Barcelona: Institut Universitari de Lingüística Aplicada (IULA), Universitat Pompeu Fabra.

Cabré Castellví, M. T. 1999 b. *Terminology: Theory, Methods, and Applications*, Amsterdam: John Benjamins.

Cabré Castellví, M. T. 2000 a. "Terminologie et linguistique : la théorie des portes", *Terminologie nouvelles*, 21, pp. 10-15. Online document: <http://elies.rediris.es/elies16/Cabre.html> [Last search date: May, 2007].

Cabré Castellví, M. T. 2000 b. "Terminología y documentación", in Gonzalo García, C. and García Yebra, V. (eds): *Documentación, Terminología y Traducción*, Madrid: Síntesis, 31-44.

Cabré Castellví, M. T. 2000 c. "Elements for a theory of terminology. Towards an alternative paradigm", *Terminology. International Journal of Theoretical and Applied Issues in Specialised Communication*, 6, 1, 35-57 (A). Online document: <http://www.upf.edu/pdi/dft/teresa.cabre/docums/ca00e1.pdf> [Last search date: August, 2007].

Cabré Castellví, M. T. 2001 a. "La Terminología entre la lexicología y la documentación: aspectos teóricos e importancia social", in Aguado de Cea, G. and Durán, P. (eds): *La investigación en lenguas aplicadas: enfoque multidisciplinar*, Madrid: Universidad Politécnica de Madrid.

Cabré Castellví, M. T. 2002. "Textos especializados y unidades de conocimiento: metodología y tipologización", in J. García Palacios and Fuentes Morán, M. T. (eds): *Texto, terminología y traducción*, Salamanca: Almar.

Cabré Castellví, M. T. and Estopà, R. 2002. "El conocimiento especializado y sus unidades de representación: diversidad cognitiva", Sendebar: Revista de la Facultad de Traducción e Interpretación, ISSN 1130-5509, 13, 2002, 141-153 Online document: <http://www.upf.edu/pdi/dtf/teresa.cabre/docums/ca02con.pdf> [Last search date: August, 2007].

Cabré Castellví, M. T. 2004. "¿Lenguajes especializados o lenguajes para propósitos específicos?", *Foro Hispánico - Revista Hispánica de Flandes y Holanda* 26(1). Amsterdam/New York: Rodopi, 19-34. Online document <http://www.upf.edu/pdi/dft/teresa.cabre/docums/ca041e.pdf> [Last search date: August, 2007].

Chomsky N. 1964. "Formal Discussion", in Bellugi U. and Brown R. (eds): *The acquisition of language. Monographs of the Society for Research in Child Development*, 29: 37-39.

Chomsky, N. 1965. *Aspects of a Theory of Syntax*, Cambridge. Mass: MIT Press.

Chomsky N. 1968. *Language and mind*, New York: Harcourt Brace.

Ciapuscio, G. E. 2000. "La terminología desde el punto de vista textual: selección, tratamiento y variación", *Organon*, 27.

Ciapuscio, G. E. and Kugel, I. 2002. "Hacia una tipología del discurso especializado: aspectos teóricos y aplicados", in García Palacios, J. and Fuentes Morán, M.T. (eds): *Texto, terminología y traducción*, Biblioteca de Traducción, Salamanca: Ediciones Almar, 37-73.

Clear, J. 1992. "Corpus Sampling", in Leitner, G. (ed.): *New Directions in English Language Corpora*, Berlin/New York: Mouton de Gruyter, 21-31.

Clear, J. 1997. "Technical Implications of Multilingual Corpus lexicography" in *International Journal of Lexicography*, vol. 77(2), 165-187.

Codina, L. 2000. "Evaluación de los recursos digitales en línea: conceptos, indicadores y métodos", *Revista española de documentación científica*, vol. 23, 1, 9-44. Online document:<http://bddoc.csic.es:8080/basisbwdocs_rdisoc/rev0001/2000_vol23-1_pp9-44.htm> [Last search date: January, 2006].

Coleman, J.S. 1990. *Foundation of Social Theory*, Cambridge, MA: Harvard University Press.

Condamines, A. 1994. "Terminology et Représentation des Connaissances", *Didaskalia* 5: 29-43.

Cop, M. 1988. *The Function of Collocations in Dictionaries*, paper presented at the EURALEX Third International Congress, Budapest.

Cowie, A.P. 1981. "The Treatment of Collocations and Idioms in Learners' Dictionaries", *Applied Linguistics*, 2(3), 223-235.

Cowie, A.P. (1987. "Syntax, the dictionary and the learners' communicative needs", in Cowie, A.P. (ed.): *The Dictionary and the Language Learner*, Tubingen: Niemeyer, 183-192.

Desmet, I. 1994. "Propositions pour la recherche en phraséologie contrastive", *La banque des mots,* special number, 6, 45-59.

Dubuc, R. 1985. *Manuel pratique de terminologie*, Montréal, Linguatech.

Estopà, R. 2003. *Extracció de terminologia: elements per a la construcció d'un SEACUSE (Sistema d'Extracció Automàtica de Candidats a Unitats de Significació Especialitzada),* Barcelona: Institut Universitari de Lingüística Aplicada. (Sèrie Tesis; 2).

Felber, H. 1979. "Theory of terminology, terminology work and terminology documentation" in Fachsprache, nº 1, 20-33.

Felber, H. 1987. *Manuel de terminologie*, Paris: Infoterm.

Ferber, H and Picht, H. 1984. *Métodos de terminografía y principios de investigación terminológica*, Madrid, C.S.I.C., Instituto Cervantes.

Fernández Sevilla, J. 1974. *Problemas de lexicografía actual,* Bogotá: Instituto Caro y Cuervo.

Ferrer i Cancho, R. 2003. *Language: universals, principles and origins,* PhD thesis, Universitat Politècnica de Catalunya, Barcelona, 2003.

Firth, J.R. 1935. "The technique of Semantics", *Transactions of the Philological Society*, 36-72.

Firth, J.R. 1957. "A synopsis of linguistic theory, 1930-1955", *Studies in Linguistic Analysis*, Special Volume, Philological Society, 1-32.

Foss, N.J. and Eriksen, B. 1995. "Competitive advantage and industry capabilities", in Montgomery, C.A. (ed.): *Resource-Based and Evolutionary Theories of the Firm: Toward a Synthesis*, Boston: Kluwer Academic, 43-70.

Frawley, W.J. (editor in chief) 2003. *International Encyclopedia of Linguistics*, Volume 4, Oxford University Press.

Fries C. and Traver A. 1940. *English word lists: a study of their adaptability and instruction*, Washington, DC: American Council of Education.

Gambier, Y. 1991. "Travail et vocabulaires specialisés: prolegomènes à une socioterminologie", *Meta*, 36, 1, 8-15.

Gaudin, F. 1991. *Terminologie et travail scientifique: mouvement des signes, mouvement des connaissances*, Cahiers de Linguistique Sociale, 18, 111-131.

Gómez de Enterría, J. 1998. "Aproximación a los textos científicos. Una metodología activa", in *Actas del XVI Congreso Nacional de Lingüística Aplicada*, Logroño – AESLA.

Gómez González-Jover, A. and Vargas Sierra, Ch. (2002. "Córpora comparables y paralelos para la detección de terminología bilingüe: su explotación y uso con herramientas informáticas", CD-Rom publication (VIII Simposio Iberoamericano de Terminología), number 8. Online document: <http://66.102.9.104/search?q=cache:H77orvHdbv0J:wwwriterm.net/actes/8simposio/gomez_vargas.htm+termstar-vargas&hl=es&ct=clnk&cd=1&gl=es> [Last search date: March, 2007]

Gómez González-Jover, A. and Vargas Sierra, Ch. 2003 a. "Metodología para alimentar una base de datos terminológica desde las necesidades del traductor", proceedings of the I Congreso Internacional de la Asociación Ibérica de Estudios de Traducción e Interpretación.

Gómez González-Jover, A. and Vargas Sierra, Ch. 2003 b. "Utilización de herramientas informáticas para la elaboración de diccionarios bilingües", *Interlingüística*, 13, 269-289.

Gómez González-Jover, A. and Vargas Sierra, Ch. 2004. "Aspectos metodológicos para la elaboración de diccionarios especializados bilingües destinados al traductor", *El español, lengua de traducción. II CongresoInternacional*, Bruselas: ESLEtRA, 365-398.

Gutiérrez, B. 1998. *La ciencia empieza en la palabra*. Barcelona: Península.

Halliday, M. A. K. (2004. "Lexicology", in Halliday M.A.K., Teubert, W., Yallop, C., Cermáková, A. (eds): *Lexicology and Corpus Linguistics: an introduction*, Open Linguistics Series, London.

Harrell, R. S. 1967. "Some notes on Bilingual Lexicography", in Householder, F. and Saporta, S. (eds): *Problems in lexicography,* Indiana University, Mouton, Bloomington - The Hague.

Harris Z. 1951. *Methods in structural linguistics*, Chicago: University of Chicago Press.

Hartmann, R.R.K. 1987. "Four perspectives on dictionary use: a critical review of research methods", in Cowie, A.P. (ed.): *The Dictionary and the Language Learner*, Tubingen: Niemeyer, 246-256.

Hartmann, R.R.K. 1989. "Sociology of the dictionary user: Hypotheses and empirical studies", in Hausemann, F.J., Reichmann, O., Wiegand, H. E. and Zgusta, L. (eds): *Dictionaries*, Walter de Gruyter, 102-110.

Hasman, M. A. 2000. "The Role of English in the 21st Century", *FORUM*, 38 (1), 2-5.

Hatherall, G. 1984. "Studying dictionary use: Some findings and proposals", in Hartmann, R.K.K. (ed.) LEXeter '83 Proceedings, papers from the International Conference on Lexicography, 183-189, Tubingen.

Hockett C. 1948. "A note on structure", *International Journal of American Linguistics* 14: 269-71.

Hoffmann, L. 1985. "On the place of LSP Research in Applied Linguistics", F*achsprache*, 1-2, 2-11.

Hoffmann, L. 1987. "Language for Special/Specific Purposes", in Ammon, U., Ditmar, N. and Matheier, K. J. (eds): *Sociolinguistics. An International Handbook of the Science of Language and Society*, Berlin/New York: de Gruyter, 298-302.

Hoffmann, L. 1991. "Texts and text types in LSP", in Schröder, H. (ed.): *Subject-oriented texts: Languages for special purposes & text theory*, Berlin: W. de Gruyter.

Hoffmann, L. 1998. *Els llenguatges d'especialitat. Selecció de textos*, Barcelona: IULA-UPF.

Hunston, S. 2002. *Corpora in Applied Linguistics*, Cambridge: Cambridge University Press.

Ingram D. 1978. "Sensori-motor development and language acquisition", in Lock A. (ed.): *Action, gesture and symbol: the emergence of language*, London: Academic Press.

IULA 2006 a. "La unidad terminológica", in Grup IulaTerm, *Introducción a la Terminología,* Barcelona: IULA. Universidad Pompeu Fabra. Online document: <http:iulaonline.iula.upf.edu>, ISBN 84-89782-01-6. [Last search date: March 2007].

IULA 2006 b. "Terminología, estandarización internacional y normalización lingüística", in Grup IulaTerm, *Diploma de postgrado online: Terminología y necesidades profesionales.* Barcelona: IULA. Universidad Pompeu Fabra, Online document: <http://iulaonline.iula.upf.edu>, ISBN 84-89782-01-6. [Last search date: March 2007].

IULA 2007 a. "Terminología y Documentación", in Grup IulaTerm, *Diploma de postgrado online: Terminología y necesidades profesionales*, Barcelona: IULA, Universidad Pompeu Fabra. Online document: <http://iulaonline.iula.upf.edu>, ISBN 84-89782-22-9. [Last search date: October 2007].

IULA 2007 b. "Terminología y traducción", in Grup IulaTerm, *Diploma de postgrado online: terminología y necesidades profesionales,* Barcelona: IULA, Universidad Pompeu Fabra. Online document: <htto://iulaonline.iula.pdf.edu>, ISBN 84-89782-01-6. [Last search date: October 2007].

IULA 2007 c. "Terminología y enseñanza de lenguas", in Grup IulaTerm, *Diploma de postgrado online: Terminología y necesidades profesionales,* Barcelona: IULA, Universidad Pompeu Fabra. Online document: <http://www.iulaonline.iula.upf.edu>, ISBN 84-89782-01-6. [Last search date: October 2007].

IULA 2007 d. "Terminología, ingeniería lingüística y lingüística computacional", in Grup IulaTerm, *Diploma de postgrado online: Terminología y necesidades profesionales,* Barcelona: IULA. Universidad Pompeu Fabra. Online document: <http://www.iulaonline.iula.upf.edu>, ISBN 84-89782-01-6. [Last search date: October 2007].

Kading J. 1879. *Häufigkeitswörterbuch der deutschen Sprache,* Steglitz: privately published.

Kennedy G. 1992. "Preferred ways of putting things", in Svartvik J. (ed.): *Directions in corpus linguistics*, Berlin: Mouton de Gruyter.

Kennedy, G. 1998. *An introduction to Corpus Linguistics*, London/New York: Longman.

Khellmer, G. 1991. "A mint of phrases", in Aijmer, K. and Altenburg, B. (eds): *English Corpus Linguistics: Studies in Honour of Jan Svartvik*, London: Longman.

Kromann, H. P., Riiber, T. and Rosbach, P. 1991. "Principles of Bilingual Lexicography", in Hausmann, F.J., Reichmann, O., Wiegand and Zgusta, E. L. (eds): *Wörterbücher / Dictionaries / Dictionnaires. Ein internationales Handbuch zur Lexikographie / An International Encyclopedia of Lexicography / Enciclopédie internationale de lexicographie.* 3, Berlin-New York, De Gruyter, 2711-2728.

Lara, L. F. 1999. "Cognición y significado, ¿un proceso único?", V Simposio Internacional de Lingüística Hispánica.

Leech, G. 1991. "The state of the art in corpus linguistics" in Aijmer, K. and Altenberg, B. (eds): *English Corpus Linguistics: Studies in Honour of Jan Svartvik*, London: Longman, pp. 8-29. Online document: <http://angli02.kgw.tu-berlin.de/corpus/art.htm> [Last search date: June 2007].

Leech, G. and Fallon, R. 1992. "Computer corpora - what do they tell us about culture?", ICAME Journal 16: 29-50.

Leech, G. 1992. "Corpora and theories of linguistic performance", in Starvik, J. *Directions in Corpus Linguistics*, Berlin: mouton de Gruyter, 105-122.

Leech, G. 2002. "The importance of Reference Corpora", in Jornadas *Corpus Lingüísticos. Presente y futuro*, Donostia, UZEI.

Lerat, P. 1995. *Las Lenguas especializadas*, Barcelona: Ariel.

Levin, S. 1963. "Deviation statistical and determinate in poetic language", *Lingua*, 21, 276-90.

Lewandowski, T. 1982. *Diccionario de Lingüística*, Madrid: Cátedra.

Loening, K. L. and Sonnenveld, B.H. 1993. *Terminology*, John Benjamins Publishing Company: Amsterdam/Philadelphia.

Longman's Language Activator, the World's First Production Dictionary (1993), Essex, Longman Group UK Limited.

Lorente, M. 2001. "Teoría e innovación en terminografía: la definición terminográfica" in Cabré Castellví, M.T and Feliu, J. (eds): *La terminología científico-técnica: reconocimiento, análisis y extracción de información formal y semántica*, Barcelona, IULA, 81-112.

Malinowski, B. 1923. "The problem of meaning in primitive languages", supplement to Ogden, C. K. and Richards, I. A. (eds): *The meaning of Meaning: A study of the influence of language upon thought and the science of symbolism* London: Routledge and Kegan Paul.
Malinowski, B. 1935. "The translation of untranslatable words", in Nye, A. (ed.) (1998. *Philosophy of Language: The Big Questions*, Oxford: Blackwell.
Manning, C. and Schütze, H. 1999. *Foundationsof Statistical Natural Language Processing*. Cambridge, Mass.: MIT Press.
Marshall, A. 1925. *Principles of economics*, London: Macmillan.
Martínez de Sousa, J. 1995. *Diccionario de lexicografía práctica*, Barcelona: VOX, Biblograf S.A.
McEnery, T. and Wilson, A. 1996. *Corpus Linguistics*, Edinburgh: Edinburgh University Press.
McEnery, T. and Wilson, A 2001. "Corpus Linguistics", web pages to be used to supplement the book *Corpus Linguistics* published by Edinburgh University Press. Online document: <http://bowland-files.lancs.ac.uk/monkey/ihe/linguistics/contents.htm> [Last search date: October, 2007]
Molina-Morales, F.X. 2002. "Industrial districts and innovation: the case of the Spaninsh ceramic tiles industry". *Enterpreneurship & Regional Development"*, 14, 317-335.
Molina-Morales, F.X. 2005. "The territorial Agglomerations of Firms: A Social Capital Perspective from the Spanish Tile Industry". *Growth and Change* Vol. 36, Number 1, 74-99.
Náger, D. 2002. Periódico *Mediterráneo,* 13-Diciembre-2002.
Nida, E. 1997. "The Molecular Level of Lexical Semantics", *International Journal of Lexicography*, 10/4, 265-274.
Pedersen, P. 1995. "The identification and selection of collocations in Technical dictionaries", *Lexicographica Series Maior*, vol. 11, 60-73.
Pérez Hernández, M. Ch. 2002. "Explotación de los córpora textuales informatizados para la creación de bases de datos terminológicas basadas en el conocimiento", *Estudios de Lingüística Española (ELiEs)*, 18. Online document: <http://elies.rediris.es/elies18/index.html> [Last search date: December, 2007].

Picht, H. 1991. "Fraseología LSP(1) desde el punto de vista terminológico", *Sendebar, Boletín de la Escuela Universitaria de Traductores e Intérpretes de Granada n. 2*, Granada: Servicio de publicaciones de la Universidad de Granada, 91-105.

Picht, H. 1996. "En recuerdo de E. Wüster: la multidisciplinariedad de la terminología", in Cabré, M. T. (dir.): *Terminología. Selección de Textos de E. Wüster*, Barcelona: Universidad de Barcelona.

Posteguillo, S. and Piqué-Angordans, J. 2005. "Computer Terminology: Developing an Active Bilingual English-Spanish Dictionary", in Gottlieb, H., Mogensen, J. E. and Zettersten, A. (eds): *Symposium on Lexicography XI. Proceedings of the Eleventh International Symposium on Lexicography May 2-4, 2002 at the University of Copenhagen*. Special edition of *LEXICOGRAPHICA Series Maior*, 115, 453-473. Tübingen: Max Niemeyer Verlag.

Quemada, B. 1978. "Technique et langage", in Gille, B. (ed.): *Histoire des techniques*, Paris: Gallimard.

Quirk, R. 1960. "Towards a description of English usage", *Transactions of the Philological Society*, 40-61.

Rafel i Fontanals, J. and Soler i Bou, J. 2003. "El procesamiento de corpus. La lingüística empírica" in Martí Antonín, M.A. (coord) and others: *Tecnologías del lenguaje*, Editorial UOC, chapter 2.

Rey, A. 1975. *Essai de définition du concept de néologisme. L'aménagement de la néologie.* Quebec : Editeur officiel du Québec.

Rey, A. 1979. *La terminologie: noms et notions*, Paris : Presses Universitaries de France.

Rey, A. 1995. *Essays on Terminology*, Amsterdam/Philadelphia: John Benjamins.

Rondeau, G. 1984. *Introduction à la terminologie*. Québec: Gaëtan Morin.

Sager, J. C, Dungworth, D. and McDonald P. F. 1980. *English Special Languages: Principles and Practice in Science and Technology*, Wiesbaden: Oscar Brandstetter.

Sager, J. C. 1990. *A practical course in terminology processing*. Benjamins, Amsterdam/Philadelphia.

Sager, J.C. 1993. *Curso práctico sobre el procesamiento de la terminología*, Madrid: Fundación Germán Sánchez Ruipérez.

Sager, J.C. 1994. "What's wrong with "terminology work" and "terminology science"?", *Terminology*, vol.1 (2), 375-381.

Sánchez, A. 1995. "Organización del Corpus Cumbre", in Sánchez, A. (coord.): *Corpus lingüístico del español contemporáneo. Fundamentos, metodología y aplicaciones*, 25-37.

Scott, M. and Oxford University Press 1998. *WordSmith Tools Manual version 4.0*. Online document: <http://www.lexically.net/wordsmith/version4/manual.pdf> [Last search date: April 2006].

Sinclair, J. 1991. *Corpus, Concordance, Collocation*. Oxford: Oxford University Press.

Sinclair, J. 1996. *Preliminary recommendations on Corpus Typology*, EAGLES Document EAG-TCWG-CTYP/P. Online document: <http://www.ilc.cnr.it/EAGLES96/corpustyp/corpustyp.html> [Last search date: June 2006].

Slodzian, M. 1995. "Comment revisiter la doctrine terminologique aujourd'hui ? ", *La banque des mots,* 7, 11-18.

Stubbs, M. 1993. "British traditions in text analysis", in Baker, M., Francis, G. and Tognini-Bonelli, E. (eds): *Text and Technology – In Honour of John Sinclair*, Amsterdam/Philadelphia: John Benjamins,1-33.

Summers, D. 1993. "Longman/Lancaster English Language Corpus-Criteria and Design", *International Journal of Lexicography*, 6 (3), 181-208.

Svartvik J. 1966. *On voice in the English verb,* The Hague: Mouton.

Swales, J.M. 1990. *Genre analysis. English in academic and research settings,* Cambridge: Cambridge University Press.

Temmermann, R. 1998. "*Terminology theory and terminography in a natural language processing environment".*, *Revue frangaise de linguistique appliquée*, 3:2, 29-46.

Temmermann, R. 2000. *Towards new ways of terminology description: the sociocognitive approach*, Amsterdam/Philadelphia: John Benjamins.

Teubert, W. and Cermáková, A, 2004. "Directions in corpus linguistics" in Halliday M.A.K., Teubert, W., Yallop, C. and Cermáková, A. (eds): *Lexicology and Corpus Linguistics: an introduction*, Open Linguistics Series, London.

Thompson, G. 1987. "Using bilingual dictionaries", *ELT J.,* 41: 282-286.

Tognini-Bonelli, E. 2001. *Corpus Linguistics at Work*, Amsterdam/ Philadelphia: John Benjamins.

Torruella, J. and Llisterri, J. 1999. "Diseño de corpus textuales y orales", in Blecua, J.M., Clavería, G., Sánchez, C. and Torruella, J. (eds): *Filología e informática. Nuevas tendencias en los estudios filológicos*, Barcelona, Seminario de Filología e informática, Departamento de Filología Española, Universidad Autónoma de Barcelona, editorial Milenio, 45-77.

Vangehuchten, L. 2003. "La enseñanza del léxico económico empresarial en español lengua extranjera: ¿De qué léxico se trata?, in *La adquisición del vocabulario del español como lengua extranjera* (actas de la jornada de estudios del 14 de noviembre de 2001) / UCL, e-Montaigne. Centre d'études hispaniques.

Varantola, K. 1986. "Special Language and General Language: Linguistic and Didactic Aspects" en *ALSED-LSP Newsletter* 9/2 (23),10-19.

Vargas Sierra, Ch. 2005. *Aproximación terminográfica al lenguaje de la piedra natural. Propuesta de sistematización para la elaboración de un diccionario traductológico*, tesis doctoral de la Universidad de Alicante, Facultad de Filosofía y Letras, Departamento de Filología Inglesa.

Welte, W. 1985. *Lingüística moderna: terminología y bibliografía*, Madrid: Gredos.

Wright, S .E. and Budin, G. 1997. *Handbook of Terminology Management. Volume II: Application-Oriented Terminology Management,* Amsterdam/Philadelphia: John Benjamins.

Wüster, E. 1979. *Einführung in die allgemanie Terminologielehre und terminologische Lexikographie*, Wien: Springer (Versión española dirigida por M. T. Cabré Castellví: *Introducción a la teoría de la terminología y a la lexicografía terminológica.* Barcelona: IULA, Universitat Pompeu Fabra, 1998).

Zipf, G. K. 1935. *The Psychobiology of Language*. Houghton-Mifflin

Websites:

<http://www.spaintiles.info/esp/sector/informacion.asp> [Last search date: November, 2007]

<http://www.spaintiles.info/esp/ascer/historia.asp> [Last search date: November, 2007]

<http://ww.lexically.net/downloads/version4/html/index.html> [Last search date: April, 2006]

<http://en.wikipedia.org/wiki/Collocation> [Last search date: July, 2007]

<http://en.wikipedia.org/wiki/Mutaul_information> [Last search date: July, 2007]

<http://www.el-mundo.es/nuevaconomia/2002/152/1039171430.html> [Last search date: January, 2007]

<http://www.ipc.uji.es> [Last search date: August, 2007]

<http://www.itc.uji.es/biblioteca.php> [Last search date: August, 2006]

<http://www.star-spain.com/es/tecnologia/term.html> [Last search date: February, 2007]

<http://www.star-spain.com/es/tecnologia/term_estruct.html> [Last search date: May, 2007]

<http://www.termcat.net/centre/> [Last search date: July, 2007]

<http://en.wikipedia.org/wiki/Collocation> [Last search date: March, 2007]

<http://en.wikipedia.org/wiki/Zipf's_law> [Last search date: October, 2006]

<http://www.urbanoticias.com/noticias/hemeroteca/10113_la-industria-ceramica-espanola-incremento.shtml> [Last search date: November, 2007]

<http://www.spaintiles.info/documentos/proceso.pdf> [Last search date: March, 2008]

<http://www.eurofond.europa.eu/pubdocs/1998/32/en/1/ef9832en.pdf> [Last search date: March, 2008]

Online terminological databases:

British national Corpus
Columbia Encyclopedia
Encyclopaedia Britannica
Eurodicautom
Euro Glosary
FAO Terminology
ILOTERM (International Labour Organization)
Inter Active Terminology for Europe (IATE)
Terminological Information System (EU)
UNTERM. United Nations Multilingual Terminology Database
WTOTERM: World Trade Organization Terminology Database

Previous dictionaries and glossaries on the language of the ceramics industry:

- "Ceramic glossary": <http://www.digitalfire.ab.ca/cermac/glossary/index.php?goto=A>
- Fernández Chiti, J. (ed.) (1984. *Diccionario de cerámica.* Tomo 1, Condorhuasi.
- Fernández Chiti, J. (ed.) (1985. *Diccionario de cerámica.* Tomo 2, Condorhuasi.
- Fernández Chiti, J. (ed.) (1985. *Diccionario de cerámica.* Tomo 3, Condorhuasi.
- *Glossario ceramico italiano-spagnolo/spagnolo-italiano. Glosario cerámico italiano-español/español-italiano.* Faenza Editrice (1983).
- *Glossario ceramico italiano-inglese/inglese-italiano. Ceramic glossary Italian-English/English-Italian.* Faenza Editrice (1983).
- Glosario cerámico Geocities: <http://www.geocities.com/SoHo/Café/6895/glosario.htm>
- Guillem, C. and Guillem Villar, M. C. (1987. *Diccionario cerámico científico-práctico.*Sociedad española de cerámica y Vidrio.

- *Diccionario de azulejos cerámicos CEC (Deutsch-English-Español-Français-Italiano-Svenska)*
- Murfin, D. (ed.) (1994. *Dictionary of Ceramics Arthur Dodd,* London. The Institute of Materials.
- Perkins, W.W. (ed.) (1984. *Ceramic Glossary*, Westerville, Ohio. The American Ceramic Society.
- Schmid, V. (1997. *Ceramic Dictionary,* Freiburg.
- "Super-tek" glossary: <http://www.super-tek.com/doitap1.htm>
- "The Collector's Guide" glossary: <http://www.collectorsguide.com/fa/fa060.shtml>

Index

Linguistic Insights

Studies in Language and Communication

This series aims to promote specialist language studies in the fields of linguistic theory and applied linguistics, by publishing volumes that focus on specific aspects of language use in one or several languages and provide valuable insights into language and communication research. A cross-disciplinary approach is favoured and most European languages are accepted.

The series includes two types of books:

- **Monographs** – featuring in-depth studies on special aspects of language theory, language analysis or language teaching.
- **Collected papers** – assembling papers from workshops, conferences or symposia.

Each volume of the series is subjected to a double peer-reviewing process.

Vol. 1 Maurizio Gotti & Marina Dossena (eds)
Modality in Specialized Texts. Selected Papers of the 1st CERLIS Conference.
421 pages. 2001. ISBN 3-906767-10-8. US-ISBN 0-8204-5340-4

Vol. 2 Giuseppina Cortese & Philip Riley (eds)
Domain-specific English. Textual Practices across Communities and Classrooms.
420 pages. 2002. ISBN 3-906768-98-8. US-ISBN 0-8204-5884-8

Vol. 3 Maurizio Gotti, Dorothee Heller & Marina Dossena (eds)
Conflict and Negotiation in Specialized Texts. Selected Papers of the 2nd CERLIS Conference.
470 pages. 2002. ISBN 3-906769-12-7. US-ISBN 0-8204-5887-2

Editorial address:

Prof. Maurizio Gotti Università di Bergamo, Facoltà di Lingue e Letterature Straniere,
Via Salvecchio 19, 24129 Bergamo, Italy
Fax: 0039 035 2052789, E-Mail: m.gotti@unibg.it

Vol. 4 Maurizio Gotti, Marina Dossena, Richard Dury, Roberta Facchinetti & Maria Lima
Variation in Central Modals. A Repertoire of Forms and Types of Usage in Middle English and Early Modern English.
364 pages. 2002. ISBN 3-906769-84-4. US-ISBN 0-8204-5898-8

Vol. 5 Stefania Nuccorini (ed.)
Phrases and Phraseology. Data and Descriptions.
187 pages. 2002. ISBN 3-906770-08-7. US-ISBN 0-8204-5933-X

Vol. 6 Vijay Bhatia, Christopher N. Candlin & Maurizio Gotti (eds)
Legal Discourse in Multilingual and Multicultural Contexts. Arbitration Texts in Europe.
385 pages. 2003. ISBN 3-906770-85-0. US-ISBN 0-8204-6254-3

Vol. 7 Marina Dossena & Charles Jones (eds)
Insights into Late Modern English. 2nd edition.
378 pages. 2003, 2007.
ISBN 978-3-03911-257-9. US-ISBN 978-0-8204-8927-8

Vol. 8 Maurizio Gotti
Specialized Discourse. Linguistic Features and Changing Conventions.
351 pages. 2003, 2005.
ISBN 3-03910-606-6. US-ISBN 0-8204-7000-7

Vol. 9 Alan Partington, John Morley & Louann Haarman (eds)
Corpora and Discourse.
420 pages. 2004. ISBN 3-03910-026-2. US-ISBN 0-8204-6262-4

Vol. 10 Martina Möllering
The Acquisition of German Modal Particles. A Corpus-Based Approach.
290 pages. 2004. ISBN 3-03910-043-2. US-ISBN 0-8204-6273-X

Vol. 11 David Hart (ed.)
English Modality in Context. Diachronic Perspectives.
261 pages. 2003. ISBN 3-03910-046-7. US-ISBN 0-8204-6852-5

Vol. 12 Wendy Swanson
Modes of Co-reference as an Indicator of Genre.
430 pages. 2003. ISBN 3-03910-052-1. US-ISBN 0-8204-6855-X

Vol. 13 Gina Poncini
Discursive Strategies in Multicultural Business Meetings.
2nd edition. 338 pages. 2004, 2007.
ISBN 978-3-03911-296-8. US-ISBN 978-0-8204-8937-7

Vol. 14 Christopher N. Candlin & Maurizio Gotti (eds)
Intercultural Aspects of Specialized Communication.
2nd edition. 369 pages. 2004, 2007.
ISBN 978-3-03911-258-6. US-ISBN 978-0-8204-8926-1

Vol. 15 Gabriella Del Lungo Camiciotti & Elena Tognini Bonelli (eds)
Academic Discourse. New Insights into Evaluation.
234 pages. 2004. ISBN 3-03910-353-9. US-ISBN 0-8204-7016-3

Vol. 16 Marina Dossena & Roger Lass (eds)
Methods and Data in English Historical Dialectology.
405 pages. 2004. ISBN 3-03910-362-8. US-ISBN 0-8204-7018-X

Vol. 17 Judy Noguchi
The Science Review Article. An Opportune Genre in the Construction of Science.
274 pages. 2006. ISBN 3-03910-426-8. US-ISBN 0-8204-7034-1

Vol. 18 Giuseppina Cortese & Anna Duszak (eds)
Identity, Community, Discourse. English in Intercultural Settings.
495 pages. 2005. ISBN 3-03910-632-5. US-ISBN 0-8204-7163-1

Vol. 19 Anna Trosborg & Poul Erik Flyvholm Jørgensen (eds)
Business Discourse. Texts and Contexts.
250 pages. 2005. ISBN 3-03910-606-6. US-ISBN 0-8204-7000-7

Vol. 20 Christopher Williams
Tradition and Change in Legal English. Verbal Constructions in Prescriptive Texts.
2nd revised edition. 216 pages. 2005, 2007. ISBN 978-3-03911-444-3.

Vol. 21 Katarzyna Dziubalska-Kołaczyk & Joanna Przedlacka (eds)
English Pronunciation Models: A Changing Scene.
2nd edition. 476 pages. 2005, 2008. ISBN 978-3-03911-682-9.

Vol. 22 Christián Abello-Contesse, Rubén Chacón-Beltrán, M. Dolores López-Jiménez & M. Mar Torreblanca-López (eds)
Age in L2 Acquisition and Teaching.
214 pages. 2006. ISBN 3-03910-668-6. US-ISBN 0-8204-7174-7

Vol. 23 Vijay K. Bhatia, Maurizio Gotti, Jan Engberg & Dorothee Heller (eds)
Vagueness in Normative Texts.
474 pages. 2005. ISBN 3-03910-653-8. US-ISBN 0-8204-7169-0

Vol. 24 Paul Gillaerts & Maurizio Gotti (eds)
Genre Variation in Business Letters. 2nd printing.
407 pages. 2008. ISBN 978-3-03911-681-2.

Vol. 25 Ana María Hornero, María José Luzón & Silvia Murillo (eds)
Corpus Linguistics. Applications for the Study of English.
2nd printing. 526 pages. 2006, 2008. ISBN 978-3-03911-726-0

Vol. 26 J. Lachlan Mackenzie & María de los Ángeles Gómez-González (eds)
Studies in Functional Discourse Grammar.
259 pages. 2005. ISBN 3-03910-696-1 / US-ISBN 0-8204-7558-0

Vol. 27 Debbie G. E. Ho
Classroom Talk. Exploring the Sociocultural Structure of Formal ESL Learning. 2nd edition.
254 pages. 2006, 2007. ISBN 978-3-03911-434-4

Vol. 28 Javier Pérez-Guerra, Dolores González-Álvarez, Jorge L. Bueno-Alonso & Esperanza Rama-Martínez (eds)
'Of Varying Language and Opposing Creed': New Insights into Late Modern English.
455 pages. 2007. ISBN 978-3-03910-788-9

Vol. 29 Francesca Bargiela-Chiappini & Maurizio Gotti (eds)
Asian Business Discourse(s).
350 pages. 2005. ISBN 3-03910-804-2 / US-ISBN 0-8204-7574-2

Vol. 30 Nicholas Brownlees (ed.)
News Discourse in Early Modern Britain. Selected Papers of CHINED 2004.
300 pages. 2006. ISBN 3-03910-805-0 / US-ISBN 0-8204-8025-8

Vol. 31 Roberta Facchinetti & Matti Rissanen (eds)
Corpus-based Studies of Diachronic English.
300 pages. 2006. ISBN 3-03910-851-4 / US-ISBN 0-8204-8040-1

Vol. 32 Marina Dossena & Susan M. Fitzmaurice (eds)
Business and Official Correspondence: Historical Investigations.
209 pages. 2006. ISBN 3-03910-880-8 / US-ISBN 0-8204-8352-4

Vol. 33 Giuliana Garzone & Srikant Sarangi (eds)
Discourse, Ideology and Specialized Communication.
494 pages. 2007. ISBN 978-3-03910-888-6

Vol. 34 Giuliana Garzone & Cornelia Ilie (eds)
The Use of English in Institutional and Business Settings. An Intercultural Perspective.
372 pages. 2007. ISBN 978-3-03910-889-3

Vol. 35 Vijay K. Bhatia & Maurizio Gotti (eds)
Explorations in Specialized Genres.
316 pages. 2006. ISBN 3-03910-995-2 / US-ISBN 0-8204-8372-9

Vol. 36 Heribert Picht (ed.)
Modern Approaches to Terminological Theories and Applications.
432 pages. 2006. ISBN 3-03911-156-6 / US-ISBN 0-8204-8380-X

Vol. 37 Anne Wagner & Sophie Cacciaguidi-Fahy (eds)
Legal Language and the Search for Clarity / Le langage juridique et la quête de clarté. Practice and Tools / Pratiques et instruments.
487 pages. 2006. ISBN 3-03911-169-8 / US-ISBN 0-8388-5

Vol. 38 Juan Carlos Palmer-Silveira, Miguel F. Ruiz-Garrido & Inmaculada Fortanet-Gómez (eds)
Intercultural and International Business Communication: Theory, Research and Teaching.
2nd edition. 343 pages. 2006, 2008. ISBN 978-3-03911-680-5

Vol. 39 Christiane Dalton-Puffer, Dieter Kastovsky, Nikolaus Ritt & Herbert Schendl (eds)
Syntax, Style and Grammatical Norms: English from 1500–2000.
250 pages. 2006. ISBN 3-03911-181-7 / US-ISBN 0-8204-8394-X

Vol. 40 Marina Dossena & Irma Taavitsainen (eds)
Diachronic Perspectives on Domain-Specific English.
280 pages. 2006. ISBN 3-03910-176-0 / US-ISBN 0-8204-8391-5

Vol. 41 John Flowerdew & Maurizio Gotti (eds)
Studies in Specialized Discourse.
293 pages. 2006. ISBN 3-03911-178-7

Vol. 42 Ken Hyland & Marina Bondi (eds)
Academic Discourse Across Disciplines.
320 pages. 2006. ISBN 3-03911-183-3 / US-ISBN 0-8204-8396-6

Vol. 43 Paul Gillaerts & Philip Shaw (eds)
The Map and the Landscape: Norms and Practices in Genre.
256 pages. 2006. ISBN 3-03911-182-5 / US-ISBN 0-8204-8395-4

Vol. 44 Maurizio Gotti & Davide Giannoni (eds)
New Trends in Specialized Discourse Analysis.
301 pages. 2006. ISBN 3-03911-184-1 / US-ISBN 0-8204-8381-8

Vol. 45 Maurizio Gotti & Françoise Salager-Meyer (eds)
Advances in Medical Discourse Analysis: Oral and Written Contexts.
492 pages. 2006. ISBN 3-03911-185-X / US-ISBN 0-8204-8382-6

Vol. 46 Maurizio Gotti & Susan Šarcević (eds)
Insights into Specialized Translation.
396 pages. 2006. ISBN 3-03911-186-8 / US-ISBN 0-8204-8383-4

Vol. 47 Khurshid Ahmad & Margaret Rogers (eds)
Evidence-based LSP: Translation, Text and Terminology.
584 pages. 2007. ISBN 978-3-03911-187-9

Vol. 48 Hao Sun & Dániel Z. Kádár (eds)
It's the Dragon's Turn: Chinese Institutional Discourses.
262 pages. 2008. ISBN 978-3-03911-175-6

Vol. 49 Cristina Suárez-Gómez
Relativization in Early English (950-1250): the Position of Relative Clauses.
149 pages. 2006. ISBN 3-03911-203-1 / US-ISBN 0-8204-8904-2

Vol. 50 Maria Vittoria Calvi & Luisa Chierichetti (eds)
Nuevas tendencias en el discurso de especialidad.
319 pages. 2006. ISBN 978-3-03911-261-6

Vol. 51 Mari Carmen Campoy & María José Luzón (eds)
Spoken Corpora in Applied Linguistics.
274 pages. 2008. ISBN 978-3-03911-275-3

Vol. 52 Konrad Ehlich & Dorothee Heller (Hrsg.)
Die Wissenschaft und ihre Sprachen.
323 pages. 2006. ISBN 978-3-03911-272-2

Vol. 53 Jingyu Zhang
The Semantic Salience Hierarchy Model:
The L2 Acquisition of Psych Predicates
273 pages. 2007. ISBN 978-3-03911-300-2

Vol. 54 Norman Fairclough, Giuseppina Cortese & Patrizia Ardizzone (eds)
Discourse and Contemporary Social Change.
555 pages. 2007. ISBN 978-3-03911-276-0

Vol. 55 Jan Engberg, Marianne Grove Ditlevsen, Peter Kastberg & Martin Stegu (eds)
New Directions in LSP Teaching.
331 pages. 2007. ISBN 978-3-03911-433-7

Vol. 56 Dorothee Heller & Konrad Ehlich (Hrsg.)
Studien zur Rechtskommunikation.
322 pages. 2007. ISBN 978-3-03911-436-8

Vol. 57 Forthcoming.

Vol. 58 Carmen Frehner
Email – SMS – MMS
294 pages. 2008. ISBN 978-3-03911-451-1

Vol. 59 Isabel Balteiro
The Directionality of Conversion in English: A Dia-Synchronic Study.
276 pages. 2007. ISBN 978-3-03911-241-8

Vol. 60 Maria Milagros Del Saz Rubio
English Discourse Markers of Reformulation.
237 pages. 2007. ISBN 978-3-03911-196-1

Vol. 61 Sally Burgess & Pedro Martín-Martín (eds)
English as an Additional Language in Research Publication and Communication.
259 pages. 2008. ISBN 978-3-03911-462-7

Vol. 62 Sandrine Onillon
Pratiques et représentations de l'écrit.
458 pages. 2008. ISBN 978-3-03911-464-1

Vol. 63 Hugo Bowles & Paul Seedhouse (eds)
Conversation Analysis and Language for Specific Purposes.
2nd edition. 337 pages. 2007, 2009. ISBN 978-3-0343-0045-2

Vol. 64 Vijay K. Bhatia, Christopher N. Candlin & Paola Evangelisti Allori (eds)
Language, Culture and the Law.
The Formulation of Legal Concepts across Systems and Cultures.
342 pages. 2008. ISBN 978-3-03911-470-2

Vol. 65 Forthcoming.

Vol. 66 Linda Lombardo (ed.)
Using Corpora to Learn about Language and Discourse.
237 pages. 2009. ISBN 978-3-03911-522-8

Vol. 67 Natsumi Wakamoto
Extroversion/Introversion in Foreign Language Learning.
Interactions with Learner Strategy Use.
159 pages. 2009. ISBN 978-3-03911-596-9

Vol. 68 Eva Alcón-Soler (ed.)
Learning How to Request in an Instructed Language Learning Context.
260 pages. 2008. ISBN 978-3-03911-601-0

Vol. 69 Domenico Pezzini
The Translation of Religious Texts in the Middle Ages.
428 pages. 2008. ISBN 978-3-03911-600-3

Vol. 70 Tomoko Tode
Effects of Frequency in Classroom Second Language Learning.
Quasi-experiment and stimulated-recall analysis.
195 pages. 2008. ISBN 978-3-03911-602-7

Vol. 71 Egor Tsedryk
Fusion symétrique et alternances ditransitives.
211 pages. 2009. ISBN 978-3-03911-609-6

Vol. 72 Cynthia J. Kellett Bidoli & Elana Ochse (eds)
English in International Deaf Communication.
444 pages. 2008. ISBN 978-3-03911-610-2

Vol. 73 Joan C. Beal, Carmela Nocera & Massimo Sturiale (eds)
Perspectives on Prescriptivism.
269 pages. 2008. ISBN 978-3-03911-632-4

Vol. 74 Carol Taylor Torsello, Katherine Ackerley & Erik Castello (eds)
Corpora for University Language Teachers.
308 pages. 2008. ISBN 978-3-03911-639-3

Vol. 75 María Luisa Pérez Cañado (ed.)
English Language Teaching in the European Credit Transfer System:
Facing the Challenge.
251 pages. 2009. ISBN 978-3-03911-654-6

Vol. 76 Marina Dossena & Ingrid Tieken-Boon van Ostade (eds)
Studies in Late Modern English Correspondence. Methodology and Data.
291 pages. 2008. ISBN 978-3-03911-658-4

Vol. 77 Ingrid Tieken-Boon van Ostade & Wim van der Wurff (eds)
Current Issues in Late Modern English.
437 pages. 2009. ISBN 978-3-03911-660-7

Vol. 78 Marta Navarro Coy (ed.)
Practical Approaches to Foreign Language Teaching and Learning.
297 pages. 2009. ISBN 978-3-03911-661-4

Vol. 79 Qing Ma
Second Language Vocabulary Acquisition.
333 pages. 2009. ISBN 978-3-03911-666-9

Vol. 80 Martin Solly, Michelangelo Conoscenti & Sandra Campagna (eds)
Verbal/Visual Narrative Texts in Higher Education.
384 pages. 2008. ISBN 978-3-03911-672-0

Vol. 81 Meiko Matsumoto
From Simple Verbs to Periphrastic Expressions:
The Historical Development of Composite Predicates, Phrasal Verbs, and Related Constructions in English.
235 pages. 2008. ISBN 978-3-03911-675-1

Vol. 82 Melinda Dooly
Doing Diversity. Teachers' Construction of Their Classroom Reality.
180 pages. 2009. ISBN 978-3-03911-687-4

Vol. 83 Forthcoming.

Vol. 84 Maria Grazia Guido
English as a Lingua Franca in Cross-cultural Immigration Domains.
285 pages. 2008. ISBN 978-3-03911-689-8

Vol. 85 Erik Castello
Text Complexity and Reading Comprehension Tests.
352 pages. 2008. ISBN 978-3-03911-717-8

Vol. 86 Forthcoming.

Vol. 87 Carmen Navarro, Rosa Mª Rodríguez Abella, Francesca Dalle Pezze & Renzo Miotti (eds)
La comunicación especializada.
355 pages. 2008. ISBN 978-3-03911-733-8

Vol. 88 Kiriko Sato
The Development from Case-Forms to Prepositional Constructions in Old English Prose.
231 pages. 2009. ISBN 978-3-03911-763-5

Vol. 89 Dorothee Heller (Hrsg.)
Formulierungsmuster in deutscher und italienischer Fachkommunikation. Intra- und interlinguale Perspektiven.
315 pages. 2008. ISBN 978-3-03911-778-9

Vol. 90 Henning Bergenholtz, Sandro Nielsen & Sven Tarp (eds)
Lexicography at a Crossroads. Dictionaries and Encyclopedias Today, Lexicographical Tools Tomorrow.
372 pages. 2009. ISBN 978-3-03911-799-4

Vol. 91 Manouchehr Moshtagh Khorasani
The Development of Controversies: From the Early Modern Period to Online Discussion Forums.
317 pages. 2009. ISBN 978-3-3911-711-6

Vol. 92 María Luisa Carrió-Pastor (ed.)
Content and Language Integrated Learning: Cultural Diversity.
178 pages. 2009. ISBN 978-3-3911-818-2

Vol. 93-96 Forthcoming.

Vol. 97 Sylvie Hancil (ed.)
The Role of Prosody in Affective Speech.
403 pages. 2009. ISBN 978-3-03911-696-6

Vol. 98 Marina Dossena & Roger Lass (eds)
Studies in English and European Historical Dialectology.
257 pages. 2009. ISBN 978-3-0343-0024-7

Vol. 99 Forthcoming.

Vol. 100 Maurizio Gotti (ed.)
Commonality and Individuality in Academic Discourse.
398 pages. 2009. ISBN 978-3-0343-0023-0

Vol. 101 Forthcoming.

Vol. 102 Nuria Edo Marzá
The Specialised Lexicographical Approach: A Step further in Dictionary-making.
316 pages. 2009. ISBN 978-3-0343-0043-8

FSC
www.fsc.org
MIX
Papier | Fördert
gute Waldnutzung
FSC® C083411

Kolibri 360 GmbH
Ferdinand-Jühlke-Straße 7
99095 Erfurt, Deutschland
produktsicherheit@kolibri360.de